Phillips Brooks

Letters of Travel

Phillips Brooks

Letters of Travel

ISBN/EAN: 9783337135430

Printed in Europe, USA, Canada, Australia, Japan

Cover: Foto ©Andreas Hilbeck / pixelio.de

More available books at **www.hansebooks.com**

BY
PHILLIPS BROOKS
LATE BISHOP OF MASSACHUSETTS

NEW YORK
E. P. DUTTON AND COMPANY
31 WEST TWENTY-THIRD STREET
1893

PREFACE.

THESE letters of travel of the late Bishop Brooks have been selected from his correspondence with members of his family. They relate to two journeys, of more than a year in duration, taken in 1865-66 and in 1882-83 respectively, — the former when he was Rector of the Church of the Holy Trinity, Philadelphia, the latter when he was Rector of Trinity Church, Boston, — and to shorter summer trips, generally of about three months in duration. The circumstances under which they were written are sufficiently evident from the letters, and call for little comment.

Several of these series of letters Bishop Brooks regarded in the light of a record of his travels and experiences, and after his return reclaimed them, and found frequent enjoyment in the reminiscences of his journeys which they awakened.

Further details of these same journeys and other letters relating to them will appear in the forthcoming Life of Bishop Brooks. But before that is given to the public, it seemed possible and desirable to put in shape these letters of travel, which give an important chapter of his life that was always of the greatest delight to him, and in which are represented many of his most striking personal characteristics.

An interesting journey taken in 1887, which included his attendance at the Queen's Jubilee Service and his last meeting with Robert Browning and Matthew Arnold, as well as his second visit to Tennyson, is unmentioned, for the reason that he was accompanied on that journey by members of his family to whom the writing of those letters which should contain the continuous record of the summer was committed. For the same reason, one letter alone appears in this collection to represent a journey made in 1890, when, in addition to a trip to Switzerland, he visited parts of England including Cornwall and Devonshire, which are associated with Kingsley's Westward Ho! and also Andover, the name of which is so closely connected with the life of the Phillips family in America.

The letters retain the familiar character which belonged to them as being intended for the members of his own family. It will be seen that in no other form could they have been given to the public, and they are thus enabled to convey not only an interesting story of travel, but also something of that personal charm and ready wit and genial appreciation which those who were nearest to him loved so well. His warm remembrance of friends from whom he was absent will be evident in all these letters, and his nature will be seen in its sunniest and most playful mood.

October, 1893.

CONTENTS.

	PAGE
FIRST JOURNEY ABROAD, 1865–1866	1
IN THE TYROL AND SWITZERLAND, 1870	139
SUMMER IN NORTHERN EUROPE, 1872	154
FROM LONDON TO VENICE, 1874	172
ENGLAND AND THE CONTINENT, 1877	181
IN PARIS, ENGLAND, SCOTLAND, AND IRELAND, 1880	187
A YEAR IN EUROPE AND INDIA, 1882–1883	191
ENGLAND AND EUROPE, 1885	325
ACROSS THE CONTINENT TO SAN FRANCISCO, 1886	343
A SUMMER IN JAPAN, 1889	355
SUMMER OF 1890	374
LAST JOURNEY ABROAD	376

LETTERS OF TRAVEL.

FIRST JOURNEY ABROAD.

1865-1866.

STEAMER SCOTIA,
Monday P. M., August 14, 1865.

DEAR MOTHER, — My first letter from abroad shall be to you. It will not be much of a letter, for nobody feels like doing anything on shipboard, and especially this afternoon, when the ship is rolling worse than it has yet. We have had a splendid passage so far; I have not been seasick for a moment since I came on board, and we are now more than half-way across. Father and William gave you my biography up to the moment of sailing. They came pretty near having to go to Europe themselves. The first days out were very smooth, and we were well used to the motion of the vessel before the rough sea began. There has been considerable seasickness aboard.

We spend almost all the time on deck. I have scarcely been below except for meals and sleep. It is the nicest, laziest, and pleasantest life in the world. We breakfast at 8.30, lunch at 12, dine at 6, and sup at 7.30. There is the funniest collection of people here: English, French, Germans, Portuguese, Jews, and Secessionists; lots of Southern people going to foreign parts to hide their shame. I have made some very pleasant friends, especially a nice English family, whose son has been in our army. They live in Cheltenham, England, and have invited me to visit them.

We had service yesterday; the Captain (Judkins) read service and a sermon. It was quite interesting. I thought of you all at home, and felt that you were praying for us. It is hard to count these things, though, for we have gained already two hours on you, and are getting farther and farther to the eastward all the time. We have not had the sensation of danger yet, except the last two nights, when it has been very foggy, and we have run along blowing our whistle almost all the time, not knowing what ship or iceberg we might run into any minute. As yet all is safe.

It is wonderful how fast the time goes here. The days have not dragged at all, though there is next to nothing to do. We read a little, and walk the decks, and look for ships, and the hours slip by delightfully. Father told you, I suppose, that the Langs were on board. I am burnt up as brown as a berry, and never was so well in my life. It is a splendid beginning of my tour.

How I would like to look in on you at home, or rather how I would like to have you all here! You would enjoy it intensely. It would not be so agreeable if one were sick, but everybody says the voyage has been most remarkable.

I leave the next page to be filled up between here and Queenstown.

Wednesday Morning, August 16.

It is still beautiful and delightful. Just a week since we sailed, and the most splendid week I ever passed. Last night on deck, with a high wind, clear starlight overhead, and the phosphorescent water below, was glorious! I shall be almost sorry to land, except for the nights, which are very disagreeable in these miserable little berths. My room-mate is an Englishman, just returning from a tour around the world. He is intelligent and civil, but I see very little of him. They say we shall be in at Queenstown on Thursday night. I will mail this on board to-morrow, and then write again to you from Dublin.

Thursday Morning, August 17.

All has gone well, and we shall come upon the coast of Ireland to-night. To-morrow morning I go from Cork to Dublin, where I shall stay till over Sunday. Perhaps this letter will reach you a little earlier by being mailed on board, so I will close it here. You may consider our voyage as prosperously over, and me as safely into the Old World. No stranger ever got into it easier. When I write again, there will be more incidents to record. Now I only ask you to thank God with me for my safe voyage. Give lots of love to all the household, beginning with father and going down to Trip. How I shall depend upon your letters at London.

Your loving son, PHILLIPS.

GRESHAM HOTEL, SACKVILLE STREET, DUBLIN,
Friday Evening, August 18, 1865.

DEAR WILLIAM,[1]—Safe in Dublin. Is n't it funny? The Scotia arrived at Queenstown at four this morn-

[1] His brother, William G. Brooks.

ing, and we at once went ashore. I breakfasted at Queenstown, and then took the train for Cork, where I spent three hours wandering up and down the queerest city that was ever made. It is one universal Sea Street and Fort Hill. The source whence all the Biddies and Patsies have flowed over the Atlantic was evident at once, and there are plenty more of the same sort to come.

At twelve o'clock we took the train for Dublin, and rode all the afternoon through the loveliest country that ever was seen, — endless fields with their green hedges and rich crops, and men and women together harvesting them. I reached here at six o'clock, and got a room in Gresham's Hotel, a good house which you will see marked upon the picture. It has been a perfect day, especially after the long confinement of the voyage.

How strange it seems to be here! The old town, so far as I have seen it to-night, looks like Boston. To-morrow I shall see the great Exhibition and all the lions, and call on one or two people to whom I have introductions. The Archbishop (Trench), I am sorry to hear, is out of town. I shall stay here till over Sunday, and leave on Monday for Belfast and the Giant's Causeway; but I only meant to say I am here safe. God bless you all!

Affectionately,   PHILLIPS.

JEDBURGH, SCOTLAND,
Wednesday P. M., August 30, 1865.

DEAR FATHER, — See if you can find this little place upon the map, and then picture one of the Brooks boys set down at the Spread Eagle Inn (the picture of a little English or Scotch inn), after an

English dinner, to tell his adventures to the family in the back parlor of 41 Chauncy Street, Boston. Let me show you how I got here. Get the big Atlas which we had out on the Sunday night before I left, and trace me on from point to point.

The last time I wrote I was in Dublin. I spent two days there; saw the great Exhibition (whose only very striking point is the collection of pictures), the college, and the other sights of the dingy old town. I spent Sunday there, and went to service at St. Patrick's Cathedral, where we had the whole cathedral service in its most splendid style. Sunday afternoon, having failed in town to see Archbishop Trench, whom I was most anxious to see of any man in Ireland, I went down to Bray, a watering place near Dublin, where I heard he was to officiate. I did not find him there, and so came back to Dublin; whence I started the next morning and went by the way of Belfast up to Port Rush on the northern coast, where I spent Monday night. Tuesday, I drove over to the Giant's Causeway and inspected it thoroughly. It was most interesting, — more wonderful in its formation than I had imagined. Then back to Belfast, and on Tuesday night took a crazy little steamer, called the Lynx (about as big as the Nelly Baker, — not quite), for Glasgow, where contrary to all reasonable probabilities and amid all sorts of discomforts we were landed for breakfast on Wednesday morning. Spent the day there. It is a fine city, and puts one right into the midst of "Rob Roy." Nichol Jarvie lived close by the hotel, and I was inclined to run over and congratulate the good bailie on his safe return from the Highlands. There is a fine old cathedral there, in whose crypt, you may remember, one of the finest scenes in "Rob Roy" is laid. Thursday morning was clear and lovely, and I took the train early for the foot of Loch Lomond (Balloch), and then the steamer up the lake; it is a glorious sail, different from anything I know in America, and full of romantic interest; then across by coach to Loch Katrine, and down that beautiful lake by steamer. This is the one celebrated in the "Lady of the Lake," and you pass right by Ellen's Isle. Then by coach through the Trossachs, a splendid mountain gorge, to Stirling, where I spent Thursday night; saw the great castle and the old home of the Scottish kings. This brought me to Edinburgh on Friday morning. Of Edinburgh I cannot say enough. It is the queen of cities, the most romantic, picturesque, un-American, old-world town that ever was. I have been there till to-day, and would like to have stayed a week longer; its beauty is not forgettable, and its quaint sights are past all description. I went to church there on Sunday: in the morning to one of the plainest of all plain Scotch Presbyterian churches, where you sat on a board as wide as three matches, and heard a sermon of an hour long; and in the afternoon to an Episcopal church, where the service was intoned.

How strange these old towns are! You do not think of them as belonging to these days. They seem to have done their work in the world, and handed it over to us, and crept under their glass cases where they are kept for shows. Still, let me say for Edinburgh that I found it practical enough to get there a traveling suit of fine Scotch tweed, for which I paid only five pounds, which is less than half what it would have cost me in America. Monday I went down to Abbotsford and "Fair Melrose." It is like a dream to see these places. Sir Walter, the splendid old fellow, seems to walk and talk with you. It was the day I had been looking for, ever since I first read your old Lockhart's Life some fifteen years ago. It will always be one of my memorable days. Yesterday I was at Roslyn Chapel and Hawthornden, both beautiful, the chapel a wonderful little gem of sculpture; then back to Edinburgh in the afternoon and up Arthur's Seat, the famous hill which overlooks Edinburgh.

I am on my way now to the English lakes, and have stopped here over night to see the old abbey, and a Scotch family to whom I have a letter of introduction. I have seen a good deal of Scotchmen. Their thrift and intelligence demand respect, but they are cold. I spent the evening in Glasgow with the family of a professor there, who all talked the broadest and most unintelligible Scotch. The professor insisted that Pennsylvania was a city, but was pretty well informed about our war and politics, — an Abolitionist and a Northern man. I wish that you could see this queer little town. It is Scotland in a nutshell.

Thursday P. M.

I was broken off here, and must close my letter hastily to make sure of Saturday's steamer. I am very well, and enjoying everything very much indeed, as you can see. To-day I have spent about Jedburgh with the Andersons, to whom I had a letter, and who prove to be very pleasant people. Sunday I expect to spend at Windermere on the lake; after that I shall begin to get towards London, reaching there in about ten days.

. . . Love to everybody. How I should like to

see you all! I shall depend on getting a letter at London. Your affectionate son,

PHILLIPS.

QUEEN'S HOTEL, MANCHESTER,
Tuesday, September 5, 1865.

DEAR MOTHER, — My last letter was directed from Jedburgh, Scotland. This, as you see, comes from Manchester. I have reached England since I wrote, and seen something of it already. From Jedburgh I went to Kelso and Berwick-on-Tweed; thence to Newcastle-on-Tyne, and to Durham, where I spent a few hours and saw one of the greatest and best of the English cathedrals; then to the little village of Barnard Castle, where I spent the night, and on to Windermere in Westmoreland. My present enthusiasm is the English lakes. They are very beautiful. I walked from Windermere to Ambleside at the head of Lake Windermere, and spent Sunday there, a thorough English Sunday. I attended service in the parish church. At Ambleside, or rather close by, at Rydal, are the old homes of Wordsworth and Dr. Arnold, and a few miles off, at Grasmere, the homes of Hartley Coleridge and De Quincey. From there I went on Monday, by coach, through a splendid lake and mountain region, to Keswick on Derwentwater, where Southey lived and is buried, and then by rail via Lancaster to Manchester, where I arrived last night. Here I came across Americans again. I have seen three or four already from Philadelphia. This hotel is one of the great resorts of Americans in England. I am going to make one or two calls here, and then shall be off to York.

Wednesday Morning, September 6.

I spent last evening at Mrs. Gaskell's. She is an authoress; wrote the Life of Charlotte Brontë and several novels; a charming lady and most hospitable. I had a letter to her from Philadelphia. She knows all the literary people in England and told me a great deal about them. I met there a Mr. Winkworth, brother of the lady who did the "Lyra Germanica." He is the most intelligent Englishman about our affairs that I have seen. This was the pleasantest meeting with English people that I have had. Mrs. Gaskell promised me a letter to Ruskin, in London, with whom she is very intimate.

YORK, Thursday Evening, September 7.

You see I began this sheet all wrong, and so you will have to make its order out by the dates. When I left off I was at Manchester. I left there yesterday forenoon, and reached here about two o'clock. Here, you know, is the greatest of the English cathedrals. I went all over it yesterday afternoon, and attended the evening service. The music was very fine. This morning I took the train early and have spent the day at Ripon, where there is another fine cathedral, and at Fountain Abbey, which is the oldest and most complete of the old monastic establishments. I am back here to-night, and shall start in the morning for Lincoln, Ely, Cambridge, and so to London. I should like very much to stop at Boston, just for association's sake, and shall, if I have time.

York is, I suppose, the oldest city I have seen yet. Here we get our first sight of the old Romans, who had a splendid town here, and whose old wall still remains.

I am afraid my letters sound very much like guide-books. You must forgive me, but remember that I have nothing to write except what I see and hear. You can see that I am going all the time, and from morning to night. There has not yet been one stormy day, and I have enjoyed everything hugely. I have been well all the time. So far, I have seen hardly anything of Americans, for I have been off their routes. I have talked with Englishmen in the trains and at the hotels. I had no idea till I came here what a tremendous American I was. I have n't seen a New York paper since I left. How I shall revel in all your letters next week. Good-by. God bless you all. PHILLIPS.

GOLDEN CROSS HOTEL, CHARING CROSS, LONDON,
Sunday Evening, September 10, 1865.

DEAR FATHER, — At last communication is resumed. I arrived here yesterday, and found at Barings your noble, long letter, in which I reveled. I hope to get others to-morrow by the steamer which arrived yesterday. How good it was to get in sound of you again and hear the wheels in Chauncy Street moving on as smoothly and pleasantly as ever. By this time you are all together again except Fred, and he will be there soon. How I wish that I could sit down with you!

My last I mailed at Lincoln. From there I went to Boston. How strange it seemed! As we rode over the marshes (fens, they call them here) that surround the town, and saw the bricky mass rising before us, it was easy to believe that we were coming in over the Back Bay and would be with you at supper. It is a pretty little town of about 11,000 people. You walk up from the station through Lincoln Street to the church, which is the principal object of the town. It is a fine old piece of architecture. The sexton, who showed me through it, was very civil, especially when I told him where I came from. The vicar was away, or I should have called on him. I left my card for him. The Cotton Chapel is a nice little room, well restored; you see it on the right, or south side of the church, in the exterior one of the views that I send you. They still use the old John Cotton pulpit, but the sexton told me that they thought of getting a new one and giving the old relic to the American Boston.

I went then to Peterborough, where I meant to spend the night and go to Cambridge the next day, but Peterborough was so full, owing to a great sheep-fair, that I could not find lodgings, and concluded to come right through to London and go to Cambridge by and by; so this is my second day in London. I am right in the centre of the City at the head of the Strand, close to Trafalgar Square and Westminster Abbey. It is a fascinating place, for there is not a step that is not full of association. I have seen little yet in detail. To-morrow I begin. To-day I went to hear Spurgeon, and found myself in an immense crowd and rush. He is not graceful nor thoughtful nor imaginative, and preached a great deal too long, but he is earnest, simple, direct, and held the hosts of plain-looking people wonderfully. I believe with all his rudeness and narrowness and lack of higher powers that he is doing a good work here.

Thursday Evening, September 14.

This must go into the mail to-morrow, so I shall finish it to-night. Since Sunday I have been seeing London, and have been very busy. Let me see: Westminster Abbey, St. Paul's Cathedral, the British Museum, the Tower, the National Gallery, the Sydenham Crystal Palace, Regent's Park and its Zoölogical Gardens, the Tunnel, with lots of lesser sights, and the greatest sight of all which one has always in wandering about the streets of this great Babel. To-day I took the steamer on the Thames, all the way along past the City, and through its old bridges. Every rod here has some interest of its own. Yesterday I dined at Mr. Adams's at half past seven o'clock, a very pleasant dinner, and both Mr. and Mrs. Adams were very cordial and hospitable. Mrs. Adams was especially full of inquiries about you and mother. Their son Henry, and daughter, and one or two others were there. On Monday I go down into Hampshire to visit Mrs. Kemble. I have a very kind and pressing invitation from her. From there I shall very probably keep on into the Isle of Wight. I do not know how to find time enough for England, especially for London, as I must leave here by the 10th of October. I have left the hotel and gone into lodgings at Mrs. Dekker's, No. 1 A, Craven Street, Strand. It is a little cheaper and a great deal more comfortable.

I was very much disappointed at not getting letters from any of you by the last steamer. I do hope the next will bring some. Don't forget me.

I am so tired, to-night, as every night, that I can hardly write, so you must forgive the poorness of this letter. I think of you all and home constantly. Tell Fred to write. I have a letter from Franks, who

talked of going to Boston with him. I hope he did.
God bless you all. Affectionately,
PHILLIPS.

WARNFORD COTTAGE, BISHOPS-WALTHAM, HAMPSHIRE,
Wednesday, September 20, 1865.

DEAR WILLIAM, — To-day's letter must be to you. You certainly deserve it for the splendid long epistle which I received last Saturday, for which I cannot thank you enough. I am glad that you had so pleasant a visit at Trenton and Saratoga, and I enjoyed your account of it exceedingly. Certainly, so far as mere natural beauty is concerned, I do not believe there is any need of one's leaving America.

I am writing this before breakfast (they don't breakfast till half past nine) at the window of a little English cottage which looks out on as perfect an English scene as you can imagine. There is a piece of lawn like velvet in front, with gorgeous flower beds spotted over it; then a hawthorn hedge shutting out from view a little winding lane, beyond which are the broad, smooth hills of Warnford Park, with splendid great trees grouped about over it, and the Hall in the distance, which owns and rules the whole estate. Is n't that English? I am staying here with Mrs. Kemble, who occupies this little cottage close to the large estate of her brother-in-law. He owns the Hall. I came here on Monday, and have enjoyed my visit very much. Mrs. Kemble is, as I expected, very bright and interesting, very kind, hospitable, and courteous. The family is only herself and one daughter, who is just as bright as her mother. Yesterday I drove out with Mrs. Kemble to Winchester, about twelve miles, where I saw the cathedral, in some respects one of the finest in England, and called on one of the canons, to whom I had a letter from Bishop McIlvaine. The drive there was very beautiful, over the Downs, as they call them, a soft rolling country, spotted over with the sheep who are to supply the Southdown mutton, which you know is the great product of this part of England. To-day I shall leave here and go to the Isle of Wight, getting back to London on Friday, and then I shall get ready at once to go on the Continent. I find it is impossible at this time of year to see people or institutions in England to advantage ; so I propose to go to Germany and the East a little earlier, and thus secure time in the spring to run over here when everything is in full blast and I can do it more satisfactorily. I have seen most of the "sights" of London. After I wrote to you I went to Hyde Park and the Kensington Museum, where is the best collection of modern English pictures, Reynolds and Hogarth, and Wilkie and Leslie, etc. There is the original of the "Blind Fiddler" over the nursery mantelpiece at No. 41. The whole museum is very interesting. Mrs. Gaskell sent me a letter to Mr. Ruskin, and I drove out to Denmark Hill, where he lives, to present it. He was not at home, so I only had the pleasure of seeing his house, but I shall see him, I hope, by and by. The house is a very pretty suburban mansion ; a fine picture of Turner's was over the mantelpiece. I saw a good deal of the Adamses. Mrs. and Miss Adams came to my lodgings and left a card, "The Minister of the United States." Sunday I dined with them ; Sunday morning I went to the Foundlings' Chapel, where the children do some of the best chanting in London ; in the afternoon I went to St. Paul's Cathedral and heard a capital sermon from Melville, who is called one of the best preachers in England. I called on Dean Milman with Mr. Winthrop's letter, and had a very pleasant visit. He lives in a curious old deanery close to the cathedral.

My next will be dated somewhere the other side of the Channel. All goes well with me so far, as you see. I am in capital health and spirits. Just now I think of you all together at home; how happy you must be. Do write to me every week, for steamer day is always looked for eagerly. It has been very hot here, but is cooler now, and England is the most beautiful thing you can conceive. Good-by. God bless you all.

PHILL.

HOTEL GOLDENER STERN, BONN,
Monday, October 2, 1865.

DEAR MOTHER, — Is n't this a funny place from which to write you? I wish you could see it, you would think it funnier still; but you would have to allow that it is very pretty. It stands on the Rhine just before you come to the Seven Mountains, where the beauty of the Rhine commences, and is one of those queer old German cities which we have always pictured and know so little about until we have seen them. But I might as well go back to where I was at my last writing. I told Fred to send you my letter from London, so I will begin there. On Tuesday morning I went by rail to Dover, and thence by boat to Ostend. Everybody expects to be seasick on the Channel, but I was disappointed. We had a four hours' sail, as quiet and gentle as if we were going down to Hingham. It was most charming, and not a soul on board suffered from the sea. We came up to the wharf at Ostend, and felt at once that we were in Europe. I brushed up my French and went ashore, passed the custom-house examination, and took train by Bruges to Ghent, a queer old town full of historic interest; from there to Brussels, a lively French town. I found it right in the midst of its annual fête of national independence. The streets were illuminated, fireworks everywhere, and people sitting at tables drinking beer in honor of independent Belgium. I found all the best hotels full, and was crowded into a poor one, and jabbered my French for the first time to waiters and chambermaids. I went from Brussels to see the field of Waterloo. Everybody does, though it was n't much of a battle by the side of Gettysburg and Antietam. They run an English mail-coach out there every day. Then I saw the Brussels streets and churches. From Brussels to Antwerp, a dear old city, full of Rubens's pictures and the quaintest old Flemish houses and costumes. From Antwerp to Rotterdam, part by rail and part by steamer, up the Maas, through miles of dykes and windmills into my first Dutch town. Such a language as they talked there! I have n't half an idea what anybody said to me. I made a tolerable show of French and got along splendidly in German, but the Dutch was too much for me. I could only smile blandly and point what I thought was the nearest way to the next town. From Rotterdam to the Hague, a nice old place with canals instead of streets, and fine old pictures of Rembrandt and Rubens, and a lot of others; then to Amsterdam, where all is canal and not street again, and the horrible Dutch tongue still. I went to the New Church (built in 1408) and heard them sing two verses of a hymn in their language. That was enough, and I ran down the nearest canal to the English church and heard our own dear liturgy and a sermon from the English chaplain instead. From Amsterdam to Düsseldorf, where the pictures come from and where many splendid ones are still, to Cologne, where the great unfinished cathedral is, at which they have been working six hundred years; and from there, here. To-day, I have come into Germany, where they speak German and charge you for your dinner in thalers. I like the Germans much. I respect the Dutch, but I would not live among them for a million a year. To-day, too, I have come into the region of Romish churches and relics. I have seen the skulls of the Three Wise Men, the thorns of Christ's Crown, the wood of the True Cross, one of the water pots of Cana of Galilee, the steps of Pilate's Judgment Seat, and a church lined with the skulls and bones of the eleven thousand martyred virgins of Cologne. Of course you are expected to believe in them all, and isn't that pretty well for one day? But the cathedral is very noble, by all means one of the great sights of the world.

That brings me to Bonn. From here trace me to Coblentz, Mayence, Heidelberg, Frankfort (where I have directed my letters to be sent and hope to hear from you), Leipsic, and Berlin. Am I not a lucky chap to see all this? I am splendidly well, and keep on the go all the time, and, as I said, am getting the hang of German enough to be quite at home with the people. I eschew all delicacies and rough it generally. Last night for the first time I found a feather bed for covering in my room. I kicked it off and slept like a top without it. The worst thing to me about this traveling is that you can't drink water. Think of my misery. But it is too vile to touch. However, we are now in the region of light Rhine wines. For twelve and a half groschen (25 cents) you get a bottle of good wine which answers pretty well, but I would give a dollar for a pitcher of ice water to-night. All living here is cheap, but in Holland it is very dear and very poor indeed. I think I did right in coming alone, that is, as no very intimate friend offered. I find companions everywhere, and see much more of the people than if I were with a party of my own. It costs a little more, because I have to pay all fees, which are a great expense here for one, instead of dividing them among a party. To-day I met a Philadelphian on the steps of Cologne cathedral, and last week I found a family of parishioners at the Hotel St. Antoine in Antwerp.

My dearest mother, you cannot think how strange it seems to be writing in this little German inn, and knowing that you will read it in the old back parlor at home, where you have read my letters from Cambridge, Alexandria, and Philadelphia. Johnnie will bring it up from the post office some night, and Trip will break out into one of his horrible concerts two or three times while you are reading it. Then as soon as it is over, father will get out his big candle and you will put up the stockings, and all go up the old stairway to the old chambers, and to bed. Well, good-night and pleasant dreams to you all, and don't forget that I am off here wandering up and down these old countries and thinking ever so much about you. At Frankfort, where I hope to be early next week, I shall find your letters and have a talk with you again.

And now, good-night; peace and every blessing be with you always. God bless you all.

PHILLIPS.

CASSEL, GERMANY,
Monday Evening, October 9, 1865.

MY DEAR WILLIAM,—Just before I left Frankfort-on-the-Main to-day, I went to the bankers' and found there your good letter of September 22. It was my company on a lovely ride up the country to this queer old German town, whence I answer it from the dining-room of the Romlicher Kaiser hotel. A thousand thanks for it. I shall not write so good a one, but I will try to tell you what I have been doing in a very busy week since I wrote to mother last Monday night from Bonn. I left there by the Rhine boat and landed first at Kaiserwinter, on the right bank at the foot of the Drachenfels; climbed that hill and saw one of the loveliest views in the world from the old castle at its top. We went up through vineyards and looked down on the Rhine winding past the Seven Mountains ever so far towards the sea. Kaiserwinter is a charming little German village, and on my return from the hill I heard the bells chiming, and stopped to ask what it meant. I was told it was a "Fest" or village feast, and so roamed into the village to see it. It was the most perfect German picture. The young men of the village were firing at a mark in a little wine garden, and all the hamlet were gathered to drink the new wine and look at them. By and by the bird was shot down, and the man who shot it down was thereby king of the Feast. He had the privilege of choosing the prettiest girl in town for the queen, and then, with a rustic band of music, the procession, headed by the king and queen, marched through the old streets and called on all the gentry, who treated them and gave them contributions for a feast, to which they all returned in the garden. Here they made merry through the afternoon, and closed all with a dance. It was just like a German story book.

Juch-he, juch-he, juch-heise, heise, he,
So ging der fiedelbogen.

Think of being at a dance of German peasants on the Rhine! From here I took the boat again, and sailing down past vine-covered hills topped with ruined castles, I came at last to Coblentz. Here I stopped again and climbed to the Castle of Ehrenbreitstein, where was another view of the Rhine and the Moselle, which flows into it just here. Then the boat again, past the great Castle of Stolzenfels and countless others, one on almost every height, till we came to St. Goar, the most delightful little village on the left bank. Here another stop, and then on through the region of the choicest vineyards to Mayence, the quaintest of old fortified towns. You have no idea of the beauty of this river from Bonn to Mayence. I think we have rivers whose scenery by nature is as fine, but the castles and ruins have grown to be a part of the nature, and are not separable from it, and the soft October air and sunlight of those days showed everything at its utmost beauty. The trees were gorgeous in color with not a leaf fallen, and the vineyards climbing the hills, and perching on every inch of ground that faced the southern sun, were very interesting.

From Mayence I went to Worms, where Luther dared the Diet; then to Mannheim, and so to Heidelberg. Of all beautiful places this is the most perfect.

It lies along the Neckar, and is overlooked everywhere by the noblest of old ruined castles. Here is one of the great universities which I went to see. The boys looked pretty much like Cambridge juniors, except where here and there you see one with his face all slashed up from a duel. Let us be thankful Cambridge has not got to that.

From here I went up to Wiesbaden, one of the great watering and gambling places, a splendid German Saratoga. It was in full blast, and I saw the roulette and rouge-et-noir tables in the gorgeous saloons crowded day and night. At night, a great free concert by a splendid band, and illumination of the beautiful grounds. It was a strange sight. Then to Frankfort, where I spent Sunday at the Hotel de Russie. This is a fine town, part of it very old and quaint, part very new and fine; some good pictures, some good statuary, and an old cathedral, where I went and heard a German sermon and some splendid German music. Both Luther and Goethe were born here, and their houses still stand. To-day, up from Frankfort here, through one of the richest historic regions of all Germany. This is another of those old towns to which I am getting very used, and which delight me more and more. I like the Germans immensely. They are frank, kind, sociable, and hearty. They give you an idea of a people with ever so much yet to do in the world, capable of much fresh thought and action. Their language is like them, noble, vigorous, and simple. I am getting hold of it very well. They think for themselves and unselfishly, and they believe in America. Their peasants are poor, but seem intelligent, and their better classes have the most charming civility. I have seen more pretty women than I saw in all England, and I have not seen the best of Germany. I am impatient to get to Hanover, and Berlin, and Dresden, where one sees the finest specimens.

Here, then, you have another week's biography. Is it not full enough? My next will be from Dresden. I shall spend all this month in Germany, and about the first of November leave Vienna for the East. I am splendidly well and happy all the time, but very often, to-night, for instance, I would like to look in upon you all at home, and tell and hear a thousand things that will not go on paper. As to money, you will get two drafts, one in London and one in Cologne. These currencies with their perpetual changes are great nuisances. First, in Belgium, it was francs and centimes; then, in Holland, thalers and groschen; then, in Prussia, florins and kreutzers; and now back to thalers and groschen again.

I received a weekly "Herald" to-day; many thanks. Send one once in a while, say once a month, for the only paper on the Continent that pretends to give American news is the London "Times."

It is two months to-day since I sailed. How they have gone! And to me they have been the fullest months of my life. Not a day without something that I have longed all my life to see. So it will go on till I see the sight that I shall be most glad of all to see, you and father waiting on the wharf to see me land, as you came down before to see me sail.

Good-by; love in lots to father and mother, and Arthur and John and Trip, and Fred when you write. God bless you all. PHILL.

BERLIN,
Tuesday, October 17, 1865.

DEAR FATHER,—I will begin a letter here and finish it in Dresden, where I go to-day. I have been here since Friday, the longest stay I have made anywhere since I left London. Let me see, my last was to William from Cassel, a week ago yesterday. From there I went to Eisenach, where Luther's prison is in the old Wartburg Castle; then to Weimar, where Goethe and Schiller lived; then to Leipsic, where the great fair was going on; then to Halle, where the university is, and where I stayed and called on several of the professors, to whom I had letters. They were very cordial and pleasant, and I enjoyed my visit there very much; then to Wittenberg, which is the great shrine of Luther: his house just as he left it, the church where he preached and nailed his Theses to the door, his grave, his monument, and countless other memorials of him. Melanchthon lived here too, and his house is still preserved. Thence to Magdeburg, a fine old town with a fine old cathedral, and then to this Berlin, the Prussian capital, one of the brightest and most beautiful of all the great cities of Europe. I am staying at the Hôtel du Nord, in the street called Unter den Linden, right opposite the splendid statue of Frederick the Great, and in view of a dozen noble buildings, the palace, museum, university, etc. Here is one of the great picture galleries, which I have explored thoroughly and know well. I have been to several private collections besides. There are many Americans here. I went to a soirée on Saturday evening at our minister's, Governor Wright's, and met some fifty. I have also seen a good deal of the family of Dr. Abbott, to whom I had a letter, and who is a capital fellow. I have dined there two or three times, and have met his father-in-law, Mr. Fay, formerly our minister to Switzerland, who has given me a good letter to Motley in Vienna. You see I do not lack for company and friends. I found that the Germans were much interested in our freedmen, and I got quite back into my last winter's harness, in making a speech on the subject to a meeting of German gentlemen at the American embassy. Tell Fred I used him. These Germans are with us out and out. The professors at Halle are Abolitionists of the strongest sort. It is very refreshing to be with them after being in England. Berlin is a charming city, the headquarters of art and science and music. I went to a capital concert here last night. I almost hate to leave the town.

I get no letters since I left Frankfort, and shall not now till next week, when I arrive at Munich. I have ordered them sent there. You have no idea what eras in a traveler's life are his arrivals at places where his letters meet him. I always rush to the banker's for them the first thing.

MUNICH, Thursday Evening, October 26.

I beg pardon most humbly for this long gap. The truth was I got as far as that, and then went to dinner, my last day, at Dr. Abbott's, and right after dinner left Berlin for Dresden, and since then have been so busy that letter writing has been neglected. I reached here yesterday, and found letters from father and mother and Fred and Franks, all in one bundle; and to-day I dropped in at the banker's again and found William's letter of the 3d; so now I certainly must write, and will go back to where I left off in Berlin a week ago last Monday. I rode direct to Dresden, where I spent two days; and such days! Oh, if you could see the picture gallery there! it has the picture of the world which I have waited years to see, Raphael's Madonna di San Sisto. I will not say anything about it, because there is no use trying to tell what a man feels who has been wanting to enjoy something for fifteen years, and when it comes finds it is something unspeakably beyond what he had dreamed.

The other rooms of the gallery are rich in the great paintings of the world. Then I took the train to Prague, passing into Bohemia and showing my passport to the inquisitive Austrian officials at Bodenach. Prague is the queerest old Austrian town, with splendid views, grand old churches, some good pictures, fine palaces, and the strangest old synagogue in Europe. Then to Nuremberg, the oldest-looking town on the Continent; old without an admixture or intrusion of the new, to-day as completely a town of three hundred years ago as it was then. Tell William to read you Longfellow's poem of "Nuremberg" aloud to-night, and you will know just what I saw and how I felt. From Nuremberg to Ratisbon, another of the very old towns, with one of the most perfect cathedrals and the Valhalla or Temple of Fame, on the banks of the Danube. Here was my first sight of the great river. Then from Ratisbon here, where I am sitting in my room of the third story of the Vierjahreszeiten (that means "Four Seasons") Hotel, writing this letter to you. Munich is in its beauty a new town, but splendidly full of interest. Let me see. Here is the great Gallery of Old Pictures, the Gallery of Moderns, one of the great sculpture galleries of the world, the great royal foundry, the second greatest library, the largest bronze statue, the finest church glass, and the noblest public buildings in Europe. Is that enough, and is n't this last a week to cross the Atlantic for? Dresden, Prague, Nuremberg, and Munich! I will say no more about them, but be sure I am very well contented with my lot.

Your letters were delightful to get. I could see you all sitting around the table writing them and talking as the work went on. How you must have enjoyed your visit from Fred! I am very glad that Franks went on with him. He is a nice boy, a great pet of mine, and more than that, a fellow of a great deal of earnestness, ability, determination, and sterling character. You may well be glad to have given him so much enjoyment as he seems to have had in Boston. Of course, before this they are both hard at work again in Philadelphia.

I shall be here one day longer, and then leave for Salzburg, Vienna, Pesth, and Trieste, whence I expect to sail on the 10th of November for the great East. You will gather from my letter that all goes well and I am very happy. There has not been an hour since I left New York that has not been full of pleasure, not a day that has not been lighted up by seeing some of the sights for which I have longed. And all the East and Italy and France and much of England and Switzerland is yet in store. Hurrah!

This place is full of English and Americans. I had a discussion at the table d'hôte yesterday with an English gentleman, during which lots of American secessionists got up and left. General McClellan is in Dresden, but I did not see him, and slept soundly in the same city with the great Coppery hero.

I have a letter from Mr. Coffin, who reports all well

in the church matters. He says Dr. Butler is doing everything there is to do, so I feel easier to be wandering about here in this delightful way.

And now good-night. Before you get this I shall be on my way to the Lands of the Sun. Think of me, pray for me, and write to me. God bless you, and keep us all, and bring us safe together again by and by. Lots of love to all. PHILLIPS.

Poor Trip!!

STEAMBOAT FRANCIS-JOSEPH, ON THE DANUBE,
Sunday, November 5, 1865.

DEAR WILLIAM, — This is the funniest yet. Here I am fairly on my way to the East. I am sitting in a little cabin, with a perfect Babel about me. Every language except English is in my ears, German, Italian, French, Hungarian, Greek, and I know not how many more besides. Outside it is raining guns. The old river is broad, shallow, and vilely muddy. The banks are low and gravelly, except where here and there the great Carpathian Mountains gather down about the stream and make a grand gorge where the river goes whirling and dashing through. We have just done breakfast, which is served at ten o'clock, with meats and poor Hungarian wines. Every now and then we pass a miserable little Turkish village, with its dirty, strange-dressed peasants. It is not much like Sunday morning, but I must make the best of it, and do not know how I can use it better than by writing home, so here goes.

You have kept the run of me, I hope, as far as Munich, the most beautiful of German cities. From there I took the train to Salzburg, where I spent two days. One of them was occupied in a long excursion to the Königsee, a lake in the Styrian Alps, shut in by snowy-topped mountains, with glaciers all down their sides. The lake itself is lovely, with its deep green waters, and picturesque Tyrolese boatmen row you up to its head and back again. Then you stop and dine at a little Alpine cottage inn at the foot, and after dinner drive to Berchtesgaden, where the great salt mines are. Here you dress up in full miner's rig, and walk a mile or two into the heart of a mountain, and then, sitting down on two parallel bars with a man in front to hold your legs, you slide like lightning down into the bowels of the earth and come to a great salt lake (lit up by hundreds of lamps) which you are rowed across by two subterranean beings who look like fiends; then another walk and another slide bring you to a vast temple, nobody knows how far under ground, with a dome of infinite darkness, where some more fiends are drawing up the salt rock from unfathomable depths still below. All the way, as your lamp shines on the walls or ceilings, they sparkle all over with the precious crystals; then some more avenues, till you reach the salt grotto where the choicest specimens have been collected, and there you sit down on a little railway car, which plunges along with you through the mountain till it whirls you at last out into daylight, and your visit to the great salt mines is over. It is one of the most unique and splendid things to do in Europe. I would n't have missed its interest and beauty for anything. My second day in Salzburg was Sunday. I went to all the churches and heard their services and music, and saw the people in their holiday dress. Of course it is all Roman Catholic; there is nothing Protestant in the town. In the afternoon I went up to the great castle and saw the view, which is one of the noblest on the Continent. Then I hunted up the grave of old Paracelsus, the middle-age magician, and his house, where I amazed an old German lady by insisting on seeing his room, which I succeeded in doing and in which I was much interested. Then to the houses where Mozart was born and where he lived, and wound up by following a funeral procession, which went chanting with banners and incense through the town, into an old graveyard behind one of the churches.

From Salzburg by Linz to Vienna. What shall I say about Vienna? Here is another of the great picture galleries, with its Raphaels, Titians, Rembrandts, Rubenses, and countless others, whom one learns to know and admire in these splendid collections. Pictures and churches are the two great attractions of these old towns. Vienna has a grand old cathedral with the most beautiful of Gothic spires. I was there on All Saints' Day and heard high mass, with an old cardinal officiating, and a full band and splendid choir of men and boys doing the music.

The next day was All Souls', when the Romish Church commemorates the dead. All the churches were draped in mourning, masses were sung, the graveyards were full of people, and in one of the churches the vaults were thrown open and the coffins of the Austrian emperors from time immemorial were shown to hosts of people, who crawled down to see them, among whom was I. In Munich they do better still, and show you the very corpses of their emperors preserved in glass chests full of spirits. I did not see their majesties, but I saw an old saint, six hundred years old, kept in this way in one of the churches. Vienna is great in relics. A piece of the tablecloth of the Last Supper, a piece of John the Baptist's robes, St. Anne's arm-bone, nails from the Cross, a large piece of the Cross, and lots of others, — all these are used at the coronations of the emperors. I dined at Vienna with Mr. Motley of the "Dutch Republic," who is our minister there, and found him full of hospitality and very pleasant. I had a letter to him from Mr. Fay in Berlin. I stayed here three days, and bought my last outfits, thick boots, blankets, etc., for the East.

At Vienna I met Dr. Leeds of Philadelphia (formerly of Salem), who is also for the East, and we joined company for the present. It is almost necessary, and certainly a great deal cheaper, to have some company in Syria. We left Vienna on Friday, and concluded to go down the Danube to Constantinople, thence by steamer to Beyrout, thence through Syria to Jerusalem, getting to Bethlehem at Christmas, when there is a great service there; then to Jaffa, and thence to Egypt; then Greece, and so back to Italy. We took rail to Pesth and then to Baziasch on the river, where we took a steamer which carries us to Tchernavoda, whence we cross by rail to Kustenji on the Black Sea, where another steamer meets and takes us down to Constantinople. (Can you find these places on the map?) We have begun to find the delays and the irregularities of Eastern travel. Already we have changed our steamer three times as the river became shallower or deeper. Last night we reached Orsova at about dusk, and to our surprise found that the boats did n't travel after dark, so we laid up there till morning. We shall probably reach Constantinople on Wednesday night instead of Tuesday morning, as we were told. I think it very probable that our course may be so slow that I shall give up Egypt and sail right from Jaffa to Greece, but I cannot tell. I don't worry ahead. Italy is before me all the while, and I must get a great deal of time there. I do not care as much for Egypt. I certainly shall not go up the Nile, so tell mother she need not worry about the Pyramids.

My next letters from home will not reach me till I get to Alexandria or Athens, so I am shut off from communication with home till then, but you will hear from me. I received yours and father's and mother's letters in Vienna, and am glad to hear of all being so well. Keep on writing; I shall get them some time or other. I believe none have missed me yet, and if you could see how glad I am to get them, you would not mind writing.

We crossed the Turkish line this morning, so we are in the Sultan's dominions now. Our passports bear his stamp, and we feel already like Turks. How far off it seems! I shall not have a chance to mail this till we get to Constantinople, and before you get it I shall be in the Holy Land. Think of me there, and be sure that I am thinking of you all.

I am perfectly well and ready for anything. Three months next Thursday since I sailed. What a three months they have been. Nine more like them, and then I will come back to work again. May God keep us all.

PHILL.

IN THE BOSPHORUS,
Thursday, November 9, 1865.

I open this to tell you that with many delays and disappointments we have come thus far. We finished our sail on the Danube on Tuesday about noon, and landing at Tchernavoda took the railway across the Peninsula to Kustenji. It was funny to find an English-built railway here, with English conductors and engineers in turbans. We had gone about five miles when we came down with a thump, and found that the train had run off the track and broken the rails to pieces, so we had to wait there all day till another train could be sent for, and we did not reach the Black Sea till nine o'clock at night. We took ship at once, and yesterday had the most pleasant sail down to the Bosphorus, which we entered just at four o'clock, and sailed as far as this place, whose name I can't find out, about halfway down the Bosphorus, where we were quarantined last night, and this morning are waiting for the fog to clear away to go on to Constantinople, which is only an hour off. Think of that! This will be mailed from among the minarets, and before to-night I hope to see the Mosque of St. Sophia and look upon the dancing dervishes.

Before you get this, Thanksgiving will have come and passed. I hope you had a pleasant one. I suppose I shall be only just in time if I wish you now a merry Christmas. So I do with all my heart. I shall spend mine in Bethlehem.

CONSTANTINOPLE,
Sunday, November 12.

There has been no mail before to-night, so I open this again to say we have been three days here in Constantinople. They have been very full of sightseeing. It is the strangest life to look at, and like a dream every hour. I have seen St. Sophia, the bazaars, the howling dervishes, the dancing dervishes, the Sultan, and much besides, of which I will tell you some other time. To-morrow we leave for Smyrna. I received the American papers from our minister here, and shall get your letters when I reach Alexandria, or Athens, about New Year's.

I have met here a young Mr. W. S. Appleton of Boston, son of Nathan Appleton, I believe, who joins us in our trip to Syria. He is a good fellow, so with our dragoman and servants we shall make a strong party. Good-by for the third time. Love to all.

PHILL.

SMYRNA, Sunday Afternoon,
November 19, 1865.

DEAR MOTHER, — I will just begin a letter now, though I do not know whence or when I can send it to you. It will seem a little like talking to you to be writing it, at any rate. I am here in Smyrna, and just now especially full of the trip I made yesterday to Ephesus. So I will begin with that. They have a railway to within three miles, and we took the train early in the morning to Ayasoluk, a miserable little Turkish village, whose only interest is an old ruined castle, and the remains of a mosque which is built on the site of the church where St. John the Evangelist preached, and under which he is said to be buried. We cannot, of course, be sure of it, but it seems by no means unlikely; and I chose, as I stood there, to believe it true. Then we rode on horseback across a broad plain, where the great city once stood, and where now there is not a trace of life save here and there a poor Turk straggling about in the lazy way of this wretched people. We came finally to a pass between two hills, and here the ruins began. We had only two hours to examine them, and many of the sites are doubtful. The great Temple of Diana is altogether gone; but the one thing most certain of all, about which there can be no doubt, is the theatre where the great meeting was held, in the Book of Acts, and where Paul tried to go in to the people. There it is, a vast amphitheatre in the side of the hill, in ruins of course, but as clearly and evidently the theatre as it was the day he saw it. Then there is the market-place where Demetrius addressed the craftsmen; and they point out also the School of Tyrannus, where Paul taught.

They show you also the tomb of Mary Magdalene, but this is uncertain. The theatre is the one certain building which is referred to in the Bible story. Many of the ruins of other buildings, temples, race-courses, gymnasia, etc., are very beautiful, and the situation of the old city must have been charming. Was not this worth seeing? Even coming a good way for? And now to tell you how we came here. Our steamer left Constantinople last Monday afternoon, sailed down the Sea of Marmora, through the Dardanelles, past the plain of Troy, where you see the whole scene of the old war, and the funeral mounds still standing on the shore, by the islands of Lemnos, Imbros, and Tenedos, keeping inside of them. The sea was very rough, and we were at last obliged to come to anchor in a little bay between Mitylene and the mainland. (St. Paul stopped at Mitylene, you know.) Here we had to stay thirty-six hours, waiting for smoother weather. We went ashore and roamed about, but there was not much to see,—Turks, and their huts and camels and donkeys.

We sailed on Thursday morning again, and Friday morning landed here at Smyrna. I wish you could see this town; it is the strangest mixture in the world. Turks, Greeks, and Armenians, in their strange costumes, fill the little dirty streets. The bazaars are full of cross-legged merchants praising their wares in all sorts of gibberish: Persian carpets, shawls, slippers, with figs, fruits, and spices, all of the East, Eastern. Every now and then a long caravan of camels laden with bales goes winding through, just arrived from Persia, with its wild-looking drivers shouting and screaming to make way for them. This morning, we went to the English chapel, which is at the English Consulate, and heard a sermon from the old chaplain who has been here for thirty years. This afternoon, to the Armenian church, where there was a strange sort of service going on in their native language. The strangest services I have seen were those of the howling dervishes and the whirling dervishes in Constantinople. They are a kind of order of Mohammedans; the former make all their worship consist in working themselves up into frenzy by roaring and screaming; the latter, by whirling round and round their church till they are dizzy. I saw both, and shall never see anything more curious in the way of religious service. In Constantinople, I went all over the great Mosque of St. Sophia, the greatest of mosques, originally built for a Christian church, and still having many crosses and other Christian symbols uneffaced upon its walls. It is very curious and impressive, and very sacred among the Mohammedans. Here, and in all their sacred buildings, you have to take off your shoes and enter in stocking-feet.

We live oddly here. Our fare everywhere is a mixture of French and Turkish diet, and as unlike home as you can conceive. On board boat we rise about eight, and find a cup of coffee waiting in the cabin.

That is all till ten, when we have a full meal, fish, meat, pastry, fruit, and wine. Then at five or six a dinner of about the same, and in the evening tea, so you see we do not suffer. Traveling here in the East is very slow and very expensive; but now that I am here, I had better do it thoroughly, and it is all interesting. We were two days behind time in reaching this place, and shall be slow in getting to Beyrout. The Ægean is the most uncertain sea in the world, but I shall certainly spend Christmas at Bethlehem, and Thanksgiving probably at Damascus. I am quite well off for company with Dr. Leeds and Mr. Appleton, who joined us at Constantinople. I am perfectly well and am having a splendid time.

ON BOARD STEAMER GODAVERY,
Monday, November 20.

We came aboard the steamer this morning to sail for Beyrout. She is a French steamer just arrived from Marseilles, and going to Alexandria. I wish you could see this bay of Smyrna, this lovely morning. Everything is as perfect as a picture, and the air on deck is like the softest summer. We shall be four or five days on board, if all goes well, and I look forward to it with much enjoyment. This morning, as we sat at breakfast, you would have liked to see a big mulatto come in and be greeted by the captain and officers with immense respect as "Pasha," and take his seat alongside of my friend Dr. Leeds, and eat his breakfast with us in the most composed and matter-of-course way. I wondered what they would have said to it in Philadelphia?

Wednesday, November 22.

We are still pushing along towards Beyrout. The weather so far has been delightful, and the sea not at all rough. The scenery is perfect, as we go winding along among the many islands, every one of them a place of some old associations, the most interesting we have seen, but I was sorry to pass by Patmos (where St. John was banished and wrote the Revelation) in the night, so that we saw nothing of it. Yesterday we stopped two hours at Rhodes, but the quarantine is in force there at present and we were not allowed to land. Just enough cholera remains hanging about these parts to keep the quarantine alive, and that is the only danger from it now. I hear there is a ten days' quarantine in Greece, which will seriously inconvenience me if I go there. The fear seems to be that the cholera will just linger along through the winter, and then break out with more violence next summer. However, I am in no danger now, nor shall be while I am in the East.

Thursday, November 23.

Here we are, laid by for a day to discharge and receive cargo at Messina, which you will find almost at the very northeast corner of the Levant. The place, which we can see plainly from the ship, is a little straggling village with its mosque. Lines of camels are continually winding in and out, carrying back into the interior the goods we bring. The only interest of the country is, that just behind those hills there lies the old town of Tarsus, where St. Paul was born, and where there still stands an old church, which they say he built. We have no time to go there, and must be content to know just where it lies. In the distance the

Taurus Mountains, covered with snow, are very grand. The weather is superb, as soft as June. Last night was the most gorgeous starlight I ever saw.

Saturday, November 25.

I must finish this letter now, for to-night we shall be at Beyrout, and I must mail it. All day yesterday we were lying in front of Alexandretta (Iskanderoon), the port of Aleppo, where we discharged part of our cargo and took on board a lot of cotton. We went ashore and wandered about the picturesque and dirty little Turkish town. It had a quaint old bazaar, as all these places have, where the business of the place is carried on. Palm-trees, camels, and women muffled in white with only the eyes looking out, and all sorts of odd male costumes, made it a very Eastern picture. The day was oppressively hot, like August in Boston.

We sailed at night, and arrived early this morning at Latakia, a pretty little town among the trees, with mosques and minarets and an old castle. Here we only stayed two hours, and then started again for Beyrout. We stopped once more at Tripolis. At Beyrout our voyage ends. There we shall get a dragoman and horses, and ride down the coast to Sidon and Tyre; then by the mountains up northeast to Baalbec; from there to Lebanon and the Cedars; then down to Damascus; thence across to the Lake of Galilee and Tiberias, to Nazareth, to Mt. Carmel on the coast; from there to Samaria, and thence down to Jerusalem. That is our route now, but it may be altered. Does n't it sound interesting? It will take in all about three weeks, and I will write again from Jerusalem. Now good-by. I am very well, and think much of you all.

DAMASCUS.

God bless and keep you all, and bring us together again. Love to all. Your loving son,
PHILLIPS.

GRAND HÔTEL DE DAMAS,
Sunday Evening, December 3, 1865.

DEAR FATHER, — Here I am in Damascus. I have reached the most easterly point of all my travels. I am in the oldest city of the world, and will write you how I reached here and what it looks like. My last, which I suppose was sent from Beyrout, was written on the steamer from Smyrna. We landed at Beyrout a week ago to-day, and went to church in the morning at the American mission, and in the afternoon at the English consulate. We had a host of dragomans about us, and selecting one, we set him at work to make his preparations for our long Syrian journey. We engage him to take us to Jaffa, paying all charges at an expense of five pounds ten shillings per day for the party. Monday we spent in making our arrangements, trying horses, getting our contract with the dragoman certified before the American consul, etc., etc.

Tuesday morning early our party might have been seen mounting and making ready for departure at the door of the Hôtel de l'Orient, surrounded by a great crowd of curious natives. Let me tell you of what our caravan consists. Remember, we are to travel thirty days or more, dependent almost wholly upon what we carry with us. First, of the animals: there are six horses, six mules, and two donkeys. The six horses are ridden by Dr. Leeds, Mr. Appleton, and François his French courier; by P. B., and Ibrahim Amatury, our native dragoman, an invaluable person, who speaks many languages and does all sorts of things; and Achmet, the muleteer, who owns the horses and goes with us to look after their welfare. Scattered about among the animals come our other attendants, namely, Antonio, the cook, a native of Bagdad, and Luin his waiter, Ibrahim, Luttuf, a boy from Damascus who sings Arabic love songs, Hoseim, and Elias, these last four, mule drivers and general servants. So our whole corps, you see, is twelve. Our baggage always starts off first, and we follow in an hour or two. Then we stop to lunch at midday, and let them get ahead again, and arrive at our camping-place for the night to find the tents all pitched and dinner ready. Our horses are good. I am mounted on a bay horse (not quite as big as Robin), which would n't make much show on the Mill Dam, but has stood it splendidly, so far, over these hard roads.

We left Beyrout early this morning on the road which a French company have built all the way to Damascus. We kept this road all day. We wound up Mt. Lebanon by slow degrees, through olive groves and mulberry-trees, with the snowy summits of the highest peaks looking down upon us, passing several monasteries, which swarm all along these hills. At noon we made our first halt, and lunched at the Khan Sheik Mahmoud, a rude sort of lodging-place halfway up. About three in the afternoon, we reached the top of the range, and began to descend into the valley between Lebanon and Anti-Lebanon, called, of old, Cœle-Syria. Here Mt. Hermon first loomed in sight, with its great round snow-covered top off to the southeast. At the foot of Lebanon we came to the little village of Mecseh, just outside of which we pitched our first camp and spent the night. We were a very picturesque group, I assure you, by our night fire, with our Syrians in their striking costumes and the wild mountain rising behind us. We have two large tents: Dr. Leeds, Appleton, and I sleep in one, and the rest of the company in the other. We live well, our cook is firstrate, and provisions are plenty. The middle of the day is intensely warm, the nights very cold, but the weather so far splendidly clear.

Wednesday morning we were off again early, and leaving the French road soon struck off through the town of Zahleh, and so along up the valley towards Baalbec. We stopped a few minutes at a little village to see what they call "Noah's Tomb," which is a queer thing in a long house; a kind of grave, about fifty yards long, in which they say the patriarch was buried. He must have been about as long as St. Paul's church. It is a sacred place and covered all over with offerings. We stopped this day to lunch by an old mill on the river Litâny, and then, after a long, hot afternoon ride, about five o'clock we saw before us the ruins of Baalbec. We galloped in, pitched our tents in the great court of the Temple of the Sun, and ate our dinner in sight of the grand remains. I cannot describe to you the splendor of the moonlight that night, as we roamed about and saw the Temple of the Sun, with its enormous columns, and the Temple of Jupiter close by it, both in ruins, but both sublime. We slept well in the old temple court. Our guides told us of a jackal prowling around at night, but I cannot boast of having seen him. I wish I had. Right opposite we saw the snowy hills on which the Lebanon cedars grew, but had no time to visit them.

Thursday, Thanksgiving Day, we thought much of

America and home. We spent the forenoon in carefully going over the ruins, which are immense and very beautiful. At noon we took horses, and now began, striking for Damascus, to cross the Anti-Lebanon range. We lunched under a fine old walnut-tree, two hours from Baalbec, in the midst of a hot and stony plain. Then crossing another ridge, on the top of which we saw the mosque which contains the tomb of Seth, the son of Adam, we came by a steep, zigzag Roman road into the loveliest little green valley, up which we rode to the town of Sigâya, where we encamped that night, and while our Thanksgiving dinner was getting ready roamed about the little town, to the great wonder and bewilderment of the people, who came about us in crowds. These Syrian villages are the most miserable places on earth. As soon as you enter one, the children turn out at your heels, crying, "Backsheesh," and the squalid, half-dressed men and women creep to the doors and gaze vacantly at you. The houses are of mud and stones, one story high, so that you see the tops of the houses as you ride, with sometimes a Moslem on them saying his prayers towards Mecca, or a lazy group cooking themselves in the sun. Our Thanksgiving dinner was a great success. We had brought a turkey especially from Beyrout, and a choice bottle of wine. Antoine made us a superb plum pudding, we drank everybody's health at home, and were supremely patriotic. Then we smoked our pipes and went to bed, and I for one dreamed I was in America.

Friday morning early, off again up the valley of Sigâya, past several little villages, over hot stones, till we lunched by a heap of rocks in an open field, the only shade for miles and miles. Then in the afternoon we began to get into a deep gorge, and soon came to a fine waterfall, and so felt we were getting somewhere near Damascus, because this was the river Barada, formerly the Abana. ("Are not Abana and Pharphar, rivers of Damascus, better than all the waters of Israel?")

We kept along this stream, passed the old town of Abila, the scenery growing finer and finer all the afternoon. On a hilltop close by we saw the old tomb of Abel, the son of Adam, and so about dusk came to the beautiful fountain of El Fijeh, where we camped. It is a spring gushing out of the rock, over which stand two ruined temples, surrounded by deep groves. It is one of the sources of the Abana. We slept here, and the next morning left early, crossed the last range of Anti-Lebanon, and, as we climbed the final peak and stood beside a little ruined dome upon its top, there was Damascus in the valley, with its beauty all about it. No city ever looked so lovely; a broad girdle of gardens encircles it, and its domes and minarets fill up the picture within, while the Abana on one side and the Pharphar on the other come bringing their tribute of waters to it. We were soon down the hill, and a quick trot carried us through the gardens, thick with pomegranates, oranges, and citrons, into the town itself, where for a day or two we exchanged tent life for that at the Grand Hotel.

Now about the town. This is the most picturesque of Oriental cities, where you see nothing but Orientals, no Frank hat but your own; where Bedouins fresh from the desert crowd you in the streets; where you sit in the court-yard of your hotel, hear the fountain splashing in the centre, and see the orange-trees around it; where the promenade is on the house-top, and the narrow streets are full of dogs, donkeys, and camels. It is a delightful town; and then its history! Here is the street called "Straight," where Judas lived, keeping its old name (see Acts ix). They show you the house of Judas, where Paul lodged, and the house of Ananias. On the wall you see the place where Paul was let down in the basket, and even the place of his conversion is kept by a tradition; nay, more, the old house of Naaman the Syrian is shown, with a hospital for lepers close by it. The poor creatures came and begged alms of us as we were looking. And the old mosque which was once a Christian church is said to have been, further back, the "House of Rimmon" of the old Testament. At any rate here is the old town, and all these things were here, and the life in this old stagnant East is just about the same to-day that it was then.

This morning I went to the Greek church and saw a miserable mummery. This was my only church-going. There are not enough English here to keep up an English service. The English consul, Mr. Rogers, called on us last night, and says he is almost alone here.

You will wonder why I have written you all this. The truth is, I have written partly for myself. I don't dare to hope that it will all interest you, but I want to keep a pretty full account of this Syrian trip, and so put it down day by day. Please keep my letters. To-morrow we leave for Cæsarea and Tyre. You will see our route is somewhat changed since I wrote to mother. I hope to get letters from you all at Jerusalem at Christmas. I am perfectly well, with good spirits and lots of appetite, but sometimes I think how good it will be to get home again and think this over. I wonder how you all do, and I pray you are well. Good-by; I don't know when you will get this, probably not till after New Year's, when I shall be in Egypt or in Greece. I am thirty years old next week. God bless and keep you all.

PHILLIPS.

IN TENT AT RASCHEYA, SYRIA,
Tuesday, December 5, 1865.

DEAR WILLIAM, — I wrote to father from Damascus on Sunday, and I will continue my plan of a journal while I am in Syria. I want you to keep the letters, for they will be all that I shall have to recall the details of my route. Let's see, then. Monday morning, early, we went out with the janizary of the British consul, who was kindly loaned for the occasion, and went over the great mosque. Except for its history, there is not much of interest about it, but it is curious here, as in St. Sophia and elsewhere, to see how in changing a Christian church to Moslem purposes they have left ever so many Christian emblems uneffaced; the communion cup is still upon the bronze doors, and the outside has a walled up doorway with the inscription, "Thy Kingdom, O Christ, is an everlasting Kingdom, and thy Dominion endureth from generation to generation." After the mosque, we roamed about the bazaars, especially a dim little picturesque hole where the silversmiths of Damascus do their beautiful work.

At two o'clock we were on horseback again, and riding out on the French road, through the gardens that girdle the city, along the sparkling Abana. We said good-by to Damascus, and encamped for the night at Dinas, a little village about twelve miles off in the

Anti-Lebanon mountains. The night was very cold, and early this morning we were off, and have ridden eight hours to-day, still over the Anti-Lebanon. We passed an old castle and temple in ruins about noon, perhaps one of the old Baal temples which abounded in this region of Hermon. Then we stopped and lunched under a little group of trees by the wayside, and at last, after a hard day's ride, came to our camp-ground. It is a larger village than usual, but very forlorn. There is an old castle on the hill, to which we wandered before dinner and saw its Turkish garrison. This was one of the towns where the massacre of the Christians by the Druses was most terrible in 1860, and much of it is still in ruins. But the most interesting thing of all is Mt. Hermon. There it lies to-night above the town, with its broad top covered with snow, — a splendid old hill, the northern limit of Palestine. We have had it in sight from time to time for a week, and here we are close to its feet, and, sitting among our Syrians round our fire, we fancy we can see the old Israelites doing "their idolatry on this one of the high places," where the old altar still stands. Here, just now, came the commander of cavalry from the pasha of the town, to offer the Franks his profound regards and any help they wanted. You should have heard the palaver that went on between us with our good Ibrahim for interpreter.

CAMP AT CÆSAREA PHILIPPI.
Thursday Evening, December 7.

Here we are, encamped in a grove of old olive-trees close to Banyas, which is on the site of the old Cæsarea Philippi on one of the southern spurs of Mt. Hermon, and close to the source of the Jordan. Yesterday morning we broke up camp at Rascheya, and started across the Anti-Lebanon mountains to visit the great gorge and natural bridge of the Litâny. It was a terrible day's ride. We were in the saddle ten hours, over the most abominable road. We reached the gorge about three o'clock, and were well repaid. The river is very fine, and the great chasm through which it breaks its way is bold and picturesque. We then went to Hasbeya, whither our mules had preceded us by a shorter route, and where we arrived after dark. This morning we rode from there over rough hills, till at last we came out into the Jordan valley, and saw far off before us the waters of Lake Merom, through which the Jordan flows. It was a pleasant ride then around the spur of Mt. Hermon, which we are getting to know like an old friend, over fields full of the crocus, or, as our dragoman called it, "the lily of the field," which was very beautiful, and neither sowing nor spinning, till we came in sight of the great castle on the hill and soon rode into this little village.

Here we lunched, drinking the Jordan water, and then spent the afternoon in wandering about where the sacred river bursts out of a deep cave on which was built first the Temple of Baal, then of the Greek god Pan, then of the Roman Cæsar, and now there stands there a little white Mohammedan mosque. The whole scene is very beautiful. The Jordan runs in many streams among the ruins, and is overgrown with laurels and olives. The present village is miserably mean. Its inhabitants are Mohammedans, and in the mountains around are the wild Bedouins. This is the first night we have kept watch. This, you know, is the place where Christ had the conversation with

St. Peter, and many put the Transfiguration on some one of the spurs of Hermon which surround us. This is the first spot that we have touched where Christ himself has been, and it is full of interest. Our weather is still perfect, and to-night soft and warm, with gorgeous starlight. An English gentleman and his sister, going from Jerusalem to Damascus, are encamped close to us.

TYRE, Sunday Afternoon,
December 10, 1865.

Please get your Bible and read Ezekiel's Prophecy, and then imagine me set down among the ruins of this old Queen of the Seas. Friday morning we left Banyas and rode across the plain of Huleh or Merom. Here we stopped and saw another of the fountains of the Jordan at Laish or Dan. You will find all about it in Judges xviii. It is a beautiful spot, a little hill with springs bursting out all around its roots, and running in many channels down the fertile plain towards Lake Merom. Now we have reached the northern border, and may look over into Palestine from Dan towards Beersheba. Out of the plain we struck again into the mountains, and lunched by a picturesque little bridge over the Litâny, under the shadow of a splendid great Phœnician castle, famous in Crusaders' history, which overlooks all the country from a lofty hill. We spent that night at the village of Nabatiya. It was our first rainy night, and what with the tent pins giving way and the Syrian floods pouring down through the thin places of our tent roof and the high wind making the sides rattle terribly, we had an exciting night of it. Next morning we were off in the rain, striking right for the coast. About noon we saw the sea, and lunched on a hill that overlooks it, near the little village of Toosa. Then it cleared up, and our afternoon's ride was glorious. We wound down the hill, crossed our old friend the Litâny near its mouth, and so saw the last of it, and then kept down the shore with Tyre right before us, reaching it in about three hours. It used to be an island, but Alexander built a causeway out to it, and the water has heaped up the sand on both sides of the isthmus till it is a broad-necked peninsula. It is the most ruined of ruins. An old church, once splendid, in which Origen and Frederick Barbarossa were buried, is the only building they ever pretend to show and that you can hardly make out at all. Everything else is gone.

The seashore is lined with piles of splendid marble and granite columns, worn out of shape by the waters and half sunk in the sand. The place where Hiram lived in magnificence may have been this poor little house which we have hired to spend Sunday in. It has one big room through which the family of queer-looking people whom we have dispossessed circulate continually, and where we three sleep and eat while our cookery goes on in the yard outside. The whole island is only about three quarters by one half mile, and half of this now is utterly covered with rubbish. But the view is splendid to-day. On one side we look out upon the noble Mediterranean, and feel (at least I do) as if the stretch of waters established some sort of communication with home. On the other side stretches the long coast, with the hills of Lebanon skirting it, and old Hermon with his snowy top, the watch-tower of all this country, glistening in the sun beyond. Just round that point up the coast lies Sidon, the mother-city of this Tyre, and the little white mosque on the hill this side of it marks the place of Sarepta, the town where Elijah met the widow.

All our yesterday's ride was through the coasts of Tyre and Sidon, and any spot our horses passed may have been the scene of Christ's meeting with the Syrophœnician woman. "What city is like to Tyrus, to the destroyed in the midst of the sea." Being the only Franks in town, we make some little sensation. All day the Star-Spangled Banner has been seen flying in our honor on the house of an old gentleman who acts here as our consular agent for the transaction of nobody knows what business, and this afternoon he sent us word that he would be glad to have us visit him. We went, of course, taking Ibrahim for interpreter, and were soon squatted on a divan around a room whose only other furniture was the rugs on the floor. Narghilehs and coffee were brought, and then we made civil speeches to each other, which were duly translated, and left with lots of salaams and wishes for eternal prosperity. Then our quarters have been besieged all day with natives small and large, male and female, bringing "Antikers," as they call them, rings, coins, seals, etc., dug up among the ruins, for us to buy at big prices. Fortunately Appleton is a coin collector, and so satisfies them for the party.

These last two weeks have been like a curious sort of dream; all the old Bible story has seemed so strangely about us, — the great flocks of sheep that we meet everywhere, wandering with their wild shepherds over the hills; the lines of loaded camels that go laboring across the horizon; the sowers in the field scattering their seed, half on the stony ground (it is almost paved with stones), and half among the great thorn bushes that grow up every-where; the little villages, half a dozen every day, with the people on the house-tops; the wild men of the desert, who come suddenly in your way among the hills; and the families with mules and asses, women and children, who seem to have no purpose in their traveling but just to fill up your picture for you. Far off to the east, from time to time the high hills, the hills of Bashan. (Think of being in the dominions of that old Og whom we have always read of in the Psalter.) Olive-trees, palms, fig-trees and pomegranates, all this, and Lebanon, Damascus, Hermon, Jordan, Cæsarea, and Tyre; it certainly makes a strange two weeks. The next two will be fuller still from here to Jerusalem. You shall hear of it. . . .

I shall send this from Acre. I hope you will get these Eastern letters. Good-by now. God bless you all.

PHILL.

HAIFA, AT THE FOOT OF MT. CARMEL,
Monday Evening, December 12, 1865.

DEAR MOTHER, — I sent a letter to William from Tyre, which I hope he received. I will carry on my story from there. We left Tyre early yesterday morning, and as we rode out saw the fishermen spreading their nets on the rocks, as the old Prophecy of Ezekiel, you know, foretells. It was a lovely morning, and the seashore was sparkling in the early light as we came across on to the mainland and struck down the coast. We passed, yesterday, a group of fine old fountains and pieces of moss-grown aqueducts, where the city of old Tyre stood, and a beautiful little spring on a hill where was once a town called Alexandros Kyne, or Alexander's Tent. It is said the great conqueror lodged there on his way to besiege Tyre. In the afternoon we climbed over a great white cliff which runs out into the sea and is called the Tyrian Ladder. It is the southern limit of Phœnicia, and below it Palestine begins. Soon after, we came to our camping-place at the little village of Eszib, whose old name was Achzib, which you will find in Judges i. 31, and was one of the towns given to Asher, but never captured by them. We camped close by the well, and all the evening women were coming for the water, which an old man, sitting on top of the well, drew for them; the scene was very picturesque, but the town, except for one or two splendid palm-trees and a noble sea coast, is forlorn.

To-day we have been riding down the coast. The scene is all changed. We are in the plain of Acre, a rich country, the very sight of which lets you understand how Asher "dipped his foot in oil" and "his bread was fat, and he yielded royal dainties." All along the coast are the creeks and bays where he lingered when Deborah reproached him with "abiding in his breaches." We rode past golden orange orchards, and ate the fruit fresh from the tree. About noon we came to Acre, an old city formerly called Ptolemais, whose principal history belongs to the Crusades and to Napoleon's time. We went through it; saw the fortifications and the ruins of an old church, but there was not much to look at. After it, came a long beach of twelve miles, stretching from Acre to where Mt. Carmel runs out its grand promontory into the sea. We crossed this rapidly, and just before we reached Carmel came to the mouth of a swift river, where we sat down under a palm-tree and lunched.

It was "that ancient river, the river Kishon." It comes up from the plain of Esdraelon and passing through the Carmel Mount runs into the sea near this town of Haifa, which lies at the foot of the hill, and in which our tent is now pitched. The old stream looks strong enough to sweep away another Sisera, but Carmel is what we came here for. There it is with all its " excellency," a long ridge running far out into the sea and back into the rich country, with Sharon on its south and the plain of Acre on its north. There is the place where Elijah and the priests of Baal had their trial, and there is the ridge where his servant went up and looked seven times till he saw the little cloud rising out of that bright Mediterranean, which has not had a cloud on it to-day. All is clear as if we saw the prophet's altar burning. This afternoon we climbed the cliff to where the convent stands overlooking the sea. The Carmelite brothers received us hospitably. They are jolly, comfortable-looking fellows, with brown coarse coats and cowls. In their church they take you down under the high altar and show you the cave where Elijah hid from Jezebel. It is fitted up in their tawdry style with a small chapel. Halfway down the hill is another, larger cave, called the Cave of the Sons of the Prophets, where it is said Elijah received the chiefs of the people. This is in the hands of the Mohammedans and is fitted up for their worship, so curiously are things mixed up here. But the mountain itself, and its glorious view, is just what it was in Elijah's time, wooded to the top, looking out on beauty and richness everywhere. Westward, over the blue sea, north along the splendid bay of Acre, over the great fertile plain to the Lebanon hills in the distance, with Hermon's white head looking over them, east into Galilee to the hills of Kedesh-Naphtali and the fertile plain of Esdraelon, and south along the beautiful coast over the smooth pasture-land of Sharon, what a place for a prophet, and what a scene for the great trial of his faith! Below, the Kishon runs through the plain as if it were still telling to-night of how he took the prophets of Baal and slew them there. We sleep under the shadow of Carmel. I am very tired, and all is still, except the jackals screaming in the distance. Good-night. I wish I were going to bed in that back room at home.

NAZARETH, Wednesday Evening,
December 13, 1865.

We are encamped on this my thirtieth birthday in a group of olive-trees just by the fountain of Nazareth. We left Haifa early this morning and rode along the base of Carmel for several hours, then struck across the plain, crossing the Kishon by a deep and rapid ford. Soon after we came to the first of the Galilee hills, and climbing it saw Mt. Tabor, the great mountain of Galilee, before us, and the plain of Esdraelon stretched out between it and Carmel. It was just the landscape which I have always expected in Palestine, — low, round, wooded hills, and rich plains between. Tabor is the finest, most beautifully shaped of the sacred hills, a soft smooth cone with wooded sides and top. We rode on all the afternoon through hills and glens, till about four o'clock, when we came suddenly to the top of a steep hill, and there lay Nazareth below us. It was a strange feeling to ride down through it and look in the people's faces and think how Christ must have been about these streets just like these children, and the Virgin like these women, and to look into the carpenters' shops and see the Nazarenes at their work. The town lies in a sort of gorge, halfway up the side of a pretty steep hill. As soon as our horses were left at the camp, we climbed the " hill on which the city was built," and saw what is perhaps the finest view in Palestine. I thought all the time I was looking at it how often Jesus must have climbed up here and enjoyed it. There were the Lebanon hills and Hermon to the north, Tabor to the east, and a line of low mountains, behind which lie unseen the Sea of Tiberias and the Jordan; beyond them, the hills of Moab stretching towards the south. On the southern side the noble plain of Esdraelon, the battle-field of Jewish history, with Mt. Gilboa stretching into it, where Saul and Jonathan were killed. Jezreel lies like a little white speck on the side of Gilboa, and Little Hermon rises up between. On the west, the plain is closed by the long, dark line of Carmel, stretching into the sea, and the sight that His eyes saw farthest off was that line of the Mediterranean over which His power was to spread to the ends of the world. It is a most noble view. The hill is crowned with ruins of the tomb of some old Moslem saint. It is the same hill up which they took Jesus, to cast Him down from the cliff. The scene was very impressive in the evening light.

When we came down we went to the village fountain, where the women of the town were drawing water. Such a clatter and crowd! Some of them were quite pretty, and the sight was very Oriental, as they walked off with their water-pots upon their heads. The Greeks, by their tradition, put the Annunciation at this fountain; the Latins have a grotto for it, which they say was Mary's house. This is a good place to keep a birthday, is n't it? Our tent fire is burning bright, and I shall sit by it a little while and then to bed.

TIBERIAS, Thursday Evening,
December 14, 1865.

Our tents are pitched to-night by the Sea of Galilee, in the ruins of the old castle of Tiberias. We spent this forenoon in continuing our survey of Nazareth. First, we went to see the place of the Annunciation. We entered the church of the Franciscan monastery while service was going on. After it was over, a monk took us down under the altar into a cave, fitted up richly for a chapel, under the altar of which is a black marble cross, to mark the place where Mary stood. Opposite it are two stone pillars, between which the angel came. One of them is broken through, so that a piece hangs from the ceiling, and a piece stands up from the floor. They say the Moslems tried to break the cave down, and could n't. From this cave a stairway leads up into another, a second room of the house. Over the altar of the Annunciation is a good picture of the scene, and around the cross are ever-burning silver lamps. It is a pretty and impressive spot, and there is no impossibility about its being the place.

We went then to the carpenter's shop of Joseph, and the synagogue where Christ preached. Both are modern churches, and there is nothing interesting about either. Then to the church where the Greeks celebrate the Annunciation. They place it at a fountain under a tawdry old church, and take you down into a cave, where they have *their* lamps around *their* cross, and a well from which a monk draws up water and gives you to drink out of a silver cup. The old church was very prettily full of birds flying about. These are the sights of Nazareth, but its old streets and the view from the hill are its true interest, and those I shall never forget. We said good-by to it, and left it lying among the hills, where Jesus must have looked back upon it the last time He went out.

A quick ride of five hours brought us here. We lunched at Cana of Galilee, at least at a little village which one legend calls so. There is another claimant to the name which we saw in the distance; either may be the place. Both are so situated that you can picture Jesus and His mother going out from Nazareth to a near town to attend the marriage to which they had been invited. Ours was a forlorn little town, in which we stopped at a wretched church, where a cross-legged master was teaching twenty cross-legged boys to read their Arabic. Against the wall were built in what looked like two fonts, about the size of that in my church. This is said to be the house of the marriage. Then we rode on through a rolling country which Jesus must have often walked, on His way back and forth between Nazareth and the lake. The whole country, every hill and valley, seemed marked with His foot-prints. At last we came to a broad plain with one round hill rising out of it. Here the last great battle of the Crusades was fought, and Saladin finally conquered the Christians. Legend calls the hill "The Hill of the Beatitudes," and says it is where the Sermon on the Mount was preached. Perhaps it is. Opposite is another hill, where they say Christ fed the multitude, but that must have been on the other side of the lake. Another ridge climbed, and there was the "Sea of Galilee, which is the Sea of Tiberias." There it lay in the soft afternoon light, blue among the purple hills. There were the waves He walked, the shores where He taught, the mountains where He prayed. With Hermon's white head to the north, with the steep Moab hills coming to its brink on the east, with its low western shore where the old city stood, with Safed "the city set on a hill" off to the northwest, it was a sight not to be forgotten. I have hardly ever enjoyed an hour more than the one we spent in winding down the ridge into Tiberias. The town lies on the lake shore; it is miserable and dirty. It has a population of wretched Jews, who are rascally-looking creatures in black felt hats, and long elf locks. The women are horribly tattooed with ink. "Every prospect pleases, and only man is vile." So ends a most interesting day. By the way, looking into a house-door at Nazareth, this morning, I saw "two women grinding together at the mill" sitting together on the floor, and working the upper millstone round upon the lower by a handle, which they both grasped.

Our weather is still splendid, and to-night is soft and warm as June. Good-night.

TIBERIAS, Friday, December 15, 1865.

To-day has been a perfect day, cloudless and warm, and we have spent it in seeing this wonderful lake. We were ready early, and our horses were brought out because there was a fresh wind blowing and the timid fishermen would not venture the one boat, which is now the only craft of the lake, upon the water. So

TIBERIAS. 59

we must ride. We left the old walls of Tiberias behind us, and rode northward along the western shore. Tiberias itself is a miserable town, but its walls show that it was once fine, and it was new and at its best in Jesus' day. After crossing one or two ridges, with their intervening valleys, we came out on a plain three miles long and extending back a mile or two, flat and fertile, from the beach. This is the "land of Gennesaret." Just as we entered it from the hills, we came to a little group of twenty or thirty dirty huts with a ruined tower near them. This is Magdala, the native town of Mary Magdalene. The Arabs still call it Medjel. We rode across the plain, through the oleander bushes that skirt the shore, and at its other end came to an old ruined khan, a fountain gushing out under an old fig-tree, and an acre or more covered with old foundations and heaps of stones. Right in the midst was a wretched burial ground, and three poor Bedouins were digging, as we passed, a grave for a body that lay wrapped in its blankets on the ground beside them. This is Capernaum, the home of Christ after Nazareth rejected Him. "And thou Capernaum." Passing this, we climbed a cliff, and, keeping a narrow road cut in the rock, came by and by to another beach, and beyond it to a snug little cove, just the place for fishing-boats to be drawn up, with nothing on the shore but some old ruined aqueducts, and some reservoirs, one of them now used for a mill. Not a living soul was there. This is Bethsaida, the city of John and James, Peter and Andrew. We kept along then a mile or so farther, and came to another heap of ruins interspersed with miserable huts, and the black tents of Bedouins, who are in temporary occupation. This is Chorazin. There are ruins of some fine buildings here, columns, capitals, etc., but this is probably later than Jesus' time. Here we lunched, sitting in the shadow of one of the huts, with the Bedouins gathered on its roof, staring at us. They seemed harmless, but would be bad enough if they had the chance. There were some good faces among them. I noticed especially one sweet-looking little girl, whom it seemed hard to leave in such keeping. These are the cities "wherein many of His mighty works were done,"—all ruined and gone. We turned back here; our dragoman would not let us go farther, for fear of Bedouins. We saw in the distance where the Jordan enters into the lake, and then riding back to Tiberias, made the fisherman take us out to row on the lake. It was strange to see him, as we reached the middle, and the hour of prayer arrived, leave his rudder, and spreading his cloak on the floor of the boat, kneel towards Mecca and with many gestures say his evening prayers. All this on the lake of Gennesaret. But religions are all mixed up here. We had the Tiberias fish for breakfast this morning, but they were so bad we could only taste them. Tomorrow we leave the lake, but I shall never forget how it has looked to-day.

NAZARETH, Saturday Evening,
December 16, 1865.

We have returned here to spend Sunday. Our road from Tiberias was different from the one we took in going there, and was arranged to take in Mt. Tabor. It has been a hard day's ride, nine hours and a half on the way. The only point of interest was Tabor. After keeping it in sight all the forenoon, we reached its foot about twelve o'clock, and climbed it slowly. The ascent is not long, and there is a sort of road, but very rough. You wind up through oak-trees, scattered among the rocks, and about an hour brings you out on the top, where there are the ruins of an old town, and a convent of Greek monks. The view is noble, though not equal to the Nazareth hill. The beautiful plain of Esdraelon stretches to the west, with Carmel closing it in. On the south lies Little Hermon, " the Little Hill of Hermon," with Endor and Nain upon its sides, and the mountains of Gilboa showing their heads beyond. To the west you can just see a bit of the lake, and trace the valley where it lies and where the Jordan runs, with the table-land of Bashan stretching out beyond, and the blue hills of Gilead farther off still. To the northwest there is old Hermon, still with his snow, so that we have the two great mountains associated. "Tabor and Hermon shall rejoice in Thy name." You know that Tabor has been held to be the mountain of Transfiguration. There is no authority for it but tradition, and I for one am well convinced that some one of the ridges of Hermon is far more likely to be the place. But Tabor is very beautiful, and has been always one of the sacred places. We met on the top a poor Abyssinian priest, who had come all the way hither on a pilgrimage, and now clings about here, living on charity. He kissed my hands and called down unintelligible blessings when I gave him five piastres. A hard afternoon's ride brought us to our old camping-ground, surrounded by hedges of cactus, among the gnarled old olive-trees beside the fountain of Nazareth.

Here we shall rest ourselves and our horses for a

day in this old town, which with the sea of Galilee has more attraction for me than anything else that I have seen. Next week to Jerusalem.

I put you in two "lilies of the field" from Mt. Carmel, and two purple oleander blossoms from the "land of Gennesaret," between Magdala and Capernaum.

Sunday Evening, December 17, 1865.

I have had a very pleasant, quiet Sunday here at Nazareth. This morning I went to the Greek church and heard their usual boisterous and disagreeable service. The forenoon we spent in reading and resting. It was warm as summer, the tent curtains wide open, the babble at the fountain all day. This afternoon to the Latin church, where a very impressive mass was performed before the altar of the Annunciation. The chanting with an organ (the first I have heard since Vienna) and boys' voices was very fine. A strange group of Bedouins, women, children, and all odd costumes, kneeling on the altar stairs. After service Appleton and I took a walk into the country, and saw what we have seen all along, the shepherds leading (not driving) their flocks and carrying the weak ones in their arms. All day the people have gathered round to look at us. It is touching to hear the poor people tell of how they suffered from the locusts in the spring. They came in clouds, covering the ground half a foot deep, as large as sparrows; all the shops and houses were closed for days. Every green thing was eaten up. It sounded like a chapter out of Joel. It is sad, too, to hear them talk of their government. All spirit is gone out of them, and they only wait the inevitable dropping to pieces of the rotten thing, which all expect. The English missionary here called to see us this afternoon.

JENIN, Monday Evening,
December 18, 1865.

To-day has been very interesting. We were off bright and early, and left Nazareth behind us among its hills. Crossing a very bad, rocky ridge, we came down into the great plain of Esdraelon and crossed its eastern end, between Tabor and Little Hermon, where Deborah and Barak gathered their troops before the battle with Sisera. Keeping part way up Little Hermon, we came to a forlorn village. The people were a little dirtier and more rascally looking, the hovels a little viler, than any yet. We rode through it up to a large cave in the hillside, some twenty feet deep, with a spring in it and a fig-tree beside it. The village is Endor, and this cave is shown as the place where the witch called up Samuel. Certainly, the town looks as if it had had a crop of witches ever since, and were growing another for the next generation. We left it with the whole population crying out for "backsheesh" and throwing stones at us. Keeping along the side of Little Hermon, in about an hour we came to Nain, another wretched collection of some twenty huts, where you could imagine the beautiful scene of the miracle at the gate. Thence around the end of Little Hermon to its southern slope, where we came to Shunem, the scene of the pretty story of the Shunammite woman and Elisha. The village is a little larger than usual, with more bad smells and dogs. Below it, in the plain, lay the fields where the boy went with his father to see the reapers; and far off is Carmel, to which the mother rode to fetch the man of God. There is a reality about these things here which is very enjoyable. An hour's ride, now across the plain, brought us to the fountain of Jezreel, a spring and great pool of water at the foot of a steep rock. This, you know, was the scene of two great events: first, the destruction of the Midianites by Gideon (here is the very pool of which his soldiers drank or lapped), and the defeat of Saul by the Philistines. Here is where his army lay. The Philistines were opposite, at Shunem. Over that ridge of Little Hermon he went the night before the battle to consult the witch. Behind us rise the mountains of Gilboa, in whose high places he was killed, and down the plain towards the Jordan you see the ruins of old Beth-shan, where his body was exposed. We lunched by the fountain, and then rode along the side of the Gilboa range to its western slope, where is Jezreel, the palace of Ahab, the home of Jezebel, the place where her body was thrown out to the dogs. The wretched creatures were prowling about there still, as we passed through. It is a miserable village of huts now, but you look across the plain and see where, after the miracle on Carmel, Elijah ran before Ahab "to the entrance of Jezreel."

From here we have been keeping all the afternoon along the southern slope of Gilboa to this point. The hills of Samaria have been full in view. Far off across the plain, by Carmel, are dimly seen Taanach and Megiddo, the towns of Deborah's song. The white mosque of Jenin came in sight at five o'clock, and here we are in tent again. This place is prettily situated, but has nothing remarkable. It is the old En-gannim of Joshua xxi. 29. The day has been overcast, but no rain; to-night is clear, and I am very tired. Four months to-day since I landed at Queenstown. I have not forgotten that this is George's birthday.

NABLOUS (SHECHEM),
Tuesday Evening, December 19.

Another very interesting day. The days become more interesting as we approach Jerusalem. We were to go from Galilee to Judea, " and must needs pass through Samaria." Shortly after we left Jenin, crossing a range of hills, we saw, two miles on our left, a small " tell " or hill which is the old Dothan, whence Joseph went to seek his brethren, and where they sold him to the Midianites. We rode on all the morning, over hills and plains, the hills occasionally opening to the east, and letting us see the plain of Sharon and the blue sea beyond. About noon we saw before us the terraced hill of Samaria, and lunched by and by among the olives on its northern side. It is full of the interest of Elisha, and the old Israelite kings, and the visit of Philip in the Acts. I read over 2 Kings vi. and vii. on horseback. The place is full of ruins of the old Roman time, when it was rebuilt by Herod and called Sebaste. Countless columns are scattered around, and some standing. The prophecy seems strangely fulfilled. Some are rolled down the hills, and the husbandmen were ploughing among them, all over the old site. The present village is miserable; we rode into it after dinner, and were surrounded by the population like fleas. There is an old church of St. John in whose ruins is now a wretched mosque. A long quarrel and fifteen piastres " backsheesh " gained us admission, and in a little subterranean room, whose walls were covered with defaced crosses, they showed us what they called the tomb of John the Baptist. It is a very old tradition. As we rode out of town, we were chased by the children, with much dirt on them and very little clothes, screaming what Ibrahim told us meant " Ho, Christians! Ho, Jews! May the Lord leave not a bit of you."

The afternoon's ride was lovely. The fields dark green with young wheat and barley, dotted with the light gray green of the olive-trees. And here we are now at Shechem. Before us is Mt. Ebal, behind us is Mt. Gerizim. Here is where Jacob bought " the parcel of ground ; " where the curses and the blessings were pronounced from hill to hill across this ampitheatre, where the town lies and where the Ark stood. Here is where Joshua collected his tribes for his last charge, and more than all, here is where Jesus came and lived two days after his conversation with the woman at the well which we shall see to-morrow. The city itself is large and charmingly old and quaint. There are about fifteen hundred Samaritans left, the only remnant of their people. We have been to see their synagogue, a dingy little hole, where a splendid old priest, in red turban and gray beard, showed us their famous roll of the Pentateuch, which they claim is thirty-two hundred years old, and written by the son of Eleazer, son of Aaron. There is a very fine old mosque too. As we passed through the streets, the small boys cursed us and spit at us. Think of that for a free American citizen to stand. Two days more to Jerusalem. To-night we sleep under the shadow of Gerizim. Good-night. It will be good to get your letters by next Thursday.

PHILLIPS.

JERUSALEM. 67

MEDITERRANEAN HOTEL, JERUSALEM,
Friday Morning, December 22, 1865.

I add another half sheet, just to say that we are in Jerusalem. We arrived last night about five o'clock, and I am writing now, before breakfast, with my window looking out on the Mount of Olives. I can hardly realize that I am here. Our day's ride yesterday was rocky and tiresome. "The hills stand about Jerusalem" and make the approach slow. The only especially interesting places were Bethel, a poor little village, on a plateau surrounded by hills. There is nothing attractive in the site, and nothing in the town; but every association makes it interesting. Ramah stood up on our left, a village with an old square tower. In the middle of the afternoon, Neby-Samuel, the old Mizpah, where Samuel is buried, rose high on our right, and just before we saw Jerusalem we crossed the side of a high hill, which is the old Gibeah of Saul.

It was about four when we rode up the slope of the hill of Scopus, and got all at once the full sight of Jerusalem. It lies nobly surrounded by its mountains, and overlooked on the eastern side by the Mount of Olives, which, though only a hill, is higher than I thought. Between it and the city is the valley of Jehoshaphat. We entered the city on the north by the Damascus gate. The first sound I heard in it was the muezzin on a minaret calling the Moslems to prayers. The interior of the city is like all Eastern towns, filthy, narrow, noisy, and when the novelty is off disgusting, but I am not going to write about the city now. I am here, and there is the Mount of Olives right before me.

I fear a little of my first enthusiasm on arriving at

Jerusalem may have been in the prospect of a temporary return to some of the luxuries of civilization, a bath, a bed, and a shave. We found them all good at this hotel, and then the letters! No less than ten, and a half dozen newspapers. I reveled in them all the evening, and rejoiced to hear of you all well. They took me back home for the night. Another glorious day to begin to see Jerusalem. We shall have plenty of time here, for there is no steamer for Alexandria till January 4. And now, again, good-by, and God bless you all always.

JERUSALEM, Saturday Evening,
December 23, 1865.

DEAR FATHER, — This comes from the Holy City. I suppose you have heard by mother's letter of my arrival here, day before yesterday. Two days have been spent now in sight-seeing. Yesterday, the Mount of Olives, Gethsemane, the valley of Jehoshaphat, and the Brook Kidron, the city walls in the afternoon, the weekly sight of the poor Jews wailing outside the old Temple wall. To-day, the Mosque of Omar, the site of the great Temple, the valley of Hinnom, the pool of Siloam, again the Mount of Olives, the Jews' synagogue, the tombs of Zechariah, the Virgin, St. James, and all the others, and the church of the Holy Sepulchre, which includes within itself the Tomb and Calvary. Are not these names enough? We lodge here on the Via Dolorosa, near what is said to be the top of Calvary. But, ah! monkery has been so busy manufacturing all sorts of holy sites that one knows not what to believe. Calvary is at the top of a dirty paved street, in a chapel of a gaudy church; Gethsemane is a flower-garden with a high wall, redeemed only by eight very old olive-trees; only the great general aspect of the whole, Mount Zion, Mount Moriah, Mount Olivet, and the deep ravines, these are past all doubt and full of inspiration. They have been two rich days.

Saturday, December 30, 1865.

My energetic letter-writing has paused for a week. I take it up again to tell you of my tours around Jerusalem. Last Sunday morning we attended service in the English church, and after an early dinner took our horses and rode to Bethlehem. It was only about two hours when we came to the town, situated on an eastern ridge of a range of hills, surrounded by its terraced gardens. It is a good-looking town, better built than any other we have seen in Palestine. The great church of the Nativity is its most prominent object; it is shared by the Greeks, Latins, and Armenians, and each church has a convent attached to it. We were hospitably received in the Greek convent, and furnished with a room. Before dark, we rode out of town to the field where they say the shepherds saw the star. It is a fenced piece of ground with a cave in it (all the Holy Places are caves here), in which, strangely enough, they put the shepherds. The story is absurd, but somewhere in those fields we rode through the shepherds must have been, and in the same fields the story of Ruth and Boaz must belong. As we passed, the shepherds were still "keeping watch over their flocks," or leading them home to fold. We returned to the convent and waited for the service, which began about ten o'clock and lasted until three (Christmas). It was the old story of a Romish service, with all its mummery, and tired us out. They wound up with a wax baby, carried in procession, and at last laid in the traditional manger, in a grotto under the church. The most interesting part was the crowd of pilgrims, with their simple faith and eagerness to share in the ceremonial. We went to bed very tired.

Christmas morning, we rode up to town and went to service. It rained all that day, and we stayed in the house. The next morning we were off for our trip to the Jordan. Passing out of St. Stephen's Gate, we rode past Gethsemane, and around the southern slope of the Mount of Olives, the same road by which Christ made his triumphal entry from Bethany. The point at which He must have first come in view of the city, with the multitude throwing the branches under His feet, is very clearly seen, and very interesting. Passing round the hill, in about an hour we came to a little village hid away in a fold of the valley, as quiet and out of the way a place as one can imagine. This is Bethany; a poor little town now. They show still the tomb of Lazarus, — a cave, deep and dark and tomb-like. All the afternoon we rode on over the hills. This is a dangerous region, and we had a guard with us, a sheik, and three soldiers from the government of Jerusalem. However, we saw no robbers; plenty of Bedouins, but very harmless. Towards night we came out into the great plain of Jordan, wide, green, and beautiful. We crossed the "Brook Cherith" of Elijah and the ravens, and went to the site of old Jericho, where is the fountain which Elisha changed from bitter to sweet. Then across the plain to the site of the later Jericho, which Christ entered. This is the old Gilgal. They showed us the house of Zaccheus. We camped here, and after dinner the Bedouin women came and danced their wild dances and sang their wild songs and got their backsheesh. Next morning, we rode down the plain to the river, the Jordan! We came to it just " over against Jericho," where the Israelites may have crossed, and just where tradition says that John preached and Jesus was baptized. The stream was swift and turbid; about as wide as the Shawsheen where you cross it going from Mr. Tompkins's to grandmother's. We saw the place where the hosts of pilgrims came to bathe at the Passover.

From the Jordan we rode an hour and a half to the Dead Sea, and stood on its desolate, dreary shore, and tasted its dreadful water. The view was wild and melancholy, and still appeared full of the story of the old catastrophe. In the afternoon, we rode across the hills toward the Greek convent of Mâr Sâba. The views were splendid. We were in the wilderness of Judea. On our left was the Desert of Engedi, where David fled from Saul. A terrible hail and sleet storm came up and wet us through, and we were glad enough, passing along a splendid ravine, through which the Kidron flows, to find a picturesque old Greek convent, where sixty monks live their miserable, useless life. They were useful for once, however, for they took us in and made us comfortable for the night. I wish you could have seen us among the brethren, disturbing their quiet life with the many wants of tired, wet, and hungry men. The convent was built about the grotto of an old hermit years ago, and is surrounded by the deserted caves where hundreds of hermits used to live. Thursday morning, we said good-by to the monks and left them working in their garden, and took up our way toward Hebron. We had to go first to Bethlehem again. We passed a very striking encampment of Bedouins, with their black goat's-hair tents in the valley, and riding through the fields of the shepherds and Ruth, came into the little town. The people, who are very handsome, gathered about us to sell relics. I saw some very beautiful faces in the church among the women, on the night of the service; they wear a peculiar red robe, and in general seem decidedly superior to the ordinary inhabitants of the country. We went into the church again and saw it more thoroughly. The place of the Nativity is in a little grotto like the one at Nazareth. The manger is in an altar opposite. The grottoes of St. Jerome and his fellow-anchorites, SS. Eustasia and Paula, are close by. Each of the three convents has a passage-way down to the altar of the Nativity. We rode on from Bethlehem along an old aqueduct, which leads by a beautiful green valley, in which Solomon had his gardens and country houses, to the "pools of Solomon," three immense reservoirs, built to supply Jerusalem with water, but now long out of repair and use. He says in Ecclesiastes that he made him " pools of water." From here to Hebron, the oldest city in Palestine, the home of Abraham and the kings, which lies in a broad valley five hours from the pools. What a ride we had to get there. It rained, and rained, and rained. The rocks were slippery, it grew dark, the horses were tired out, and glad enough we were to get to the town and find a little room in a Jew's house (there are no Christians, only Jews and Moslems in the place), and try to get dry and get through the night.

JERUSALEM.

The next morning, the storm was just as bad, or worse, but we started. There is not much to see in Hebron except the place itself, and that we could not see. The cave of Machpelah is in a mosque, where they don't admit Christians, so we looked at the outside. Then we rode by a splendid great oak at Mamre, which they call the oak of Abraham. This is the valley of Eshcol. And then, in rain and cold and discomfort, we struggled back to Jerusalem, lunched at the pools with some Nubian soldiers, who are there as guard, passed by the tomb of Rachel, just outside Bethlehem, and reached our hotel at five o'clock, glad enough to be here. This is the sketch of our trip, which we enjoyed in spite of its discomforts. It is about our last. Next Tuesday, we shall leave for Jaffa, to catch the steamer of the 4th for Alexandria.

And now, what about Jerusalem? I believe I know it thoroughly. I have seen all its sights, have walked about it, and marked the towers thereof, till I understand its shape and spirit pretty well. It is not large, but it is crowded full of interest. Everywhere you get striking views, — Olivet, with the little mosque on its top, the great mosque on Moriah, David's tomb on Mount Zion, the Holy Sepulchre, with its broken dome, on Calvary. You cannot get away from some of them. Do you know that they have the Holy Sepulchre and Calvary all in one church? You go up a flight of a dozen stairs from one to the other. But I must not attempt to describe Jerusalem. I will tell you all about it when I get home. Our consul here and Bishop Gobat of the English church have been attentive. It is sad to see how Moslem power rules here. The very keys of the Holy Sepulchre are kept by the Mohammedans.

I need n't say I was delighted to get letters here, and hear that you are all well. I have read them over and over, and now am looking for more at Alexandria, where we hope to arrive on Saturday next. The least items from home, you know, are interesting to us away off here. Tell mother her letters are most welcome. To-morrow is New Year's Day. A happy New Year to all of you! Good-by, God bless you all.

JERUSALEM, Monday, January 1, 1866.

I must wish you all a happy New Year. It is a good way off, but I am sure you all know that I am doing it this morning, and I can almost hear you wishing it back to me. May it be a happy year to all of us. Before it is over, God grant we may be together again safe. Two more days in Jerusalem! Saturday, I went out to see the old cave tombs, which are all about the city, the tombs of the Judges and those of the Kings. Yesterday, I went to the English church in the morning, and heard Bishop Gobat. In the afternoon, a lovely bright sunny day, I walked out to Bethany and back; over the summit of Mt. Olivet, the way that David went when he fled from Absalom, back around the southern ridge of the hill where Christ came in on his triumphal entry. It was a delightful walk.

Appleton received a bundle of Boston Advertisers yesterday afternoon, which were very refreshing. They told us all about the elections, etc.

Tell mother I put in this letter for her the head of a reed which was "shaken by the wind" on the brink of the Jordan, and two flowers which I picked in Gethsemane.

JAFFA, Wednesday Evening, January 3, 1866.

So far westward. Yesterday morning we left Jerusalem, seeing our last where we saw our first of it, from Mt. Scopus. Then we rode to the hill of Nebi-Samwîl, the ancient Mizpah, where Samuel is buried. There is a splendid view from the top; an old minaret crowns it. Down thence through Gibeon and Beth-horon and the valley of Ajalon, where Joshua's great battle came to pass, and the sun and moon stood still. The ride was over hill and valley, very interesting. Late in the afternoon, we came down into the great coast plain of Philistia, and passed through Lud, the Lydda of the Acts, an old town with the remains of a fine church. Another half hour brought us to Ramleh, where we camped last night. It is a place famous in Crusaders' history. From there, a three-hours' ride brought us here to-day, with no accidents, except my horse tumbling into a ditch and muddying me from top to toe. Jaffa is the old Joppa, and we went to see the house of Simon the tanner, "by the seaside," where Peter lodged. It is a pretty likely-looking sort of place for a tanner. Mr. Kayat, the British consul, came to see us this afternoon; we went to see his orange gardens, and ate lots of the ripe fruit off the trees. We are lodged in the Russian convent. Was n't it funny to find our chairs here in our room, rocking-chairs and all, marked " M. L. Gates, 66 Commercial Street, Boston ?" So our Syria is over, and if the steamer is up to time to-morrow, we are off to Alexandria.

JAFFA, Wednesday, January 10, 1866.

Here we are still, after a week of dreary waiting and discontent. The day after we arrived, a storm came up and has lasted until to-day, with strong west wind. Not one of the three steamers that ought to have touched here has arrived, and we have no news of either of them. Even if they had come, we could not have got aboard, for the harbor is rough and the sea runs very high. We have lost a week in waiting. We have had all sorts of plans: sometimes, to go by land up to Beyrout, and try to get aboard there; sometimes, to take camels and go across the desert direct to Cairo, but the torrents of rain have hindered our moving. We could not travel now without getting swept away with the full streams, so we must wait and wait. To-day is bright and pleasant, but the high wind still blows on shore and no news of the steamer.

STEAMER EGYPTO, between Jaffa and Alexandria,
Sunday, January 14, 1866.

We are off at last. Yesterday morning, there came along an Austrian steamer bound for Alexandria, and as the wind and sea had moderated, we went aboard her and shall be in Alexandria to-night. We have had a very pleasant and smooth passage so far, and are glad to be out of Jaffa, which has nothing to boast of but its oranges. They are splendid, and did n't I eat them!

STEAMER MŒRIS, January 23, 1866.

DEAR WILLIAM, — This is one of the times for letter-writing. I am on a four days' voyage from Alexandria to Messina. The first two days the sea was terribly rough, and this French boat, being a screw steamer, rocked horridly, so that it was out of the question to think of writing, or anything else, except holding on and not getting washed overboard, or pitched downstairs. They were days when, in the elegant and expressive language of Artemus Ward, it was hard for the passengers " to keep inside their berths or outside their dinners." Still it was the first very bad sea I have had anywhere, and I must not complain. To-day is calm and still, and we are getting on fast towards Sicily.

On arriving at Alexandria, after our long imprisonment at Jaffa, I found a host of letters, and received some more the day I left. You may guess they were welcome. The latest was yours of Christmas Day, and none better deserves an answer. I will tell you in a few minutes about what I saw in Egypt. My stay in Egypt was short. Alexandria was the meanest place I have seen yet. Enterprising, busy, but perfectly unattractive. Too Western to be good Eastern, and too Eastern to be good Western; too old to be good new, and too new to be good old. A bad mixture. Cleopatra's Needle is an obelisk in a cow-yard. Pompey's Pillar is an old column on a hill overlooking lake Mareotis. It has nothing in the world to do with Pompey, and is principally interesting from some American sailors flying a kite over it once, as recorded in the pages of the American First Class Book. But if Alexandria is detestable, Cairo is delightful. I could write pages, yea, a book, about the dear old place, with its bazaars, mosques, gardens, palm forests, palaces, donkeys and donkey-boys, its great old river, and its Pyramids. But I won't. Let it be enough that one morning I straddled a diminutive long-eared creature, about as big as the family rocking-horse, with a brown, bare-legged boy running behind, poking the donkey and screaming at him all the way; I rode through Cairo, was ferried over the dreamy old Nile, and then rode across its gorgeous green valley, climbed to the top of the Pyramid of Cheops, and looked out on the Desert. The usual army of wild Arabs dragged me to the top. The ascent is not hard, but they insist on giving you their hand and pulling you up from step to step. The easiest way is to let them do it. All the while they chant a wild stave in the Hiawatha measure, something like

>Good Howadji ! Great Howadji !
>Strong Howadji ! Lots of money !
>Give us Backsheesh ! Plenty Backsheesh !

When you get to the top, you do give them as much backsheesh as will stop their tongues and let you enjoy one of the strangest and most memorable views that the world has to show. I sha'n't attempt to describe it. One must get on the top of that Pyramid before he can know anything about it. When I got down, I went and stood in the shadow of the Sphinx, and looked up into her vast stone face. If the Pyramids are great in their way, she is a thousand times greater in hers, as the grandest and most expressive monument of a religion in the world. But I am writing a letter about Egypt, and I did n't intend to. The mosques of Cairo are very attractive, vaster and more gorgeous than any elsewhere, and containing some of the most interesting specimens of old Arab architecture, in which are the germs of a good deal of modern European. Then we went out to visit the viceroy's gardens and palace, and saw something of Egyptian luxury. It was a place that Anthony and Cleopatra might have reveled in. While we were in Cairo, the season of Ramazan, the Mohammedan Lent, began. They fast all the daytime, and carry on all night. Their worst privation is from tobacco. It is terrible to go through the bazaars and see the poor old fellows looking so melancholy and cross, holding their pipes all ready filled, awaiting sunset to light up. The nights of Ramazan are gorgeous with lights and feasting. But I positively won't say anything more about Egypt.

HOTEL TRINACRIA, MESSINA,
Tuesday Evening, January 23.

My letter was cut short this morning by finding how near we were to our port. I went up on deck, and there was the coast of Italy, the sole of the "boot" on one side, and Mt. Etna, with its great white sides and little spire of smoke, upon the other. About one o'clock we arrived here. I had some hopes, in coming here, of meeting the boat for Greece, and making my visit there now. But she passed us going out, about three hours before we came into the harbor. There was no connection from Alexandria to Greece for ten days, so I did not wait there. I shall go to Naples to-morrow, and next week to Rome, where I shall stay till after Carnival, then make a trip to Greece and be back by Holy Week. I am alone again. Dr. Leeds stayed in Egypt, and Mr. Appleton has gone on to Paris. He will probably join me to Greece. My whole scene has changed. Italy is all around me. This is a delightful old town, with a quaint old cathedral and square, and pictures of Italian life at every step. I am depending, with all my heart, on Naples and Rome.

Tell Mr. John that I expect him to appreciate my brotherly attention in going to the Egyptian post-office, in Cairo, and at an expense of much gesticulation buying a full set of the new Egyptian postage stamps, which I am told are rare in America. I think they deserve a letter at least. I was glad to hear how Christmas passed with you. Before this you have heard how I passed mine. I saw lots of " Little Wanderers " in Syria and Egypt, and now Italy seems as full of them as either.

ON BOARD STEAMER IL COURIER DI SICILIA,
Wednesday P. M., January 24.

I have been all the morning seeing Messina. It is a delightfully Italian town, lying along the shore, backed by a wilderness of green hills. They have a lovely old cathedral, full of elaborate carvings and mosaics, and the views everywhere of the straits and the hazy Italian shore opposite are beautiful. The great show of the town I have missed. It is an autograph letter which the Virgin Mary sent them once, with a lock of her hair. She is their special patroness. The priest who had the key of the cathedral was out, so I could not see it. Now we are on our way to Naples, just passing between Scylla and Charybdis. We are going through the old peril safely, I think. This little steamer was built at Glasgow in Scotland. We are leaving Sicily and Messina behind us. Messina, you know, is the town of " Much Ado about Nothing." There Benedict and Beatrice courted, and walking out last evening I saw honest Dogberry " comprehend a vagrom man " in the streets.

HOTEL VITTORIA, NAPLES,
Sunday, January 28.

Three days, now, in this most beautiful spot on earth. No one can wonder at people's enthusiasm about

Naples. I have seen some things in my travels which were not up to the mark, but of the beauty of Naples and its bay, the half has not been told, simply because it can't be. As I look out of my window now, I can see the blue bay, with Capri lying off in front, the promontory of Baiæ, and Puteoli stretching its arm around it, the green hills covered with olive groves and vineyards shutting in the land side, and the bright gardens of the Villa Reale, with their fountains, statues, and gay promenaders, lying in the foreground; the whole in a climate such as we have in our best June days, and an atmosphere such as we never have. I have seen something about Naples. One day to Puteoli, where is a very perfect old amphitheatre, and where Paul landed to go up to Rome; to Baiæ and Cumæ, Virgil's Elysian Fields, Lake Avernus and Sibyl's Cave, up as far as Cape Misenum. Another day down the coast to Salerno, thence to Pæstum, where are the most perfectly preserved Greek temples in the world. That is one of the greatest things to see in Italy. The road there is very beautiful, a little given to banditti, so that we had to take a guard of soldiers. We had no adventure, and got home safe. The two greatest wonders of Naples I have yet to see, Pompeii and Vesuvius. The mountain, which is not vast or grand, but simply beautiful, overlooks you everywhere you go, but I have not yet seen even a whiff of smoke out of his great pipe. Etna is a much more splendid mountain, and so is Stromboli, which we passed the other day coming up from Messina. You see Italy is beginning with even more fascination than anything yet, and my next three months are going to be very full. I am afraid my letters will not be quite so long now. I shall have no more sea voyages to write in, and shall have employments for my evenings out of doors. I will try my best, and you must allow I have done splendidly for the last three months. For the present, this is all. I am very well, and in first-rate condition every way. Shall probably go up to Rome next Saturday. I hope to get some more letters there. Good-by; give love to all, and don't forget your affectionate brother, who expects to get home in September. PHILLIPS.

ROME, Sunday, February 4, 1866.

DEAR MOTHER, — In Rome at last, at the place of all others in Europe that I have most wished to reach. I got here last night about seven o'clock, and this morning before breakfast went down the Corso to the Capitol, and through the Forum to the Coliseum. It is exactly as I have always pictured it, only a great deal more interesting. This is really all I have seen of the city yet. I went to service at the American embassy this morning, and found the place crowded with Americans, lots of people that I knew.

Since my letter went to William I have been having a great time in Naples, seeing everything in that most beautiful of cities. One long day I spent at Pompeii, which is most wonderful, with its old streets and houses, uncovered just as they were left the day that the great eruption came and buried them. Then I went up Vesuvius, and saw where the eruption came from, ventured down into the crater, which is very grand, and stood on the hot ground, where another eruption is cooking, to burst out by and by. Another day I went down to Sorrento along the shores of the bay, spent a night there, and then crossed over to Capri, the beautiful island where the old Roman emperors had their palaces and lived their horrible lives. I spent a day at the great museum of Naples, where all the statues and other antiquities from Pompeii and Herculaneum, and the other ruins in that neighborhood, have been collected into the most enormous repository in the world. It is very rich and very beautiful. On the whole, Naples has delighted me, and I put it along with Edinburgh, Constantinople, and Damascus as one of the four great cities of the world in beauty. There is a railway from there here, taking about seven hours.

Thursday Evening, February 8.

I have been very busy all the week, and now am so sleepy I can hardly keep my eyes open, but I will send this off to let you know that I am well and enjoying every moment. Rome is so much greater and fuller than I had ever dreamed of. I have seen a great deal, but when I think what there is right about me, it seems as if I had seen nothing; I have wandered all through St. Peter's, spent a long day in the wilderness of the Vatican, another in the great museums of the Capitol, and followed the banks of the Tiber, skirted with ruins of the old temples, palaces, and theatres of this wonderful race, roamed through some of the picture galleries of the great palaces, found my way into a few of the numberless gorgeous churches, and to-day have been from one to another of the studios of our own living artists. All this has swallowed up many hours.

Then the Carnival is in full rage, and every afternoon it is hard to keep away from the Corso, where every old gray palace is hung with bright red, and the balconies are filled with gay people full of fun, pelting with flowers, sugar-plums, and confetti the queerest-looking crowd, in every sort of wild harlequin disguises, that is running riot in the street below them. Really, while I am in Rome you must not look for any more long letters of the Syria sort. I will tell you about it some day. The city is full, too, of Americans, and lots of people that I know are here. I have made some very pleasant acquaintances among the Americans who are living here, and who know Rome well. The state of the country is terrible, and the poor Pope is in a most miserable position. I saw his Holiness the other day, driving in splendid state, but had no good look at him through the carriage windows. The swarm of priests and monks of many sorts in the streets is horrible. I have n't heard from you since I left Alexandria. I hope to get letters to-day.

Friday, February 9, 1866.

No letters to-day. What has become of you all? Well, this must go. It is a poor letter to send from the Eternal City, but it is so hopeless in a place like this to try to tell you what one sees. One does n't know where to begin. To-day, for instance, I spent the morning in two of the great picture galleries, in the Borghese and Corsini palaces, then two or three hours in the sculptors' studios, among others Rogers's, who has by far the best bust of Mr. Lincoln that has yet been made; and the afternoon among the ruins, which are exhaustless. So make allowance for shortcomings and forgive me. This will do at any rate to tell you that I am splendidly well and happy, and love you all as much as ever. I wish you could see, feel, and taste this glorious soft Italian weather. Good-by. God bless you all. Six months more and I shall be almost home. Your loving son,

PHILLIPS.

ROME.

ROME, February 19, 1866.

To the Sunday-Schools of the Church of the Holy Trinity and Chapel, Philadelphia:

MY DEAR CHILDREN, — When I think how near Easter is coming, I think also how pleasant it would be if I could spend that day at home in Philadelphia; and particularly, I wish I could be with you in the Sunday-school and at your Easter service. As I have no chance of that, I want to write a few words which I hope Mr. Coffin will find time to read to you some time in the course of the day, as my Easter greeting. For of all my friends in America there are none by whom I should be more sorry to be forgotten, or whom I should be more sorry to forget, than the circle who make up our schools and classes. I do not mind telling you (though of course I should not like to have you speak of it to any of the older people of the church) that I am much afraid the younger part of my congregation has more than its share of my thoughts and interest. I cannot tell you how many Sunday mornings since I left you I have seemed to stand in the midst of our crowded schoolroom again, and look about and know every face and every class just as I used to; nor how many times I have heard one of our home hymns ringing very strangely and sweetly through the different music of some far-off country. I remember especially on Christmas Eve, when I was standing in the old church at Bethlehem, close to the spot where Jesus was born, when the whole church was ringing hour after hour with the splendid hymns of praise to God, how again and again it seemed as if I could hear voices that I knew well, telling each other of the "Wonderful Night" of the Saviour's birth, as I had heard them a year before; and I assure you I was glad to shut my ears for a while and listen to the more familiar strains that came wandering to me halfway round the world.

But I meant to write you an Easter letter, and to give you an Easter greeting. As I have gone to Palestine once in this letter already, let me take you there again. In the Holy City of Jerusalem, you know, Christians built ever so many years ago a noble church directly over the place where it is believed Jesus was buried, and right under the dome of this grand old church, they have built up a little temple of marble which incloses what is believed to be the real tomb where the Saviour lay — and this, of course, is a very holy place; and when I was in Jerusalem I used to go and stand by the side of that cold stone and watch the endless stream of worshipers that came up there to pray. They were pilgrims from every quarter of the globe; in all kinds of dress, with all kinds of faces, and all shades of color. First an old man that seemed to have used almost the last strength that was in him to crawl from his far-off house in frozen Russia to see the Holy Sepulchre before he died; then a young girl with her face full of enthusiasm, who had apparently given all her youthful strength away and came pale and weary, but full of joy, to the place that she had longed for by day and dreamed about by night; then a mother would come with her child and press its little lips against the cold marble, while the baby would shrink back and look up in her face as if he wondered what it meant. It was a very touching sight to me. They crept on their knees through the little low doorway into the tomb, that is always lighted with countless lamps of gold and silver; and as if there were no way strong enough for them to express the feeling that had brought them so far to see this holiest of all places, they cast themselves upon the stone and covered it with kisses, and cried as if their hearts would break for joy. It was a strange and very touching sight. But when I recall it now in connection with Easter Day, the one thing I think of most is the emptiness of that tomb in Jerusalem, and the ways we have of doing honor to Jesus which are so much better than making pilgrimages to the place where he was once buried. You remember what the angel said to the disciples on the first Easter morning, when they made their pilgrimage to the Holy Sepulchre : " Why seek ye the living among the dead ? He is not here. He is risen." It seems as if one heard those words all the time he is walking about in Jerusalem. Let us, my dear children, rejoice together on Easter Day in the great Easter truth that Jesus our Saviour is to be found and worshiped, not in any cold tomb, but in any heart, no matter how young and humble, that is warm with his love, and bright with the constant cheerful effort to do whatever duty He desires. That is the happy temple in which He loves to live, and I hope every one of us, this happy Easter Day, will find this Saviour very near to us, risen from his tomb and come to live with us, and help us, and be our friend and brother, in every joy and sorrow of our lives. That is the Easter prayer which I pray with all my heart for each one of you.

I must not write only to the members of our schools and classes at the church and at the chapel. I must not and do not forget the teachers, who are laboring on in their good work. My dear friends, let me bid you Godspeed out of a heart full of sympathy with you and with your work. May your Easter be a day of renewed courage, and hopefulness, and love. May God help you in your happy work, now and always. It will be a happy day for me when I stand once more among you to be your fellow-worker.

I suppose we shall none of us meet this Easter without thinking of the last. What a sad day it was! You remember we had to take all our flowers down and hang the church in black, and our celebration, with its cheerful carols, was given up, for it was just then that we heard the terrible news of our good President's murder. We shall never, any of us, forget that day. Every Easter will always bring it back. And especially this year, I am sure, none of us will keep the holy day without thanking God that the cause which our President died for has been so victorious, that peace has come back to us, that the great rebellion has been defeated, and that men and women can no more be slaves in America forever. We must be very thankful for these things, and pray God earnestly to keep our dear country always from these two great sins of rebellion against the government and oppression of any of its people.

But my letter, which meant to be very short, has forgotten itself, and wandered along over all these pages. There is much more that I want to say, but I must wait till I get home, and can say it myself. That will be, I hope, very early in the fall. I shall spend my Easter here in Rome, after making a short journey first to Greece. I wish I could paint for you in words the beauty of the springtime in this delightful climate, which is already blossoming into summer, while America is still shivering with the cold of its severe winter.

And now, my dear friends, good-by, and may God our Father bless and keep us all. If He spares us to meet again, I think we shall all try to work harder than ever to serve and please Him. Let us pray for one another that we may be kept from every danger and every sin. I let my mind run along our schoolrooms, and as I see you there I ask a blessing for each of you. May our Lord Jesus Christ, who rose on Easter Day, rise anew on this Easter in all your hearts, and be a living Saviour, a friend, a brother, a helper, and a comforter to you all, all the days of your lives. May He live with us until, when we have done our work, He takes us to live with Him forever. Always, my dear children,
Your affectionate friend and rector,
PHILLIPS BROOKS.

ROME, Tuesday, February 20, 1866.

DEAR FATHER, — I wonder what is the matter. Since I left Alexandria, a month ago yesterday, I have not had a single letter from America. The mails keep coming, and everybody else gets lots, but there is nothing for me. I have put off writing from day to day, because it is rather pleasanter to write when one has a letter to answer, but there seems to be no use in waiting any longer. I am afraid my letters must have been sent by mistake to Alexandria, and it will be some time yet before I get them.

I cannot tell you how much I have enjoyed these two weeks in Rome. Every moment of them has been busy, and I know the old city pretty well. I have explored it from end to end, above ground and under ground, the churches, ruins, picture galleries, the Vatican, the Campagna, everything. The first week of my stay here was the Carnival, and the town was crowded with strangers. Since Lent began they have largely gone off to Naples, and left a little room, so that one can climb up to the Coliseum, or go through a picture gallery, without being in a jam of folks so great as to take away half the pleasure of the thing.

I am going off this week for a while. I start on Friday for Naples and Messina, whence I shall sail next Tuesday for Athens; and after spending eight days there shall return to Rome, getting back here about the 18th of March. Then I shall have two or three weeks here before Easter, immediately after which I shall leave for a month in northern Italy, and go to Paris about the first of May. I am depending much on seeing Greece, though I am afraid I can visit little besides Athens, for the country seems to be in such a state now with the brigands that it is not safe to go far away from the town. I am to meet Mr. Appleton in Naples, and he will go with me.

I have met a great many people here whom I know. Two or three families of parishioners from Philadelphia, a great many Boston people, and many whom I have come across in traveling. Almost everybody who is traveling in Europe comes to Rome in the spring. There are also a great many very pleasant American families living here permanently. I have seen a great deal of the Storys, and like them exceedingly. Yesterday I spent with them, in an out of town excursion to one of the old villas, which was as beautiful as antiquity and springtime could make it. We had a capital time. Miss Shaw, sister of Colonel Shaw of Fort Wagner, is staying with the Storys, and is very charming. They have pleasant receptions, where one meets the nicest people in Rome, particularly the artists. Story is at work on a colossal Everett for the city of Boston. Edward does n't look very imposing just now, for he has only got one trouser on, and is very much in the condition of "Diddle, diddle, dumpling, my son John." It is going to be a fine thing. Mr. Story has also a fine statue of Colonel Shaw, and Rogers has a capital bust of Lincoln. I dined the other day with Mr. Hooker. Charles Adams and his wife have just arrived, and other people keep turning up. Next Friday, the 22d, there is to be a meeting of the Americans here, with a breakfast. I believe I am committed for a little speech. Won't it be funny to make a Hail Columbia address in Rome? There are lots of copperheads here, and there will be much pleasure in saying a few words to them. The Rev. Charles T. Brooks is here, and is to read a poem.

Tuesday Evening, February 20.

At last I have heard a little from you to-day. I have yours and mother's of January 2, and William's of January 8. You may be sure they are very welcome. They have been to Alexandria and back. I am glad to hear you are all well, and I thank you for your New Year's wishes. How I wish you could see and feel the spring here! It is delicious, and every day now adds to its beauty. What a winter you have had at home! I feel as if I had skipped winter altogether. I have not set foot in snow once; but I must stop. I want to put a choice collection of stamps for Mr. John into my letter. I am very well, and shall be glad when I see you all again. Good-by, love to all.

PHILLIPS.

MESSINA, Monday, February 26, 1866.

Now, my dear James,[1] we will have that little talk which we have been meaning to have so long. It is a whole month, I believe, since I received your letter. Why have n't I answered it? Simply because, my dear boy, I have been in Rome, and who can write letters there? I have had to be content with knowing that I was thinking about you, and that you knew I was thinking about you, and promising myself to write as soon as I got to some less absorbing place. So here I am, waiting for the steamer that is coming to take me to Athens. I have leaned out of my window in this Hotel Trinacria, and looked away up the straits towards Scylla and Charybdis, and there is no sign that she is coming yet; so I am sure of time for a good long talk with you. It was good to read your letter, and to hear for the first time your talks as a theological student. It was so far an accomplishment of the purposes and hopes of these last two years: it is an assurance of so much done, and so is a pleasant starting-point for the next stage. It is n't easy to run, for Hebrew Dictionary and Jahns and Hornes are not light loads to carry; but the very getting at it is a sort of inspiration, and I am sure the same Help that has brought you up to it will carry you bravely through. God bless you in it.

That is all I am going to say about your studies. I say it with all my heart, you know. I am not going to write you "a page about homiletics" or anything of the sort. I am too desirous to have my letters read for that. If you want suggestions in detail, have n't you got Fred, and can't he give them to you a great deal better than I can, way off here? I am

[1] Rev. James P. Franks.

sure you are not going to disappoint any of us, but more than fulfill all that we hope of you.

How have you and that same Fred got along this winter? From what I hear of the bitter cold, you must have been very affectionate to keep each other warm. How different our winters have been. Mine has been full of fruit trees in full fruit, and hot, sunny days; while yours has had skates, snow-storms, and all that. Yours is a great deal the best for a steady thing, but mine has been a very enjoyable luxury for this once. My last three weeks have been completely given up to Rome. Did I ever tell you that it was the one place in Europe that I was most anxious to see perfectly and know through and through? I believe I do know it well, and I shall have three weeks more to revel in it, when I get back from Greece. Do you remember the photograph of the old city that hung over my bookcase in Spruce Street? How many times I have studied and tried to understand it. Now ask me any house in it and see if I do not tell you. From the first walk down to the Coliseum before breakfast, the morning after I arrived, down to my last view of the crippled old aqueduct striding across the Campagna as I rode out to Naples, it was an unceasing and infinite delight. There are a great many pleasant people there, too, some of whom I knew at home, and many whom I learned to know well there. We had a very patriotic time on the 22d of February, and stirred up the dusty old air with national melodies of which the Cæsars never heard, and talked about loyalty and liberty, which they would not have appreciated if they had. Then there was Naples, just as bright, sunny, and gay as Rome is grim. The one is always solemn and stately, even when it is dressed in carnival scarlet. The other is always on the broad grin, and dancing like a faun. They are both perfect in their ways. And now I am going to see what Athens is like, and then come Florence, Venice, Genoa, Paris, and the biggest and best day of all, when I see Boston again, which is worth the whole lot of them together, and is the best place on the world's face to live in. So say we all of us, don't we?

Everything is going well, and it is pure good nature in the people to be kind enough to miss me when they fare so well in my absence. All this is a great relief to my mind, and lets me go on without an anxiety, adding pleasure to pleasure while my year lasts. Some time in October will see me back, if I am spared. To think that before I come Fred will have been ordained and will be at his work! Where will it be? I should so like to have had a glimpse of you together in your household life this winter. How much you must have enjoyed it, and how much you both owe to me for making you know one another!

Give my kindest regards to your mother and sister, and to my other friends in Philadelphia. As to old Fred, tell him I love him still, and ask him to write oftener, and I will pay him when he goes to Europe.

And now, my dear boy, good-by and God bless you. I think of you lots; you may make ever so many friends without having one that will like you better, or wish you every blessing more fervently than your old friend, P. B.

STEAMER GODAVERY, BETWEEN MESSINA AND ATHENS,
Tuesday, February 27, 1866.

DEAR WILLIAM, — Here I am on the Mediterranean again. Coming down from Rome to Athens, I crossed by steamer to Messina, and last night our old friend the Godavery, in which three months ago we sailed from Smyrna to Beyrout, took us up and is carrying us fast towards Athens. Appleton came from Paris, and joined me at Naples. We shall be there probably early on Thursday morning. It seems like getting back to last winter's experiences. The boat is full of Greeks, French, Germans, and what not. The familiar cabins recall the days when we were getting ready to plunge into Syria, wondering what kind of a time we should have there. The Mediterranean is as beautiful as ever. To-day is a soft, clear, warm, blue day, when one just likes to sit on deck and think what a lovely thing the sea is. Indeed, I have found this treacherous sea all winter one of the gentlest, most gracious, and best behaved of creatures.

This sea life of a day or two is quite a rest after Rome with its intense and constant interest. I cannot tell you how I enjoyed that city. I had hoped much from it, but my enjoyment far surpassed all my anticipations. It has more than any other city of those things which, once seen, become pictures to you forever. St. Peter's so vast and so beautiful, the Vatican with its labyrinth of art, the Coliseum and the Forum with the beauty of their ruin, — one does n't know where to begin to think about what there is in Rome. I paid your old High School eloquence the tribute of a thought, as I looked at the ruins of Horatius Cocles' bridge, and at the place in the Forum where

"Virginius caught the whittle up and hid it in his gown."

Some day, if you care about it, I will get out the map of Rome, and we will go over it and spell out the histories that are written there, one over the other. The mere art of Rome is infinite. Think of a city that has the Dying Gladiator, and the Apollo Belvedere, and what is called the greatest picture of the world, Raphael's Transfiguration. Do you remember seeing it for years in the copy in St. Paul's chancel? I thought it a wonderful picture when I saw the original in the Vatican; I cannot think it so great a picture as the Dresden Madonna, but the comparison of great pictures is very unsatisfactory and odious. A mere list of the other pictures of Rome that fill you with their power or beauty would crowd my paper. Of the people in Rome I saw many, some very pleasant. At the Storys' house, I met several of the best artists, and other interesting folks. I saw Miss Hosmer, Miss Stebbins, and Miss Cushman, three ladies of genius, you know, and very pleasant personally. Our 22d of February went off well. President King, of New York, presided, and his son, our minister in Rome, General King, Mr. Story, General Bartlett, and I spoke, and Rev. C. T. Brooks, of Newport, read a poem. We were very patriotic, and an Italian band played our national airs well.

I am very much disappointed about my letters; there is a mistake about them somewhere. I received none before leaving Rome, except those that had been all the way round by Alexandria. The latest was yours of January 8. Now I shall get no more till I reach Rome again, which will not be till about the 14th of March. Then I shall expect a big bundle. I don't know what the hitch is, but take it for granted that it will regulate itself by that time.

ATHENS.

HÔTEL D'ANGLETERRE, ATHENS,
Thursday Evening.

I am here on the 'Οδος Αιολου, as the street signs call it, which means Æolus Street. I go out on my balcony and look one way, and there is the Temple of the Winds and the Acropolis beyond, with the Parthenon glowing in the sunset. I look the other way, and see the Academy and the old grove where Plato taught his pupils. In front is the Piræus and the Saronic Gulf, with Salamis in the distance. Two hours ago I was on Mars Hill, where Paul made his address; the old stones of the Judgment Seat are still standing at the head of the stairs that lead up from the Agora. Then I went over to the Pnyx and stood where Demosthenes and Pericles have so often spoken to the Athenians of old. Before me was the Temple of Theseus, the most perfect of all relics of antiquity.

Friday Evening, March 2.

Here my letter came to grief yesterday, owing to the dinner bell. I spent the evening very pleasantly at Dr. Hill's. You know he is our missionary here, and the man who has done more than anybody else for the elevation of Greece, by means of education.

He told me a great deal about Greece that was interesting. To-day I have been on a very delightful ride from Athens through the Pass of Daphne, along the Thriasian Plain to Eleusis, the place where the old mysteries, the most sacred religious rites of ancient times, were celebrated. It is a very beautiful spot, in full view of the Bay of Salamis, where the great battle of the Greeks and Persians was fought, and of the height where Xerxes sat and overlooked it. Coming back, I went to the Acropolis again, wandering around to see its beauty from every point of view. The whole sweep of the landscape is glorious: Hymettus, Pentelicus, Colonus surrounding the beautiful plain; the Ilissus and Cephisus, the two classic rivers of Athens, now mere dry torrent beds, running through it, and the Acropolis, with its immortal temples standing up, the central gem of the whole.

Many things are odd in traveling here. First, we are twelve days behind time. You know the East has never adopted the change of calendar, so that leaving Messina on the 27th we arrived here on the 17th. To-day is the 19th of February on all their newspapers, so for the present, I am twelve days younger than you think. Then it is curious to hear everybody, the cabmen, shopkeepers, beggars, talking familiarly a language that we have called dead, and struggled so hard to learn years ago. The modern Greek is very like the old, and eliminating differences of pronunciation, one gets to understand it a little and say a word or two so as to be intelligible. The modern city is all very new, and far better, neater, and cleaner than any other Eastern city. On the whole, these have been two great days. Yesterday, my first in Athens, was one of the most memorable of all my journey.

Saturday Morning, March 3.

I find there is a mail leaving to-day by the Austrian steamer, so I will close this up hurriedly and send it. We are going on Monday for a little trip into the Peloponnesus, to Argos, Mycæne, and Corinth. In about ten days I shall be back in Rome, and stay there till after Easter. To-morrow I am going to preach in St. Paul's Church. Athens, for Dr. Hill. Lots of love to all; I am very well. Affectionately,

PHILL.

ROME, Saturday, March 24, 1866.

DEAR FATHER,— Since I came back to Rome, I have been so continually busy that it has been not an easy thing to get time to write. I beg your pardon very humbly. Now I will tell you a little of the much that I have done and seen since I wrote an enormous letter to Arthur from Athens, which was mailed at Naples. One of the best things was to get an immense pile of letters when I arrived here. All the accumulation of two months reached me at once, and I have had a great treat in reading them. I heard of your reception of all my letters from Damascus to Naples, and you and mother, William, Fred, Arthur, and John, with others outside the family circle, contributed to my delight.

We had a rather rough passage from Athens to Messina, and then from Messina over to Naples. I am a very good sailor by this time, but still I am not sorry to think that I have no more to do with the sea, except in crossing the Channel, until I sail for home. I did not stay in Naples, but came right on here.

Since my return, the climate of Rome has been bad, sort of New England April weather, some rain almost every day. But the country is looking beautiful, and when we have fine weather it is splendid to go about; for rainy days, we have the Vatican, the Capitol, and a dozen other galleries. One day this week I have spent at Tivoli, another in the Alban Hills, Frascati, Tusculum, and Albano. The country and people are very interesting indeed.

Rome has got to be just like home to me now. I know it through and through, and after so much wandering, my stay here has been a very pleasant change. I have made a good many acquaintances among our resident artists and the travelers. The Storys, Crawfords, Tiltons, Miss Cushman, Miss Stebbins, and Miss Foley, all of them I have seen a good deal of, and like. To-day, I am to dine with Mr. Mozier, one of our best sculptors here. I have been quite interested in visiting the studio of a colored artist. Miss Lewis, of Boston, who has recently come here, and promises very well indeed in sculpture.

Of travelers there are many; Rome is crowded, so that it is impossible to get a room. Many Philadelphians are here. Also the Morrills, Mr. Gardner Brewer, and Mr. Wales, of Boston; this is all very nice.

Next week is Holy Week, with all its great church pageants, closing with the splendid fireworks on Easter-Monday night. On Tuesday, I shall leave, and go by way of Foligno and Perugia to Florence; then to Bologna, Parma, Modena, Ferrara, Padua, and Venice. Then to Verona, Milan, the Italian lakes, Turin, Genoa, Nice, Marseilles, Lyons, and Paris. Does n't that sound good? I am depending much on Florence and Venice, and indeed all the route is very rich.

I am sick at heart about Johnson's performance; it was my first greeting when I got back to Rome, and was very depressing. It seems as if we had a narrow, vulgar-minded man upon our hands, and must take all the delay and suffering that he chooses to put upon the country. Of course, we shall come out all right at last, but it is very disheartening to come up short against such an obstacle.

I hear talk about quarantine in America this summer. Would n't it be nice to spend thirty days at Deer Island on my way home? They seem to be expecting the cholera everywhere, both here and at home.

Tell Arthur and John I was set up to get their letters. I had already written to Arthur. My next will be to Mr. John. Forgive this poor letter. . . .

PHILLIPS.

ROME, March 30, 1866.

DEAR JACK, — I will tell you where I am and what I am doing. I am up in the fifth story of the Washington Hotel, that's the where; and I am seeing the sights of Holy Week at Rome, that's the what. They began last Sunday with the great blessing of the palms at St. Peter's. It was a gorgeous service, with very splendid music. You have to dress for it, as if you were going to a party. Nobody without a dress coat is admitted into any place where you can see anything. Then yesterday (Thursday) was one of their great days. In the morning, his Holiness washed the feet of twelve priests, who stood for the Apostles, in St. Peter's, and waited on them at table. It was a very odd and ugly sight. A tremendous crowd was there, and it was as perfectly devoid of anything religious or impressive as it was possible to conceive. Then the Pope came out on the great balcony in front of the church and pronounced his benediction. That was one of the grandest sights I ever saw, — the whole vast piazza crowded, and the clear voice of the old man ringing out his blessing so that every one could hear. In the afternoon, I heard the famous Miserere in the Sistine Chapel, and whatever else may be humbug about this strange week here, that was certainly the most wonderful music I ever listened to. Now, everybody is looking forward to Easter Sunday, when the whole will crown itself with a splendid service in the morning, and the great illumination of St. Peter's dome at night. There is much that is very interesting about it, but still it is good every day to get away for a while, and wander off into the ruins; to go down the Corso, and climb up among the nests of crooked streets at its foot, till you come out on the Capitol; then go down through the Forum, and under the Arch of Titus to the Coliseum; by the Arch of Constantine to the Baths of Caracalla, the finest old bit in Rome, and out the Appian Way till you get beyond the gates on the Campagna, among the aqueducts and tombs. Last night, I was going with some folks to see the Coliseum by moonlight, but it was cloudy and we gave it up; about eleven o'clock I happened to look out, and found it was clearing and the clouds breaking away, so I started off alone, and went down and had it all to myself. Not even a guide was there. I climbed over a gate to get in, and wandered all over it, with the most splendid moon pouring down and lighting up the city on one side, and the Campagna and the Alban Hills upon the other. It was a great treat to sit there and watch it. I wish you hadn't been asleep, and could have gone with me.

I am just getting ready to leave Rome, and am dreadfully sorry to go away. I have seen everything, but want to keep seeing it over again. When you paint your future, don't forget to put your brightest colors on the days that you are to spend in Rome. Perhaps I may be ready to come again by the time you set out.

We find time, even here in Rome, to talk about home, and especially about the President and his veto. I am glad to say people generally agree with you and me, and agree with us vigorously, too. The patriotism and home interest of the best sort of Americans seem to be stronger here than ever. It certainly is a great shame that such a man should block our wheels and keep peace waiting, under the pretense of hastening it; but he can only delay things, not spoil them. To-day is Good Friday, just a year ecclesiastically from the death of Lincoln, and the real beginning of things going wrong. By the way, why is there no commission yet for a great statue of Lincoln for Boston? Mr. Story showed me his Everett yesterday. It is very fine, a colossal figure in plain citizen's dress, in the act of speaking, the right arm raised in Mr. Everett's favorite gesture, the whole very bold and simple, and successful, I think.

I send some more rare post-office stamps, all I can get now. Are there any you want especially? Let me know, and I will try. Good-by, and be a good boy, and write to me.

Your loving brother, PHILLIPS.

FLORENCE, HOTEL DE L' ARNO,
April 8, 1866.

DEAR WILLIAM, — Here I am in my third day at Florence. Before I begin to rave about the city, I will tell you how I came here. When I wrote to John, I was in the midst of Holy Week at Rome. Many of its services, such as the washing of feet and tending on table by the Pope, were disagreeable and fatiguing, But three things stand out in my recollection as very fine and impressive. One was the Miserere in the Sistine Chapel on Thursday evening, by far the most sublime and affecting sacred music I ever heard. The dim chapel, dusky old frescoes, and splendid presence joined with the wonderful music to make it very impressive. Then the great Papal Benediction on Easter Day at noon, from the balcony of St. Peter's, the vast piazza crowded full, the peasants from all the surrounding country in their strange dresses, the gorgeous background of soldiery, the perfect stillness, and the voice of the old man ringing out his blessing over them all. It was one of the sights of a lifetime. Third, the illumination of St. Peter's at night was magnificent. Every line of the majestic dome bursting out in fire, the whole standing as if it were the fiery dome that Michael Angelo conceived and tried to build.

Besides these, the moment in the Easter service was very solemn when the Host was elevated, the silver trumpets sounded in the dome, and the whole vast audience fell on their knees. Romanism certainly succeeds in being very striking in some of its demonstrations. Unfortunately, Easter Monday was a windy day, and the great fireworks had to be put off, so that I did not see them.

It was hard to leave dear old Rome; I had learned to love it, and hated to go away. My six weeks there will always be a treasure to me. I know it through and through, but it makes me sorry to think that I shall never see it again. I left on Tuesday morning by rail for Terni, where I stopped over night and went to see the famous falls. They are *made* falls, but very beautiful, with more variety of surface and effect, I think, than any cataract I know. Wednesday by rail to Foligno, and thence by Vittoria to Perugia, stopping at Assizi, where is one of the most interesting old churches of all Italy, built in honor of St. Francis, who was hermit here. It is rich in the pictures of Cimabue and Giotto, the first of modern painters,— founders of modern painting.

Perugia is a dear old town, full of the pictures of Perugino, Raphael's master. Thursday by Vittoria and rail to Florence, passing lake Trasimeno, where Hannibal gave the Romans such a whipping. Of Florence I cannot speak yet, though I have had two great days here. Think of one room in the Uffizi Palace containing the Venus de Medici (I don't like her, she is too little, physically, morally, and mentally), three Raphaels, two Titians, one Michael Angelo, and lots besides, and that will give you, when you multiply it by fifty or a hundred, some idea of what is waiting for you to see here at Florence. Go to the Athenæum and look at Michael Angelo's Night and Morning. They are here in solemn marble, over the Medicis' tomb in St. Lorenzo church. Yesterday I went up to Fiesole, and looked down on this perfect valley with its beautiful town, and this morning I climbed to the top of Giotto's Campanile in the great cathedral square, and saw the city from there. To-morrow I am going down to Pisa to see if that tower really leans, as Woodbridge's Geography said, and after spending the week here, I shall be off for Bologna and Venice. I wonder sometimes that one does not tire of the very excess of interest and beauty, but the constant change is a constant impulse, and I am fresher for enjoying things to-day than I was when I first set foot at Queenstown.

On arriving here, I found yours of March 20; it seems as if I were almost at home to get such recent dates. Now I shall hear regularly every week. Four weeks from to-day I shall be in Paris. By the way, where are your commissions for the centre of fashions? What number gloves do you wear? I am glad you think I am economical. I perpetrated one or two extravagances at Rome, a bronze, etc. I saw Miss Foley in Rome and liked her exceedingly; she gave me some pretty photographs of some of her things, which you will find with those which I sent in John's letter. I have met friends here who were large purchasers, with whose boxes my modest bundles could be easily and cheaply packed.

Now, a commission for you. I want a copy of Mr. Sumner's speech on the Representation amendment in pamphlet. I must have it. If you cannot get it any other way, do write to him direct, and ask for it. I am anxious to have it for a particular reason. The Freedmen's Union have asked me to go to London to the anniversary meetings in May to enlighten John Bull's Emancipation League. . . . Good-by, I am perfectly well, and, as you see, perfectly happy. Love to all. Affectionately, PHILLIPS.

BOLOGNA, ITALY, HOTEL SAN MARCO,
Sunday, April 15, 1866.

DEAR MOTHER, — I am spending a rainy Sunday at this old town of sausages. I believe there are other things than sausages here, but I don't know anything about them yet, for I only got here late last night, and since I woke this morning it has rained so horribly that I have n't been outside the walls of the hotel. Since I wrote to William last week, I have seen all of Florence, and been to Pisa and Sienna. I am happy to report that the tower at Pisa does really lean, just the way the picture-books have it, and you have the proper pleasant feeling of insecurity as you wind around it up to the top. It has stood crooked for a good many years, and my being safe here to-day proves that it did not tumble when I was on it last Monday. The Cathedral and Baptistery at Pisa are both very rich in old art, and the Campo Santo, where the monks, priests, and nobles lie buried in the holy earth that was brought all the way from Jerusalem for them to sleep in, with its frescoed colonnades around it, is one of the nicest, quietest burying grounds in all the world. Sienna is a charming sleepy old Italian town, with a wonderful cathedral, and a gallery of immensely old pictures. Among others, an Ecce Homo by an old man called Sodoma, which I wish you could see. It is almost the most powerful and touching face of Christ which I have seen in any picture. As to Florence itself, it is the brightest, sunniest, bluest, most delightfully pretty place in Italy. The days there were the perfection of Italian weather, when everything, from the hovels to the stars, seems to have ten times as much distinctness of color and outline as it ever gets at home. The pictures in Florence are beyond all description or calculation. You get bewildered with the wealth with which Raphaels, and Titians, and so on, are scattered through the endless galleries. There are hundreds that would be the making, any one of them, of a gallery at home, and which once seen here seem to be before your eyes all the time, and not to be forgotten forever afterwards. The mornings I generally spent in the galleries, and the afternoons walked or rode off into the country somewhere around the town, to some point where its beauty stood out in a splendid view. I shall remember my week in Florence as one of the pleasantest of all my journey. The ride from there here, across the Apennines, was very fine.

Everybody in Europe now is wondering, you know, whether there is going to be war between Austria and Prussia. If there is, as seems likely, it is impossible to say to what extent it will involve all the rest of Europe. Everything seems ready for a general upset, for there is not one nation among them that is not in some way restless and uneasy with the present state of things, and prepared to welcome a general row in hopes of something better. The Old World is very rotten, and if President Johnson would only behave himself and stop vetoing good bills, and let the United States go on and do her work, *she* might lead the universe. What a great misfortune that man is to the country! What have we done to deserve him? Did we not struggle through the war, and put down the Rebellion? and now why should the conquered South be allowed to come up and rule us still in this other form? It is very hard to understand. The last veto, I take it, is decisive as to his spirit and intentions.

I had no letters from you this last week. They have gone to Venice. By the time you get this, about the first of May, I shall be in Paris, and stay there some three weeks. I hope to meet Strong there, and shall be very glad indeed to see one so fresh from home, who has seen you all so lately. My time is drawing to its close, and, much as I have enjoyed everything, I shall be quite ready to come home. I expect to enjoy Switzerland immensely. Mr. Tilton, the artist, of whom I saw a good deal in Rome, has promised to meet me there, and we shall probably travel some together. The Storys may be there, too. So far, my whole trip has been a success. I could not ask for anything in it to be changed. But here is

AVIGNON.

my paper all gone, only room left to say good-by and lots of love to everybody, and to be, in small letters, Your affectionate and dutiful son,   PHILLIPS.

HÔTEL DE L'EUROPE, AVIGNON, FRANCE,
April 30, 1866.

DEAR FATHER, — I believe it is two weeks since I have written to any of you at home, though I wrote to Fred from Venice. My excuse must be that these have been two of the busiest weeks of my journeying. Before I plunge into Paris, however, I will let you hear of me from this queer old French town. I went from Venice to Verona, where I spent a night; a very interesting town, with one of the most remarkable Roman amphitheatres, in better preservation than any other. It is one of Shakespeare's great towns, too, " Romeo and Juliet," you know, and " The Two Gentlemen." The old house of the Capulets, where the pretty Juliet lived, is still there. From Verona to Brescia, a delightful old place, Roman remains, mediæval architecture, and pictures; everywhere the quaintness, simplicity, and unlike-anything-else-ness of modern Italy. Few places have given me more pleasure than Brescia. From there to Milan, as bright, and gay, and pretty a modern town as there is in the world. In the midst of it stands the wonderful cathedral, that everybody knows all his life in pictures, a bit of most delicate and beautiful lace work, done in white marble, a forest of statues and elaborate carvings, not done yet, and not likely to be finished for many years to come. There are superb pictures in Milan, too, and the almost-gone remains of one of the greatest pictures of the world, Leonardo da Vinci's fresco of the Last Supper. Then to Turin by a splendid road, close under the shadow of the Alps, with Monte Rosa and a hundred other white peaks looking at you all the way. Turin is a handsome town, but has not much to be seen except some good pictures. Then to Genoa, the city of palaces, splendid structures, with magnificent architecture and paintings. The whole situation of the town, too, is very striking. There I took a steamer and sailed to Marseilles. Good-by to Italy, and into the domains of Napoleon the Little; red-legged soldiers and big gendarmes everywhere. Marseilles is a big city, but not very interesting, and I was soon off to Nîmes, a French town as old as the Roman empire, and older. It has fine Roman remains, another amphitheatre, temples, etc. From there to Avignon, the place where the Popes ran in the fourteenth century, when they had to clear out of Rome, and the dearest, Frenchiest of old towns. The old Papal castle, a grim, thick-walled great affair, is now a barrack for soldiers. From here I go to-morrow to Lyons, and the next day to Paris, where you may think of me when you get this. There is this bit of my biography which you must fill out with ever so much enjoyment every day, and be thankful for, as I am.

I received letters from you at Venice to March 23. I am depending much on getting some more at Paris. You are all as good as can be about writing. I will try to pay you up when any of you come to Europe. Meanwhile, forgive my shortcomings. I see papers now more frequently; I am so glad that Congress has passed the Civil Rights Bill. Let them go on and do their duty, firmly, but without passion or exasperation, and all will be well in spite of Johnson.

All Europe is wondering whether there is going to be

war. Italy was in great excitement, and is longing for Venetia, which she ought to have. My opinion is not worth anything, for Bismarck has n't sent me word. But I believe the storm will blow over.

I expect to meet Strong in Paris in the course of a week. How long our plans will run together, I cannot tell till we meet. Only four or five months more, and I am with you. It will be a glad day. A million thanks for all your goodness in writing. You do not know how glad I am to get letters. No end of love to you all. PHILLIPS.

PARIS, May 9, 1866.

DEAR WILLIAM, — I have been in Paris now a week, and a busy week in Paris will let you know a good deal about the city. I have loafed in it from one end to the other, and have seen the bigger part of what is worth seeing in the town itself. Under these circumstances, I feel justified in deliberately asserting, and you may repeat it if you wish, on my authority, that Paris is considerable of a place. It is a great change from most of my other traveling, after Syrian tents, and Greek inns, and Italians albergos, and steamboat berths, to settle quietly down in this luxurious hotel, dine at nice restaurants, and walk all day on these bitumen sidewalks, which are the luxury of pedestrianism. I am glad I came here last. It is a better place to end than to begin with.

Paris, you know, is almost a new city. There is very little really ancient or mediæval left; even the memorials of its revolutionary days are hard to find. Everything is splendid with the lavish outlays of Napoleon III. I saw him and Mrs. Eugénie driving in the Champs Elysées the other day, and the little prince, who is said to be really a very remarkable boy, I saw driving into the Tuileries on Sunday. Paris is full of all sorts of people. Every day somebody turns up that I have known or heard of. I like it very well for a little while.

I don't know how long I shall stay here. I have some little thought of going over to London on Monday to see the very English sight of the Derby Day. I have also urgent letters from the Freedmen's friends there, who are going to have a public meeting some time this month. If I go, I shall stay in England about six weeks, and get a week or two more here before I go into Switzerland.

Father's and mother's letters by the Asia, of April 25, turned up to-day. That seems like being very near home. Tell them not to worry about the cholera. I shall keep as clear as possible of any places where it may show itself. I am delighted to hear that you are all well at home. Nothing but the war is talked of now. Things certainly look very belligerent. I did Venice just in time. Nobody is allowed to go there now.

By the way, our friend Mr. Ward is in London, and one of the active Freedmen's men. . . .

What an exceedingly disagreeable creature our chief magistrate is! I always take up a new paper now, sure that there will be another of those abominable vulgar speeches, and they are so weak and bad. If they had any strength in them, we could stand their vulgarity. Well, he can last only three years longer, and meanwhile everybody must work against him, as as they did against our other enemies.

This is not much of a letter to write from Paris, but perhaps next week I will give you a stunner about the Derby Day. Paris you must come and see for yourself. It's such an odd, splendid jumble that it can't be written about satisfactorily. However, I am well and happy, and you must take that for the burden of this letter. Affectionately,

PHILL.

LONDON, ALBEMARLE HOTEL,
May 18, 1866.

DEAR MOTHER, — I write in great haste this morning, because I do not want this week's mail to go without some indication of me. I am in London again and very well, that is about all that I have time to say. I left Paris behind me on Tuesday morning, and crossed the Channel by way of Boulogne and Folkestone. With my usual luck, I had a bright, smooth day, and none of those disagreeable scenes which are often witnessed on board the Channel boats.

I found London very full indeed, and only just succeeded in getting a room. Wednesday I went to the Derby Day. It is one of the great characteristic English sights; all the city of London shuts up shop, and goes out twenty miles into the country to Epsom, to see which of two horses will run the fastest. The excited look of the city, the stream of people of all ranks and sorts going out, the hosts who cover the grounds, the excitement of the race itself, and then the return to town at night, let you see one sort of English life as you cannot well see it anywhere else. The Prince of Wales was out there, and so was I.

This is the big thing that I have done in London this week. Besides this, I have been seeing the great city over again, and picking up new impressions of it. When I was here before, it was deserted; now it is crowded, and every excitement and fashion is at its height. You cannot think how strange it seems to get back into English ways, and in sound of our own language. Why, the very boys in the streets speak English! It seems like getting very near home again, and if it were not that I am to put off into foreign parts again by and by, I should feel as if my travelings were almost over. I hope to stay in England now till the end of next month. The country is not looking its best yet, though it is very beautiful. It seems as if you could not cut out a square mile anywhere from this England without getting a gem of a garden or a park.

About the Freedmen's business, of which I have feared that I should have a good deal when I reached here, I think I shall escape it almost altogether. The great financial crisis has interfered with their plans, and no meetings will be held. I am going to a private meeting of a Mr. Kinnaird, M. P., this evening. . . .

I called at the Adamses yesterday and saw Mr. Adams; Mrs. Adams was out. I shall see more of them, no doubt, by and by.

Strong met me in Paris and came on to London, and is now with me. I was delighted to see him and to hear about you all.

Four months more and I am with you. Until that happy day, I am always affectionately,

PHILLIPS.

ALBEMARLE HOTEL, LONDON, May 26.

DEAR MOTHER, — I must not let to-day's steamer go without a line to say that I am well. I am still in London, though I expect to leave for the country some time next week. I have promised to speak at a meeting at Birmingham, June 12, that will be my only public performance in England. Yours and father's and Arthur's reached me last Monday, and were most welcome. Tell Mr. Arthur to do it again, if he can.

London is full to the brim, and the weather is glorious. Every day has been very busy, seeing the endless sights. One day I went down to Canterbury, and spent the whole day at the cathedral and other old buildings there. It is a glorious place; next week I hope to get to Cambridge, and as soon as possible to Oxford.

Your cousins the Adamses are well and very hospitable, and inquire all about you. To-day the Scotia is in, and I hope she has some letters for me. She brings news of another veto of our precious President. English people think he is a great man.

Strong is with me, and will be, probably, most of the summer. It makes it very pleasant.

It looks now a little more as if they were going to get over the crisis in Europe without much fighting, but a little match may set the whole pile of combustibles off at any moment. This all makes it more fortunate that I came just when I did, and got through. No cholera anywhere, and don't worry about Switzerland. Lots of love to all. Affectionately,

PHILLIPS.

UNIVERSITY ARMS, CAMBRIDGE,
May 29, 1866.

DEAR FRED,[1] — I am in our Alma Mater's Mater. There is something charmingly homelike and familiar in old Cambridge. Outwardly unattractive by situation, but very lovely with old Gothic courts and build-

[1] His brother, Rev. Frederick Brooks.

ings, and all the beauty of noble old trees, perfect lawns, and blossomy hawthorns. The pretty Cam covered with college boats, the streets full of college faces and manners that might have been transplanted from the dear old banks of the Charles. The students seem to me very like indeed to Harvard boys, — the same average of age, the same general bearing, the same sort of talk. If anything especially gives them an advantage over us, it seems to be in the University system, the grouping of colleges so as to create a friendly corporate as well as personal rivalry, and the presence among them of older and mature scholars, residing on fellowships, etc., who raise the scholarly standards of the place higher than they could be set by mere undergraduate attainment.

Both of these advantages, I think, are capable of being engrafted on our system, and if they ever are, I see no reason why, in time, our greater freedom from old prescriptions and restraints should not make our University a better place than this. The beauty of the college grounds, their homey seclusion, and perfect vistas are past describing. Oxford, of course, surpasses Cambridge in all this, but Cambridge is a continual delight.

I only arrived to-day, but hope to stay a day or two, and see much more of the University life. From here I am going on a little trip to Peterborough, Ely, Norwich, and some other towns in this part of England. It is the season of seasons for its beauty. The Phillipses (this for father) came, I believe, from Raynham in Norfolk, or near it. You remember the original George, who came over and preached under a tree in Watertown, and died of an unfortunate colic. Don't you? Perhaps I have got them a little mixed up, but all those facts were among the household words of our childhood. . . .

As to my time in London, it was very full, but of a lot of things that you can get from the guide-books about as well as from me. I like London immensely. Last night I spent at the House of Commons. It was one of the great nights of the Reform Bill. By the kindness of Mr. Forster, I got admission to the Speaker's gallery. The best men on both sides spoke: Gladstone, calm, cool, clear, and courteous; Disraeli, jerky, spiteful, personal, very telling; Bright, honest, solid, indignant with the small trickery and meanness of the opposition; Mill, who holds people by sheer power of thought, as I have hardly ever seen any man do; Whiteside, Grey, and others. The government was defeated on a side issue by the manœuvring of the opposition, and the weakness of some of their own men. As to the look of the House, it certainly surprises one, who has heard their endless abuse of our legislative assemblies, which of course are bad enough. There was no such brutal outbreak as sometimes disgraces our noble representatives, but for constant and bitter personality, in place of argument, for boisterous and unmannerly carrying-on generally, Washington cannot beat them. In the middle of the evening, I dined with Mr. Forster and Mr. Bright, and had our great English friend pretty much to myself for two hours. He is a great talker, especially when he gets on to America, and he knows what he is talking about. Both he and Forster are friends worth having. Bright personally wins you in a minute by the frankness and cordialness and manliness of his greeting. Hughes, I saw, but not for any talk. The Reform Bill, little as it attempts, seems bound to fail.

One word about Venice. If I did not expatiate, it was not because I did not enjoy it immensely. It is all that your fancy ever painted. Some day I will tell you about it.

Many thanks for your photograph. It is capital, the very boy I used to see, lazily stretching his length in my chair in Spruce Street.

Strong wants me to remember him very kindly to you. We are having a great time. The new rector of the Trinity parish in Boston is to join us for Switzerland this summer. I wish you were to be the fourth.

I am to speak at a breakfast and public meeting in Birmingham for the freedmen. Probably I shall not have time to write to Boston this week, so either send them this letter, or let them know that I am well.

Be sure I shall think of you ever so much on your ordination day. God bless you. PHILL.

ALBEMARLE HOTEL, LONDON,
June 8, 1866.

DEAR WILLIAM, — There will be another very short and unsatisfactory letter, I am afraid, to-night. The fact is, I can tell you about London by and by a great deal better than I can write it, so we will put it off until I get home, which, by the way, will be on the 25th of September. I am to sail in the good steamer Ville de Paris, from Brest for New York, on the 15th of September, and shall be with you in ten days from that time. Does n't that sound near? I prefer the French steamers to the English, and this particular one is unsurpassed by any boat on the Atlantic. Look out for her.

To-day I have been to one of the great London sights of the year, the Charity Scholars' Festival, under the dome of St. Paul's, four thousand little wanderers gathered together and singing in chorus. I never heard anything so telling, the great building rang with their voices. A bishop preached the sermon. After the performance I had the pleasure of lunching with Dean Milman, a charming old gentleman. Do you not remember his "Belshazzar," that Dimmock used to spout? This evening I have spent with Browning, at the Storys' rooms (they have just come to London). He (Browning) was one of the men I wanted most to see here, a pleasant gentleman, full of talk about London and London people, with not a bit of the poet about him externally.

Last Monday I went to Eton, to their great annual festival. Do you remember Eton Montem in the "Parents' Assistant"? It was a fine day, and the country was looking very beautiful. And I saw the greatest of the great English schools at its best.

I wrote last week to Fred from Cambridge. I continued my trip to Peterborough, Ely, and Norwich, and enjoyed immensely the great cathedrals of all the towns and the perfect English country. Strong has left me for a week or two to go to northern England, to see some places which I visited last fall. I am going in a day or two, and shall be at Birmingham for a Freedmen's meeting, on the 12th; at Oxford for the great Commemoration on the 13th, and then keep west. Meet Strong again at Chester, take a run through Wales, and the southern part of England, and get back to London about the first of July, and then be off to Switzerland with your rector.

An "Advertiser" to-night with Seward's speech. So good-by; engage Robin for September 26. I am very well. Lots of love to all. Good-night.

PHILL.

WARWICK ARMS, WARWICK, June 14.

DEAR FATHER, — If a letter is going to you at home this week, it must be written to-night, and yet I confess I don't feel much like writing it. I have just reached here, am very tired, and the waiter is thinking of bringing me some dinner. Until it comes, I will try to talk to you, and you must not be surprised if you find me stupid. When I woke up this morning, I found myself in Stratford-on-Avon, where I faintly remembered arriving late last night; I arose as soon as I realized where I was, and took a walk before breakfast across the nicest and quaintest of English fields, to see the old farmhouse where Shakespeare made love, where Anne Hathaway used to live. The old cottage stands without an alteration, and is a charming little place. Then I came back to breakfast, and after that was over, went off to see the rest, — the birthplace, schoolhouse, burial-place, and all that belongs to the poet's life here, which we know very well by pictures that we have seen all our lives. Nothing in England, I think, has a stronger charm than this queer old town. About noon, I took the train for Warwick, but, finding I was too late to see the castle to-day, I looked at the church with its monuments, the finest, best preserved in all England, and then drove across the loveliest of country, stopping at Guy's Cliff, where the earliest of the Warwicks, the hero of the fairy stories, used to put up (and he had a splendid place of it), to Kenilworth, where I spent the whole afternoon among the ruins, and such an afternoon as you will never know anything about till you come over and do just the same thing. By the way, are you not making up your mind to come over to the great Paris fair of next year? It is time for you and mother to be thinking about it. Then I came down to Leamington, and spent an hour or two in the park of an English watering-place, and finally took the train back to Warwick, where I am waiting to see the noblest castle in England to-morrow morning. That is what I have done to-day. Yesterday I spent at Oxford; it was Commemoration, which is their Commencement, a strange sight,—perfect wild license of the students, and the freest liberty to chaff, and hoot, and cheer as they please. It was a picture that is not to be seen anywhere else. The day before that, I was in Birmingham, telling Britons that they had been slaves to prejudice and self-interest about America. The day before that, I was at Blenheim, the great palace of Marlborough. Do you remember Mr. Everett's splendid description of it in his Washington address? The two days before that, I was in Oxford (Saturday and Sunday) enjoying the most perfect college landscapes, and some of the kindest hospitality in the world. That takes me back about to my last letter, and accounts pretty fully for my week.

I did not get yours of last week; they are waiting for me at Chester, where I shall call for them on Monday, on my way into Wales. I hope you are all well. The Fenians seem to be restless again; I hope we shall put them down with their nonsense. And why do you not either try Jeff Davis, or let him go? It would be a great relief to foreign travelers. Before you get this, the great war will probably have begun over here, and promises to be terrible. Three months from to-morrow I sail for you all. Good-by. God bless you always. Affectionately,

PHILLIPS.

THE GOAT HOTEL, BEDDGELERT, WALES,
June 20, 1866.

DEAR MOTHER, — I am thinking that to-day is Fred's ordination day, and that you and father are in Philadelphia. Am I right? How I wish I could be with you. I wonder where the ordination is? I hope in my old church. It would always be a very pleasant thing to think of his having been ordained there; wherever it is, I wish him with all my heart every blessing and success in his ministry. Of course, you will write me about it at once.

I am in Wales. Get your map and find this little valley where we have hauled up in the rain. It lies at the foot of Snowdon, shut in by grand, bleak Welsh hills, with a little brawling picturesque Welsh stream tumbling among them. It is the place, you know, of the old murder of the faithful hound by his master, Llewellyn. Gelert's grave is in the garden of the hotel. My views of Wales are much like Jonah's, very wet; it has rained, off and on, pretty much all day, while we (Strong and I) have been driving first by coach to Llanberis from Caernarvon, and then from Llanberis here by post. Caernarvon is on the coast, with a noble ivy-grown castle of early times, where the first Prince of Wales was born. The people talk an unintelligible gibberish without vowels, and the women wear shabby hats, and all looks quaint, quiet, and thrifty. The road thence to Llanberis is very beautiful, and Llanberis itself nobly situated at the entrance of a pass, and interesting with its pretty waterfalls, and a most picturesque tower of the sixth century. It has vast quarries of slate. The schoolboys and the house roofs bid fair to be kept supplied for years to come. From Llanberis to Beddgelert the scenery is glorious. The wildest pass, with tremendous cliffs, countless waterfalls, ivied cottages, and quaint, odd-looking people everywhere. Wales delights one with its grandness and majesty, as unlike sunny England as can be.

I think I wrote you last week from Warwick; thence I traveled to Rugby, and saw the old school, and all that reminds one of Dr. Arnold, its great master. The boys were at a cricket match in the close, and all looked just as it ought. Then to Coventry, where are some of the greatest churches and quaintest houses in England, and "Peeping Tom," still looking out of a hole of a corner house, in perpetual effigy. Then to Chatsworth, the noblest private residence in England, the seat of the Duke of Devonshire, and near it Haddon Hall, a perfectly kept specimen of the old baronial hall, the best in the kingdom; then to Litchfield, where I spent Sunday. A beautiful cathedral, a lovely country, and much of interest in connection with Dr. Johnson's birth in the town, and its previous active part in the Civil Wars. Monday to Chester, where I was rejoined by Strong, and met Potter (your rector), who joined us the next day to Conway, where is a great old castle, and then to Bangor and the wonderful tubular bridge over the Menai Straits; then rail to Caernarvon, which brings my story complete. Potter left us to-day to push direct to London, where he will join us in a couple of weeks to start for the Continent. He is very well, and seems full of hope about Trinity. I think it very likely that we may return together.

So you see I jog on. Every day is full of new pleasure, and every day bringing me nearer and nearer home. I have begun to count the weeks; only fourteen more, and I am with you. Won't it be nice? This terrible war, which has begun now, will perhaps interfere with some of my summer plans. But that will be the least of its evils, and I will not complain. I have been very fortunate, and have seen, it may be, more than I can digest.

I found letters from you at Chester, but now shall get no more till I reach London, ten days hence, which is hard.

I hear from Philadelphia that all goes well, but I want to be there more than I am wanted. I had a letter from Dr. Vinton a week or two ago. How I wish I could get into the back parlor to-night, and I would tell you a great deal more about this splendid Wales. Good-by, and love to all. I am very well, and always your loving son, PHILLIPS.

ALBEMARLE HOTEL, LONDON,
June 29, 1866.

DEAR WILLIAM, — Last week's letter was sent from the heart of Wales, the foot of Snowdon. This is from the metropolis again, so I spin along. During the week I have seen and done a good deal. We climbed to the "Tip Top House" of Snowdon, and so began in a mild way our summer's mountaining. The climb does not amount to much. The view is one of the noblest I know, with infinite variety of hill, valley, and lake, and the sea in the distance. Then we took a long ride through most perfect scenery from Beddgelert to Port Madoc, down the coast to Barmouth, and thence to Dolgelly. This last stage, from Barmouth to Dolgelly, is the finest bit in Wales, and can hardly be surpassed anywhere. You must take it when you come abroad.

From Dolgelly we came across the country to Shrewsbury, then down to Hereford, where there is a fine old cathedral, on to Ross, and thence by a most beautiful ride down the valley of the Wye to Monmouth, where we spent Sunday, a pretty and deadly quiet little village. Keeping still down the Wye to Chepstowe, we passed Tintern Abbey, the most beautiful monastic ruin in England. You cannot conceive how lovely it is, with its exquisite arches, perfect windows, and immense masses of rich ivy, Chepstowe to Gloucester, Worcester, Bristol, Wells, all interesting towns, with historical associations, fine old buildings, and delightful scenery. Then to Salisbury, and there I saw what is to me the most impressive thing by far in all England, Stonehenge, the old Briton temple out on Salisbury plain. A drive of eight miles from the town, over the green, flat plain, got us there just before dusk, and we saw the gigantic ruin looking its lordliest. There was something very grand and absolutely refreshing in those enormous rude, gray stones, the symbols of old strength, and will, and worship. I would rather miss seeing anything else in England than Stonehenge. From Salisbury to Southampton, and thence to Winchester, which is full of interest, and then back to smoky, dingy, grand old London. The whole trip has been delightful, weather fine, except one or two days, and the scenery looking its best. Now I have done with England, and shall start Monday morning for Paris again, and by next week's end be in Switzerland.

I found letters here from you, for which no end of thanks. You don't know how much I enjoy them. Next Monday is your birthday. All hail to you, O thirty-two!

I met your friend, Mrs. Walter Baker, in Wales. Tell father and mother I want to know all about the ordination. Good-by, and in three months more I am with you. Love to all.

  Your affectionate brother,   P HILL.

           S TRASBURG, July 7, 1866.

D EAR M OTHER, — I have an hour or two on my hands, and will begin my next week's letter. I am on the wing again, you see, and set for Switzerland. Yesterday I was at Rheims, one of the most interesting towns of France, where all the old kings used to be crowned, and where a good many of them are buried. Its cathedral is a wonderful thing of the richest and noblest Gothic. There are old Roman remains in the town, too. These Romans are everywhere. Then I came on here. I wish you could see Strasburg; you could hardly find a better specimen of an old town, half French, half German, than this is. It is strange to hear them talking German once more. It seems like last autumn over again. This afternoon I am going to Baden-Baden, the great watering and gaming place. There I shall spend Sunday. Thanks to the submission of Austria, it seems now as if the whole Continent would be open enough to travel. Is n't the news good? All France is waving with flags for the glory that has come to her in the business. Italy will be the best monument that Louis Napoleon will leave behind him, and it will cover many of his misdeeds. I should like to be in Venetia now, and see their rejoicings.

           B ASLE, Tuesday, July 10.

I had a day or two in Baden-Baden, and then came on as far as here, where my tour of Switzerland really begins. I enjoyed Baden very much indeed. Its situation is most beautiful, and everything just now is looking its best. The great gambling-place is not quite as full as usual this year. The war has kept some away, but there is plenty of gayety there, and the tables are going from morning until night. Sunday morning, just after breakfast, I saw them at it, and I did not sit up late enough to see the end. The walks and drives through the country about Baden are charming. No wonder it is a place of such attraction. I came from there here. This is a quiet little town, with the usual old cathedral and a picture gallery, and the Rhine running through it. There is nothing particularly interesting about it. I am waiting only till this afternoon for Strong, whom I left in Paris, and who will probably overtake me here. . . .

It is getting quite warm, and no doubt we shall suffer enough from the heat in some parts of Switzerland; but there are always the mountains to retreat to, and with a glacier close at hand one ought to be able to get along.

I hope you are counting the time as closely as I am to my getting home. Only twelve weeks more, and there I am. How you will miss the chance of writing me a letter every week, and what a saving there will be in postage! I am hoping to hear, when I get to Geneva, of Fred's ordination, and perhaps of his settlement somewhere. I hope he will not be in a hurry to decide where to go. There is so much to do everywhere that he can have his choice, and it will be a great deal better if he waits till fall.

I am glad you have had a journey. I hope you went to West Point and Niagara. I depend on hearing all about it. Next year you and father must come over to the Great Exposition. Now good-by for another week. Love to all.

Most affectionately,   PHILLIPS.

CHAMOUNIX, Tuesday Evening, July 17, 1866.

DEAR WILLIAM, — I write to you to-night from the foot of Mont Blanc. I do not in the least expect the letter to be worthy of the place, but here I am in the Hotel Royal. Early this morning, George Strong and I left Geneva (about which I will not tell you anything, except that the lake is one of the loveliest things on the earth), in the back boot of a big lumbering diligence, with five horses, and set our faces towards the Alps. For five broiling hours the country was tame and dull, and nothing seemed to foretell Switzerland, except the increasing number of horrid-looking people with goitres on their necks, who came with idiotic grins to beg by the coach side. About noon, the hills began to gather round us, an occasional snow patch was seen up among the clouds, now and then a waterfall came hurling itself down, and saying something in the Alpine tongue, which we had n't yet learned to understand. At one o'clock (I want to be exact about such an important moment in my life), we drove into the little village of St. Martin, and, turning suddenly to cross the gray, small river Arve, which had been brawling at our side all the way, the driver pulled up his five horses, and there was Mont Blanc, as vast, and grand, and white as one has dreamed of it, twelve miles off, they said, though it might as well have been twelve hundred, it seemed so unapproachable and far away, although we saw its whole outline, and the ridges in its snow, and the great black needles standing up out of the white distinctly. Well, we had a pretty good lunch at the town on the other side of the bridge, called Sallanches, and then, leaving our diligence behind, took small carriages and started for Chamounix. It was awfully hot. Our brains sizzled and steamed. I have been as hot only once or twice; never hotter. And the snow peaks were looking down, and making cool fun of us all the time. By and by, we came to a steep hill, and had to get out and climb three miles. When we reached the top, Mont Blanc was nearer and plainer, and we could see the great glaciers running down the sides, and almost catch the sparkle of the intense white snow on top. Then the heat broke up in rain, and it poured down, first in great big Alpine drops, and then in sheets, for the next two or three miles. When this was over, a great rainbow came, tied itself like a sash on the white shoulder of the ridge, and fell down across its white robe to its feet.

We entered the valley of Chamounix, passed along by the foot of the Glacier des Boissons, saw the Mer de Glace in the distance, crossed a lot of boisterous little streams, that came down just fresh from the great calm snow, rattled over a bridge across the Arve again, and were in the village; secured rooms in a sort of supplement to the hotel, which is called the Crystal Palace, and found ourselves just in time for the six o'clock table d'hôte.

Chamounix as a village is principally three great hotels, with no end of little ones. All the other houses are connected in some way with Alpine tourists. It is safe to ask at any house for an alpenstock. The general appearance of the town reminds me of Gorham, only there is n't a railway, and there is Mont Blanc. It is raining guns to-night, but my pair of big shoes, with nails in the soles, are out already for to-morrow. Meanwhile, a flash of lightning every now and then cuts across a gap, through which you can look at the snow, that has laughed at some thousands and thousands of rain-storms.

There, young man, sometimes you complain that I don't tell you what I am doing. Look at that! I flatter myself nobody ever made more out of a day's ride than that; certainly you will know at least how I got from Geneva to Chamounix.

At Geneva, I found letters, all whose burden was the great Philadelphia visit. One from you, one from father, one from Mr. Coffin, and a little slip from Fred. I am rejoiced that all went off so well, and now I depend upon hearing about the new Reverend's future plans. Four months from to-day I shall be on the ocean. The Ville de Paris made a passage of nine days lately, so I think you and Robin may look for me on the 26th. Now good-by. Glory, glory, gloriation! ten more weeks before vacation.

. . . PHILL.

GIESSBACH, SWITZERLAND, August 5, 1866.

DEAR MOTHER, — To-day, I am up here in the woods, with the famous Falls of Giessbach tumbling and roaring in front of my windows, spending Sunday in what, if it were not for the great hotel, would be the most retired nook of all creation.

At Interlaken, the other day, I received three weeks' accumulation of letters; a good feast after a long starvation. I must defer all accounts of my own minor travels to congratulate you on the great achievement of your Niagara. I am very thankful that you have been there. It is certainly the greatest wonder of Nature, which remark has been made about it before, perhaps, but I want to assure your complacency by letting you be confident that the Old World has nothing to show that will compare with it. Mont Blanc is pretty grand, and there is no reason why you should not see that, too, some day, but for the present you may rest well satisfied with Niagara.

It seems lucky, with such a houseful as you have had, that one of the boys was safely out of the way in Europe.... This last week, I have been seeing the wonders and the beauties of the Bernese Oberland, as it is called, that part of Switzerland which lies about the lake of Thun. Then from Macugnaga, where I wrote last Sunday, I came down the valley of Anzasca to Domo d' Ossola, then over the great Simplon Road to Brieg, over the Gemmi Pass to Thun, down the lake of Lucerne, over the mountains, close to the splendid Jungfrau to Meyringen, and from there to this mountain side on the lake of Brienz. It has all been splendid. The beauty of Switzerland is, that it has no dull places, and one is never tired, only sometimes bewildered a little with its endless attractions. Strong and I are still together.

The great interest of your letters was what you told me of Fred's beginnings in the good work. Everything seems to be going splendidly with him, as everybody knew it would. I hear indirectly from parishioners, whom I meet here, of how great is the impression that he made in Philadelphia. I hope he will not be in such a hurry to settle far away, but that I shall see him somewhere in September.

This is a poor letter, still I am no less your loving

son, and will tell you so by word of mouth in seven weeks and a half. Good-by, love to all.

PHILLIPS.

ARONA, LAGO MAGGIORE,
Sunday, August 12, 1866.

DEAR WILLIAM, — Last week I wrote from the borders of the lake of Brienz. To-day you see I am on an Italian lake, in a different atmosphere and among a very different people. The traveler over these Swiss passes is constantly changing back and forth between two nations and climates, as different as any to be conceived of. It was very striking, the other day, as we came over the St. Gotthard. At two o'clock we were in the midst of snow fields and icy streams, bleak mountain tops and cold, bitter winds; then, as we began to descend, we came to sun, fruits, and flowers, and at five o'clock were reveling in the softest air and sunniest sky, the roads were hemmed in by endless vineyards, the girls were offering peaches and apricots at the diligence window, and soft Italian words had taken the place in the lazy-looking people's mouths of the harsher German.

Since last Sunday I have crossed the lake of Brienz, passed through the Brunig Pass to Lucerne, sailed over its lake, the most picturesque in Switzerland, climbed the Rigi, and spent the inevitable night there among its swarming tourists (the sunset was glorious, but the sun rose nobody knew when, for the dense cloud). We then drove to Andermatt, where we stopped to climb the Furca Pass and see the great Glacier of the Rhone, over the St. Gotthard, and down this noble lake to its southern point, whence I write to you. There is a feeble band playing outside the hotel, a young woman is walking across a rope over the street, and all the ceremonies of a Sunday circus are in full blast, to the great enjoyment of the population, priests and all.

We shall spend a few days here among the lakes, and then strike northward again. Our plans will be regulated somewhat by the possibility which the very unsettled state of affairs allows of our visiting more or less of the Tyrol, but we hope to come out any way at Munich, and get a day or two there before I return to Paris to sail. To-day's newspaper brings the news that the armistice is signed at last and peace must follow soon. Mr. L. Napoleon, it seems, is cutting in about those Rhine provinces, and will probably get what he wants; it is a way he has. . . .

I received a letter from you at Andermatt, and a good one, too. Is Fred still with you? I hope soon to hear something about his plans. Isn't it funny, to think that this is the last letter you will have any chance to answer? Good-night, no end of love to all.
Affectionately,
PHILLIPS.

THUSIS, SWITZERLAND,
Sunday, August 19, 1866.

DEAR FATHER, — I wrote the other day to Fred, but I suppose that will not be allowed to pass for my weekly letter. At any rate, as there are only two more to write, I won't be mean, but give you the full measure. We are beginning to see our way through Switzerland now, and there are no broken heads or legs. Last Sunday I wrote from the lower end of lake Maggiore. Since then we have seen the lakes Maggiore, Lugano, and Como; all of them, especially the last, very beautiful. Indeed, in its own sort, nothing can be more lovely than lake Como. We stayed one day at Bellagio on its eastern shore, and then sailed down to Como, where we spent a night, and then up to Colico near its head.

From here we drove over the Maloja Pass into the upper Engadine, one of the most interesting regions of all Switzerland, peculiar in climate, scenery, and customs. Their own description of their climate is that they have "nine months winter and three months cold," and as we entered their high table-land, out of sunny Italy, we put on great-coats and buttoned up to the chin against the bitter cold. The scenery is very grand, hardly surpassed in the region of Mont Blanc or Monte Rosa. We stopped at Pontresina, and from there climbed the Piz Languard, the observatory mountain of the district, and had snow-peak and glacier views of surpassing grandeur to our hearts' content. Think of that, while you were sweltering in Boston dog-days. They call their language, down there, the Ladein, and it comes nearer to the genuine old Latin than anything else in existence. It was very interesting. There is a great bathing establishment in the Engadine, called St. Moritz, with lots of visitors, among others, a Mr. G. McClellan, formerly an American general. I did not see him.

From Pontresina we drove over the Alps again by the Julier Pass to Tiefenkasten, and from there walked across one of the picturesque foot passes to this little village on the banks of the infant Rhine, at the gate of the great Splugen Pass. From here we shall explore the Splugen and its wonderful Via Mala, then go north by Zurich to Constance, through their lakes, and so on to Munich. From there a little trip into the Austrian Tyrol, then back to Paris, where I hope to be three weeks from to-day. Four weeks from yesterday my boat is on the shore, my bark is on the sea, and my foreign travels will be over.

There has been a great deal of heavy rain in Switzerland this year, but we have very happily escaped it almost all. I remember only four rainy days. It looks now a little as if it might be ugly weather to-morrow.

No letters from home lately. Some more are ordered to Zurich, where I shall get them Wednesday or Thursday. I hope you are all well and begin to have a sort of confidence that, as all has gone so capitally so far, I shall have no disappointment or bad news for the rest of my time. I hope you will have as perfect a success when you come. The Exposition, you know, is next summer.

Strong wishes to be remembered to you. I suppose he will return to Paris with me.

PHILLIPS.

HOTEL VIERJAHRESZEITEN, MUNICH,
Sunday, August 26, 1866.

DEAR MOTHER, — Here goes for my last letter but one. If you have done such a foolish thing as to keep any of my letters, you might find among them one, almost a year back, dated from this same hotel with the horrible name to it, where I am writing now. How little time ago it seems! But what a lot has come in between. It was last October, and I was just going to Vienna; since then, all the East, Italy, France, England, and now Switzerland. Yes, Switzerland is done, and except for the little glimpse that I shall get of them in the beautiful Tyrol, I have seen my last of the white hills. I look forward to nothing afterwards but a quiet week of loafing in Paris, and then the steamer. Two weeks after you get this, I hope you will get me.

I found letters at Constance from William and Mr. Coffin. William's was from that paradise on the seashore where they all went this summer. They seem to be having a splendid time, and not to envy even Switzerland. I do not wonder that they enjoyed it, for they had sufficiently varied materials for a very pleasant party. I am glad that Fred was with them, and was not rector of anything up to that date. I dare not hope that such a state of things will last long, but it makes me think that I may possibly find him not yet emigrated to any of the ends of the earth when I get back.

The great item of home news in the two last letters is one that interests me deeply. Bridget has gone! You only state the bald fact, but give no particulars about her successor, as if it were not a matter of profound interest, even to an occasional visitor under the home roof. I do not care what her name is, but what can she do? Has she any power to create those particular home dishes that have never been seen anywhere else? Or is she some new person, who will introduce another order of things, and serve up the same round of endless stuff that one gets everywhere besides? Remember, I insist on flapjacks and fishballs. As to Bridget, she never was a cheerful person; rather glum and solemn, not a sunshiny picture to have about the house; and her flapjacks for the last few years were nothing to what they were, a trifle clammy and heavy; so that I will not shed any tears over her departure, but hope the new-comer may beat her all hollow.

If this seems a foolish letter to send over the seas, just turn to my exceedingly sensible one, which I have no doubt I wrote last year, and read all you want to know about Munich. What's the use of writing when I can tell you all in four weeks? Good-by. Love to everybody.

PHILLIPS.

GRAND HOTEL, PARIS, September 6, 1866.

DEAR WILLIAM, — In answer to your last letter, here comes mine, written in a great hurry, at the last moment; you see I am so lazy, this farewell week in Paris, that I have not time for anything. My work is over, and I am just sitting here like a fellow who runs over the index of the book he has been reading, to see this epitome of all Europe and of all the world, — the cosmopolitan city, sparkling, beautiful Paris. But you will be here some day and see it for yourself, so what's the use of telling you? Since I wrote from Munich, I have roamed down into the Tyrol and back again, and seen there some of the most picturesque of scenery and life. Then I put right off for here, where I shall stay till a week from to-morrow morning, when I take the train for a sixteen hours' ride to Brest, and then on Saturday afternoon go aboard the Ville de Paris, Captain Saumon, for New York. I shall get out of New York by the earliest conveyance for Boston, and probably be with you some time on the 26th or 27th. The last trip of the steamer from New York took a little over nine days. We shall be likely, at this season, to be a little slower, but you shall see me as soon as I can get over to Boston. Will you not drop a line to New York and tell them to send the "Nation" to Philadelphia?

So good-by. When you hear the doorbell ring at No. 41, some time week after next, if you don't make haste to let me in, I will give it to you.

Your affectionate brother, PHILL.

IN THE TYROL AND SWITZERLAND.

1870.

STEAMER HAMMONIA, Thursday, July 7, 1870.

DEAR FATHER, — It rains to-day, and is very wet, miserable, and disagreeable, the second bad day we have had on our voyage. One cannot go on deck without getting wet through and his eyes full of cinders. The cabin is crowded and close, and I have slept and read till I cannot sleep or read any more; so you see it is time to begin to write home, and report myself.

We got off safely on Tuesday, the 28th, punctually at two o'clock. Monday night I spent at Potter's, and we went up to Thomas's Gardens and heard music. Mr. and Mrs. Franks met me at the station, but I suppose you have seen them before this. We were a queer set who sailed together, not many Americans, — Germans, Italians, Mexicans, Danes, and all sorts of people. It makes a very interesting ship's company. There are a lot of Jews; nobody except Dr. Derby and his wife and the Mason family, whom I ever saw before. The ship is a good one, not equal in size or speed to the Cunard or French steamers, but more convenient in some respects.

We have had a splendid passage, only two rainy days; most of the time clear, bright, sunny weather, and now moonlight nights. Being a screw steamer, she rolls pretty badly. I have been perfectly well and enjoyed it immensely. We shall be rather later than I expected; probably reach Plymouth some time to-morrow night, and Cherbourg Saturday morning. I shall go to Paris on Saturday night, and reach there about four o'clock on Sunday morning. I will mail this at Plymouth, and your getting it will show you that I am so far safe. You probably will have seen the ship reported by telegraph. It has been a most propitious beginning for my little trip.

I wonder what has happened at home since I left. Be sure and write me everything; write every week, some of you. I hope you are off to Niagara before this. Love all around.

Affectionately your son, PHILLIPS.

COURMAYEUR, ITALY,
Sunday, July 17, 1870.

DEAR MOTHER, — I have not written since I landed, of which I am a little ashamed, but I have been very busy, and it has been hard to find a place to write in. But here I am, on Sunday afternoon, sitting on the gallery of this queer hotel, in this funny old Italian town, on the south side of the Alps. In front is a tremendous mountain, with a great glacier upon its face, and at the foot an old square tower with a peaked roof, which may have been a fortress, but is now a house full of beggars; and in the street in front there is a crowd of people chattering a vile language which is half Italian and half French. This morning I went to the English service here and heard a pretty good sermon. This afternoon I thought I would rather write to you.

When I wrote to father we were still on the Hammonia. She reached Plymouth on Friday afternoon, the 8th of July, and we landed a few passengers and then sailed to Cherbourg, where we arrived very early Saturday morning, the 9th. I landed about five o'clock, and the steamer went on to Hamburg. From Cherbourg it was a ride of all day by train to Paris, from eight A. M. to six P. M. The first part of the ride was through a country wholly new to me and very interesting, — Normandy, with its quaint people, towns, and splendid cathedrals; Bayeux and Caen, and so on. I stayed over Sunday, Monday, and Tuesday in Paris, made some purchases, and enjoyed the life of the wonderful gay city. Then I rode all Tuesday night by rail to Geneva, where I met Cooper, and our Alpine trip began. First we drove to Chamounix and looked Mont Blanc in the face, from the side where I have seen him before. He was good enough to be perfectly clear, and we saw him splendidly.

The next morning we started, and had a hard day's tramp over the Col de Voza and through two of the great valleys of the Mont Blanc range, with magnificent views all the way, and spent the night way up in the heart of the hills at a mountain chalet, where the cows and sheep had the lower story and we had the upper. It smelt of them a little, and we heard their bells, but the beds were good and we were very tired. The next morning we set out at five o'clock, and walked thirty-three miles over three high passes, across snow and rocks, and finally through the Allée Blanche, the great gorge behind Mont Blanc, with its tremendous dome and its pinnacles and great rocky wall towering over us. It was splendid beyond all description. We reached here at ten o'clock well tired out, and to-day are resting. From here we go on to Aosta; then across the St. Theodule Pass to Zermatt, and shall spend next Sunday probably at Andermatt on the St. Gotthard Pass.

I have engaged passage home by the Ville de Paris, to sail on the 10th of September from Brest; the same steamer in which I returned before.

Everywhere there are rumors of wars about the Spanish business, but for three days we have been out of reach of telegraph and cannot know anything of their truth. Please tell father that I bought some bronzes in Paris, and ask him to pay the charges on the box and keep it for me.

I have none of your letters yet, and shall not have any for a week or more; but do keep writing. I hope that you have been to Niagara. Good-by, love to all. PHILLIPS.

ANDERMATT, July 24, 1870.

DEAR WILLIAM, — I wonder what you have all been about at home since I left you at the Worcester station four weeks ago to-morrow morning. I have not heard a word yet, and shall not get letters till to-morrow night, when we reach Coire, to which place I have ordered letters sent. I hope you are all well and having a pleasant summer. Last Sunday I wrote to mother from Courmayeur in Italy. Since then we have had a week of splendid weather and constant movement.

First, we rode down the beautiful valley of Aosta to Chatillon through vineyards, Italian towns, and very hot Italian roads. Tuesday we climbed up the steep and ugly valley of Val Tournanche and slept at Breuil, under the shadow of the splendid Matterhorn. Wednesday we crossed from Italy to Switzerland again by the glacier pass of St. Theodule, between the

Matterhorn and Monte Rosa, with great views of both and a hundred giants besides, and descended to Zermatt. Thursday we came down from Zermatt to the valley of the Rhone, and slept at Fiesch; Friday we climbed the Eggishorn, one of the most magnificent points of view in all Switzerland, commanding the Jungfrau and its big neighbors and the great Aletsch Glacier (the longest in Switzerland), the Matterhorn, and Mont Blanc. Yesterday we came over the Furca Pass, close beside the great Rhone Glacier, out of which the mighty river starts, and reached this quiet little German-Swiss village on the St. Gotthard road yesterday evening.

It is a lovely day, and it is good to rest for twenty-four hours. To-morrow we are off for a ramble through northeast Switzerland, and shall bring up next Sunday at Ober-Ammergau for the great Miracle Play. When that is over, I shall have five weeks still for a journey in the Tyrol before I go back to Paris to sail for home.

Meanwhile, there is war in Europe, the most unnecessary and wicked of wars that ever was made. France has been insolent and arrogant beyond herself. It probably will be short and severe. A troop of soldiers just passed by the hotel. Switzerland, of course, is neutral, but is arming her borders. We have been out of the way of the war as yet, and probably shall not see much of it.

Do write me how everything goes on at home and at the church. Give my love to Mary, and to all at home.   Affectionately,   PHILL.

ISCHL, AUSTRIA, July 31, 1870.

DEAR FATHER, — You have written me twice, and well deserve that this Sunday's letter should go to you. This Ischl is the great watering-place of Austria. Here the Emperor has his summer palace, and the great Vienna swells come hither to be under the shadow of his magnificence. Of course we Americans come, too, to see the fun. Besides this, it is one of the most beautiful spots on the face of the earth. It is at the junction of five of the most lovely wild Tyrolese valleys, and is a pretty little open piece of plain with two bright streams running through it.

We were at Andermatt last Sunday. We crossed the Oberalp on Monday, a long day's ride to Coire. There we spent a day, making a visit to the famous baths of Pfäffers. From Coire we went by the lake of Constance and by rail to a quiet little Bavarian town, called Kempten. Here we heard what we had rumors of before, that the great Ober-Ammergau Passion Play was given up on account of the war, several of the principal characters having been drafted into the Bavarian army. This was a disappointment, for it was one of the great things which I had hoped to see in coming abroad. On Thursday we pushed on to Munich. Friday morning I saw at Munich a great mass in the cathedral on behalf of the German side of the war. The King and all his court were present. Bavaria seems very enthusiastic on the German side. From Munich on Friday afternoon to Salzburg, the most picturesque of towns, where I had been five years ago, but was very glad to be again. Yesterday the loveliest ride, first by rail to the head of the Traun See; then a beautiful sail down the lake, and a ride of two hours up the valley of the Traun River to Austria, and here we are.

The preparations for war go on. They interfere with us only so far as money is concerned. At Munich we had to lose eight per cent. on a draft on Paris. We have had no disappointment yet, except Ober-Ammergau. The Masons are here. I saw the Morrills at Munich. Your letters received up to July 9th. Now we go out of reach of letters for several weeks. I am very well. Love to all.

Affectionately,   PHILL.

MALNITZ, August 7, 1870.

DEAR MOTHER, — I think you will not find this town on any map at home. Indeed, it is not easy to find when one is very close to it, for it is hidden away among mountains of the biggest kind, and is the littlest sort of a town itself. Besides this Hôtel of the Chamois, where we are staying, and the church, which, like all the churches of this region, seems unreasonably large for the population, there is not another good-sized building in the village. The streets are sheep-paths, and there is not a vehicle in the town. But the scenery is gorgeous, and the simple ways of the people are very interesting. Yesterday, we walked over a high mountain pass from Bad Gastein. It is a rough and steep road, with a good deal of snow, etc. All along the road were little shrines, put up where men at dangerous parts of the year had lost their lives by avalanches or falls, with rude pictures of the accident, and an address to the Virgin, and a horrible religious painting or carving of some sort. The people are very religious and very hospitable. It is quite pretty, the way they bless you and kiss your hand when you go away, particularly if you have paid them well.

To be sure, their bread is dreadful, and their meat is cooked in fearful and wonderful ways; but there is plenty of good milk and splendid beer everywhere, and eggs and trout abound; you always walk enough to be hungry for any food. The beds are short, and the bedclothes shorter, but one gets along with a supplementary shawl and plenty of fatigue; and the mountains, lakes, meadows and waterfalls, are glorious. We have had a splendid week. Monday and Tuesday we spent among the lakes of the Salzkammergut, the region about Ischl. There are a score of them, all beautiful, shut in by mountains, which you cross from one to another; and there is always a Tyrolese girl, ready to take her boat and row you across to start on for another.

Wednesday, we took a carriage, and for two days drove through the valley of the Salza, till, far up among the hills, we came to the very beautiful watering place of the Austrians, Bad Gastein. It is lovely as a dream,—just a deep mountain gorge with a wild cataract plunging down through it, and splendid mountains towering above; mineral baths, which are very pleasant. Yesterday, we walked across the mountains, partly in the rain, spending two hours, while it was pouring, far up in a chalet, where they were making Swiss cheese in the dirtiest and most picturesque hole you ever saw. This is the first untimely rain that we have had. This next week will be our finest mountain week.

The war goes on, but we only hear of it by occasionally seeing a week-old paper at some country inn. I hope it will not interfere with my getting to Paris and sailing on the 10th of September. That is my selfish view of it.

I shall not hear yet for three weeks, but then expect a batch of letters. I hope you are all well. Love to all. Affectionately your son,

PHILLIPS.

MERAN, TYROL, August 14, 1870.

DEAR FRED, — I have been meaning to write you ever since I came abroad; especially, I had a notion of writing to you on your birthday, the glorious 5th, but the mountains were too many for me, and every night I was so tired that I was fain to get into my uncomfortable little Dutch bed as soon as possible. I warn you beforehand, that you will have an awful time with the beds when you come into these parts. You and I are too long. I have just escaped from a bed at this untimely hour on Sunday morning, because I could not stretch out straight, or make the narrow bedclothes come over me, and that's the reason why at this present moment I come to be writing to you.

I have had five glorious weeks of Switzerland and the Tyrol, Mont Blanc, Monte Rosa, the Matterhorn, the Jungfrau, the Grossglockner, and the Marmolata. I have seen them all face to face, had splendid weather, walked myself into good condition, found the people interesting and amusing everywhere, and met with only one disappointment. That was in the giving up of the great Miracle Play at Ober-Ammergau, on account of the war, just before we reached there. It was a great disappointment, for one can never have another chance, and every one who saw it speaks of it as very wonderful.

For the last three weeks we have been in the Tyrol.

I like the people immensely, especially in south Tyrol; they seem to me to be the most cheerful, industrious, hospitable peasantry in Europe. There is a pleasant mixture of Italian and German in their character, as there is in their language, look, and dress. They have very pleasant ways of doing things. It is pleasant, instead of the horrible gong which bangs away at Alliance or Crestline, or the blowsy Irishman who howls at you, "Dinner's ready," to have a rosy, neat Tyrolese girl, as she puts down a dish of soup, wish you, "May you dine well," and as she gives you a candle at night say, "May God give you good sleep," and as she takes your fee at leaving, kiss your hand and wish you "lucky journey." To be sure, the soup is often bad, and the bread almost always horrible, in the little out of the way inns, but their dreadfulness is made more tolerable by the people's pretty ways. It is embarrassing to happen to sneeze in a group of people; every hat comes off, and the "God bless you's" are showered down in a distressing way.

Off here in the hills, we hear only stray rumors of the terrible war. The great battle of last week, with its unexpected defeat of the French, has thrown all Europe into tumult, of which we get only the echoes. In two weeks I am going to Paris. What I shall find there I do not know; unless better fortune comes to retrieve him, Napoleon must be shaken, and probably overthrown. There is a sort of revolution already in Paris. What a blessed thing for us, that big ocean between us and all this sort of thing! I wish you could be here this Sunday morning. Cleveland is pretty, but this is prettier. A lovely old valley, with vineyards at its bottom, and running up to the very tops of the high hills that shut it in. Old castles and modern chateaux looking down from every side, and in the midst this queer old town, with peasants in their picturesque Sunday clothes, strolling back and forth over the bridge that crosses the little Adige, and an Italian sky and sunlight over everything.

What a good time we had in Boston those last two days. Can't you come on in September, when Arthur will be there? I hope we shall have many Sundays together as that last in June. Good-by, and good luck to you always.   Affectionately,

PHILLIPS.

BORMIO, August 21, 1870.

DEAR FATHER, — I have received a letter from you this week, written July 26, the second that has reached me. The mails seem to be deranged, and it is not strange. I have written once a week to some of you ever since I landed. I hope long before this the stream has begun to flow, and you have received my letters regularly. This week we have been finishing the Tyrol. From Meran to Innsbruck, where we spent a day; then over the Finstermuntz and Stelvio passes, the last the grandest in Europe, till we came yesterday evening to this little Italian town, as pretty a spot as there is to find anywhere. We have had a little rain, but generally good weather, and a splendid time always.

Hence we go through a bit of Switzerland, and gradually work up to Paris. How we shall get there I hardly know, or what we shall find when we are there; but I apprehend no difficulty, and certainly no danger for a couple of peaceful travelers like ourselves. We are getting a little more into the way of news now, and can regulate our movements better. The one clear opinion seems to be, that somehow the war points to an overthrow and end of Napoleon. The disappointment and mortification of the French at their great defeat seems to be terrible, and the state of things in Paris for a few days was most alarming. Things are quieter now, but only wait for the next struggle, which must be a frightful one.

We meet no Americans; indeed, we have not seen a person we know for three weeks. Probably, as we get more into Switzerland, we shall find our countrymen there.

So old No. 41 is down, and the new store is going up. It made me quite blue to hear of it; the world changes sadly, even our little bit of it, but we certainly had a good time in the old house for many years.

To-morrow I hope to get more letters. Three weeks from yesterday I sail for home; may God bless and keep you all. PHILLIPS.

HÔTEL D'ORIENT, PARIS, August 28, 1870.

DEAR MOTHER, — We are at last in Paris, after a long week's doubt whether we should be able to get here. We arrived this morning at eight o'clock, after a seventeen hours' ride from Geneva. We met with no detention further than having to wait here and there for trains loaded with cattle and provisions for the army. No Prussians stopped our way, and though it has been officially announced that the government has taken possession of the road, the order has not yet gone into effect, and passenger trains run regularly through.

We have seen nothing here to-day to indicate that

the city is under martial law, that the Prussians are only two or three days distant, and by all reports in full march for the fortifications. There are many soldiers about, but the streets are emptier and stiller than I have ever seen them in Paris, and though there may be a row at any point at any moment, there certainly was never a more peaceful and safe-looking city. What the real state of things is, it is very hard to tell. That the Prussian army is advancing on Paris, everybody seems to believe. The French papers say that it is a movement of desperation. The Prussians call it the march of a victor. Meanwhile, the mystery which envelops the condition and intentions of the French armies at Metz and Rheims leaves one utterly in the dark. Whatever comes, there seems no probability of any danger to a stranger living here, and I intend now to stay till a week from next Thursday or Friday, when I shall go to Brest, to sail the following Saturday. What we may have a chance to see in the mean time in Paris, we cannot say. You will hear by the telegraph before you get this, but be sure that I will take good care of myself and shall not be in any danger.

We have come this week from Bormio, where I wrote last Sunday, by Tirano, an Italian town in the midst of its vineyards, over the Bernina Pass to Pontresina, in the midst of its glaciers, then over the Albula Pass to Chur, on by rail to Zurich, thence to Berne, where we had to stop to get our passports viséed by the French minister for admission into France, thence to Geneva, and so here. This ends our mountain work, almost seven weeks of as perfect and successful a trip as we could ask. Everything has gone well; no accident, no sickness, and scarcely any bad weather. I am thankful I came, and now ten interesting days of Paris will complete the journey, except the voyage home in the Ville de Paris, which I expect to enjoy exceedingly. Why cannot you time your Niagara trip so as to meet me at the ship on Wednesday, the 21st, or Thursday, the 22d, of September.

I had letters at Pontresina from you and father, which did me good. I have missed a number of your letters, and was rejoiced to get these. I also had one from Arthur about his ordination. Please write him immediately that I will gladly come to Williamsport and preach the old sermon any time in October, if he can arrange it so that the whole trip can come in between two Sundays.

It is cold and cheerless here to-day. I hope we are to have better weather for the gay city, which is bound to be gay, even if it is besieged. Love to all.

Affectionately always, PHILLIPS.

PARIS, September 5, 1870.

DEAR WILLIAM, — I write a line, which will probably not get home before I do, but I may be detained, and this will tell you that I am well and coming. Yesterday was too busy and exciting a day to write. As the telegraph will have told you, there was a bloodless revolution and we went to bed last night under a Republic. I saw the whole thing, and was much interested in seeing how they make a Government here. You can have no conception of the excitement in Paris all day.

I shall leave here to-morrow or Wednesday for Havre, and sail thence on Friday morning. There has been some difficulty in getting out of Paris, but I do not anticipate any this week. Still, at the very last there may be something to hinder, and even should the Ville de Paris arrive without me, do not be worried, but know that I will turn up soon.

Good-by, love to all. Vive la Republique!
                                                            PHILLIPS.

SUMMER IN NORTHERN EUROPE.

1872.

STEAMSHIP PALMYRA, July 5, 1872.

DEAR FATHER, — The voyage is almost over. To-morrow morning we shall be at Queenstown, where I think we shall land, to go by Cork and Dublin to London. It will be pleasanter and quicker, and probably get us to London on Sunday morning. (The ship rolls so that I cannot write straight.) We have had a very quiet passage, not much bright weather, but nothing rough to speak of. Dull skies almost all the way, with a good deal of rain. The ship is a very good and stanch little boat, rather slow, but still making steady headway, and as comfortable as she could be with her rather limited accommodations. Paine and I have found our stateroom exceedingly comfortable, and with a few pleasant people on board, the time has passed briskly. I wonder how Fred has got along? His steamer must be not very far behind us, and I expect to see him in London by Tuesday. I shall be there with him until Friday, the 12th, when we sail to Christiania. We expect to reach there on the 16th, and then shall be off for four weeks on a country trip in Norway. Paine will go with me.

. . . On Sunday, we had a sermon from an English minister, whose presence saved me from preaching. It was a lovely day, the finest we have had.

The voyage has been a very pleasant rest, and I

shall be ready for an active summer when we land. Some people get dreadfully wearied of the sea, but I find every moment of it pleasant, and never feel in better health or spirits anywhere.

I hope that you are going to have a pleasant summer. Do spend a good part of it in writing to me. I shall look anxiously for my budget of letters every week, care of Jay Cooke, McCulloch & Co., London.

I will write again from London after I meet Fred. My love to mother and all. Tell me what they are doing, and tell them all to write.

PHILLIPS.

LONDON, July 9, 1872.

DEAR MOTHER, — I will begin a letter to you, now that I have a leisure moment, while I am waiting for Fred, who reported himself at the hotel this morning when I was out, and has not yet returned. So he has arrived, but I have not seen him yet. I wrote to father just before we landed from the Palmyra. We went to Cork and spent some hours there, and drove out to Blarney Castle, through some of the loveliest country that you can imagine. It was a glorious day, and we enjoyed it hugely; then we took the train to Dublin, crossed the Irish Channel to Holyhead, a beautiful sail of five hours, and then a long night's ride by rail brought us to London, where we arrived at six o'clock on Sunday morning.

Sunday I went to hear Stopford Brooke, at St. James's Chapel in the morning, and Dean Stanley at Westminster Abbey in the afternoon. It was a beautiful day. Monday morning we went down town to the bankers, and then to the picture galleries, and in the afternoon drove in Hyde Park to see the swells. We engaged passage on the Oder for Christiania, which sails next Friday morning. We shall arrive there on Monday evening, the 15th. We also engaged passage on the Thuringia from Hamburg for New York on September 11. To-day we have been sight-seeing, — the great South Kensington Museum and the International Exhibition with the new Memorial, which has just been opened, having been built by Queen Victoria in memory of Prince Albert. It is a very gorgeous and beautiful affair.

Wednesday Evening, July 10, 1872.

Just here Frederick turned up, and from that time to this I have had his company. He is well, has enjoyed his voyage very much, and takes to traveling like a fish. He and I have scoured London to-day, called on the Archbishop of Canterbury, examined the British Museum and Westminster Abbey, visited Hyde Park, and this evening we have been to a concert at the splendid new Albert Hall. He means if possible to return with us in the Thuringia, but there is some uncertainty about getting staterooms. We shall know in a week or so.

So the two great family trips are launched for the summer, and promise to go on well. You shall hear from point to point how we are faring. I do not feel as if these few days in London were really a part of it, and shall not think that we are fairly beginning until we are aboard the steamer for Christiania to-morrow night. London seems too familiar, and, with all its strangeness, a little too much like home to be really abroad. It has grown enormously since I was here in 1865, and is simply too big to know much about in two or three years, so that two or three days in it go for very little.

I am sorry to see what hot weather you have been having in Boston. I hope it is only the working off of heat for the whole summer, and that you will have it cool the rest of the time. Here the weather is delicious, — bright, cool, sunshiny days that quite disappoint one's ordinary expectations of London.

Already I begin to feel how good it will be to get home.

LILLEHAMMER, NORWAY, July 16, 1872.

DEAR WILLIAM, — I have written to you in the course of our correspondence from many queer places, but perhaps this to-night is the queerest of them all. It is the neatest, triggest, cosiest little Norwegian inn, one day's journey from Christiania, just set in among the mountains at the head of lake Mjösen. The people in the courtyard under the windows are jabbering Norwegian and getting the horses ready for our carioles, which set out to-morrow morning at half past five. It is half past nine o'clock in the evening, and broad daylight, so that a candle would be an absurdity. Last night at Christiania, I literally read a letter in the street at eleven o'clock, as you would at noon in Boston.

But I must go back. Last Thursday evening I left Frederick in London, and went on board the steamer Oder for Christiania, which sailed the next morning at four o'clock. We had a pleasant little voyage of three days and a half across the North Sea and up the Skager Rack, touching on Sunday morning at Christiansand, and arriving on Monday at Christiania. The steamer was good, the sea smooth, and all went very pleasantly. The sail along the Norwegian coast and up the Christiania Fiord was very beautiful. At Christiania, which is a very pretty, pleasant place, we spent yesterday, got our carioles, which are the jolliest-looking traps you can imagine, this morning took them on the train, and then on the boat upon the lake to this village. To-morrow morning we mount them for our first drive into the country. I wish that you could see us pass. Much more, I wish there were a third cariole, and you were in it.

I wonder how Fred comes on. He seemed to be having a good time. I went with him to several of the great sights of London, which he appeared to enjoy, and was in good health and spirits. I hope he will find some companion for the Continent, for I am afraid he will be a little homesick sometimes, if he does not. He hopes to return with us in the Thuringia from Havre, September 14.

Will you do something for me? Will you go and see Mr. James T. Fields, and ask him (as I shall be rather later than I expected in getting home) to put my lecture on English Literature as late in the course as possible? — at the very end if he can. I think he will have no trouble in doing it.

No letters from you yet. I hope many are on the way, but we shall not get them till we come to Bergen some time next week; but do keep on writing, and tell all the news, little and great. I hope you are having a pleasant summer. . . .

Affectionately,
PHILLIPS.

AAK, NORWAY, July 22, 1872.

DEAR FATHER, — We have been spending Sunday at this remote little place in the mountains, at the mouth of the Romsdaal Valley, which is one of the most remarkable gorges in Norway. We came here in a three days' journey from Lillehammer, whence I wrote to William last Wednesday. The traveling is very odd. We have our own carioles, which we took with us from Christiania, having hired them for a month. In these we travel about fifty miles a day. The cariole is a sort of sulky, something like a country doctor's chaise, with just room for one person and a place to strap on a valise behind. The roads have stations every ten miles or so, where the people are obliged to furnish you a change of horse, which you take on to the next station. A small boy goes perched on the baggage behind to bring the horse back. In this way we are always changing horses. I have driven some twenty or thirty already, mostly strong, willing little brutes, who make very good time and do not seem to mind my overweight. The road has been very beautiful; last evening's ride, especially, was most magnificent, through the gorge of Romsdaal. There is nothing in Switzerland like it. Our weather has been generally excellent, with occasional showers which have not hurt us, nor delayed us much. It is a land where it makes not the slightest difference when you travel, for it is broad daylight all night, being literally light enough to read easily in the open air at midnight. The only trouble is to get to sleep at night with the daylight in the room, and to keep asleep in the morning.

This morning we walked about three miles to a Norwegian country church, and attended service there.

It was very interesting. The little church was crowded and the service was full of spirit. The sermon was dreadfully long, at least to us who listened to it as foreigners, and did not understand a word. After service there was a baptism of two babies, and then the catechising of the girls and boys of the parish — funny little folks they were! The people all belong to the Lutheran church, which is the Established Church of the Kingdom. They are a most thrifty, decent, poverty-stricken people, perfectly honest, and not at all handsome.

I wish that you could see the view as I look out of my window. The valley is completely shut in by mountains of the most gigantic size, and splendid in their shapes. A beautiful green river runs down through it, and the fields in the bottom of the valley are green and rich. A pair of carioles has just driven up to the little inn door, and the people are chattering in Norse about rooms and suppers in the most excited way.

To-morrow morning we take a little steamer very early to go to Molde, down one of the most beautiful fiords; then we shall keep down the coast to Bergen, exploring the fiords as we go along; from Bergen back across the country to Christiania, where we shall be in about three weeks; then to Stockholm, St. Petersburg, Moscow, Copenhagen, Hamburg; and then home. Nothing from Fred; you have heard from him of course. Love to all.

Most affectionately yours, PHILLIPS.

STEAMER FJALIR, ON THE NORD FIORD, NORWAY,
July 25, 1872.

DEAR MOTHER, — It is a rainy forenoon on a steamboat, and there is nothing pleasanter than to sit in the little cabin and write my weekly letter to you, although it is before its time. We are on our way to Bergen, running down one of the countless fiords that cut up the coast of Norway into slices. Last Sunday afternoon, I wrote to father from Aak, at the foot of the Romsdaal Valley. Monday morning, we drove in our carioles down to the head of the Molde Fiord, and there, carioles and all, went on a boat, and sailed, in the midst of the grandest scenery, to Molde, where we stopped a couple of hours and dined on salmon and lobster, which are about the only things that grow along this coast. Both are superb. That afternoon, we sailed along the coast to Aalsund, a little village with a most lovely situation, which is famous for nothing except the cod-liver oil which they make there. We passed the night in short beds, and the next day sailed up the Stor Fiord and its branch, the Geiranger Fiord, which is called the grandest in Norway. It is certainly magnificent. The narrow arm of the sea, with bright green water, is shut in between perpendicular cliffs of granite, two or three thousand feet high, over which countless waterfalls come tumbling down in every conceivable shape. The stillness and wildness is wonderfully impressive. We spent that night at a little group of fishermen's huts, and slept in a schoolhouse, because the inn, which only has six beds, was full. We called on the Pastor of the place, and spent an hour with him. He is the only educated man of the whole region, and was very hospitable and conversible, speaking very tolerable

English. Yesterday morning, we put the wheels on our carioles again, and drove all day across the country, through magnificent scenery, to a little inn called Faleide, on this Fiord, where last night we took the boat for Bergen. The cabin is full of Norwegians, talking their unintelligible tongue. There is one German family from Hamburg, who are pleasant people, and with whom, between their English and our German, we get along very well. To-morrow noon we reach Bergen, and there I hope to get my first letters from you all. After a day or two, we start again into the country, and spend two weeks more before we come back to Christiania. About the 12th of August we leave Christiania for Sweden, going to Stockholm. On the 22d we go to St. Petersburg and Moscow, returning the first week in September. We sail from St. Petersburg by Lubec to Copenhagen, and thence go down to Hamburg and take the Thuringia, either there on the 11th, or at Havre on the 14th. So all goes well. I am having a splendid time. This rain, I have no doubt, will clear up to-morrow, and with much love to all, I am always
   Affectionately ours,
          PHILLIPS.

STEAMER BETWEEN BERGEN AND CHRISTIANIA,
July 27, 1872.

Since I wrote the inclosed sheet, our plans have changed. . . . Paine has been called home. We are now on our way to Christiania, and he will stop on his way at Christiansand, go thence to Hamburg, and so home by next week's steamer. I shall go to Christiania, to take back our carioles and close up things there. I am not quite sure what I shall do afterwards; probably go to Sweden, and thence cross into Russia, and come home by way of some of the northern German cities.

We are having quite a royal progress to-day. Prince Oscar, brother of the king, is on board, and at every town where we stop, there is a boisterous welcome and farewell. Good-by again, and write often.

HOTEL RYDBERG, STOCKHOLM, August 4, 1872.

DEAR WILLIAM, — The stream of communication this summer seems to flow all one way. Since father's letter, dated just a month ago to-day, there is not a word from my beloved family, or anybody else in America. I hope they are well, but either they have not written, or Jay Cooke is faithless, or I have been running about too fast for letters to catch me. I hope Fred has been more fortunate than I. Here I am now in Stockholm, one of the nicest, brightest, gayest looking cities I have ever seen. I am very much delighted with it. It runs all about over a quantity of islands, in Venetian sort of style, and little bits of steamboats go racing back and forth. The people are bright and good-looking, and there are gardens and cafés everywhere. Friday evening, I went to the Deer Park to a concert, and the whole scene was as pretty as anything in Paris or Vienna. After I wrote last week, I came back to Christiania, and thence sailed down to Gottenburg, and thence by the Gotha canal here. It was a lovely day on the canal, and the scenery was very pretty. Yesterday, I went to Upsala, where is the great Swedish university, the old cathedral, and the oldest relics of their history. Under three great mounds, their Odin, Thor, and Freia are said to be buried.

To-morrow morning, I am going off to Gottland, where there are some strange old relics of architecture, and the whole place is said to be very picturesque and curious. It is a trip of two or three days, and then I come back here. After that, probably to Russia, where I expect to arrive next Sunday.

There are very few Americans in these parts, — a good many English, and lots of Swedes. I like the Swedes very much. They are brighter and more cheerful than the Norwegians, and very kind and willing to oblige. The country seems prosperous and happy. The environs of Stockholm are beautiful. Come here, and look at this pretty town, when you bring Mary and Agnes to Europe.

I hope they are well, and that you are not having the absurdly hot weather with which you began the summer. Already, we are within sight of the end of it. How strange it will seem to be settled down again to the old round for another winter. Paine is on his voyage home by this time. I suppose you may see him before this reaches you. If you have not written to me, pray write, and if you have written, write again, PHILLIPS.

ABO, FINLAND, August 10, 1872.

DEAR FATHER, — Did you ever get a letter from Finland? If not, then here comes your first. I write in the sincere belief that I am answering some letters of yours, although I have not received them. Somehow, I have missed everything since your letters of July 4th. I hope nothing important has happened since that time. If there has, I do not know where I shall hear of it. Perhaps at St. Petersburg, whither I am bound now. But I must wait patiently. I left

Stockholm yesterday morning, in the steamer Constantin, at two o'clock.

Steamers have an uncomfortable habit of starting at that hour all over these parts. The boat is excellent; all sorts of languages, Russian, Swedish, Finnish, French, and German, are chattering around me. There are also three or four Englishmen on board. To-day's sail has been exquisite, wandering through the islands of which this part of the Baltic is full, with views continually changing, and all pretty. At five this afternoon we came to Abo, at the mouth of the Gulf of Finland, and there we lie to-night. The steamers always lie by until two in the morning. To-morrow, we wind up the gulf among the islands. To-morrow night at Helsingfors, Sunday night at Vyborg, and Monday noon, the 12th, at St. Petersburg. The Fins are a good, dull, rude-looking people. We went ashore this afternoon and saw the strange old town. Nothing could be more foreign or picturesque. It was odd to find one's self for the first time in the Czar's dominions, but all his folks were very civil and seemed glad to see us.

I made this week a very interesting two-days' trip to the old town of Wisby and the Island of Gothland. It was a twelve hours' sail down the Baltic at night. In the morning, we reached the island, and saw the old walled town, which was once a place of great trade and importance, but now in decay. The most interesting things in it are a dozen old ruined Gothic churches, some of them quite unique in architecture, and all showing the taste and wealth of the old times. At present, the island is something of a summer resort for Stockholm people.

We took a long drive back into the country, through

rich farms and pleasant hills, the whole a picture of quiet, primitive, pastoral simplicity, which was very attractive. Another night's sail brought us back to Stockholm, which is a most beautiful city, and after another day there, I sailed on this slow and pleasant cruise for St. Petersburg.

Since Paine left me, two weeks ago, I am alone, but meet companions often from point to point. There are almost no Americans in these parts. It seems a long way from home. I shall spend two or three weeks in Russia, going to Moscow, and perhaps to Nijni-Novgorod; then to Berlin, Lubeck, and Copenhagen, and so to Hamburg, whence I sail for New York, on September 11. . . . After you get this, direct your letters to Hamburg. I shall get them sooner.

I am very well and having a first-rate time. Have not had a hot day this summer. I hope you are all well and happy, and with much love to all, I am most sincerely your son, PHILLIPS.

Moscow, August 18, 1872.

DEAR MOTHER, — Last Sunday, when I wrote to father, we were crossing the Gulf of Finland, making for St. Petersburg. We passed the great fortifications at Cronstadt, and landed at the city Sunday evening; the next three days I spent in seeing the great capital. Everything in it is on the most enormous scale. Its palaces, the biggest and most gorgeous; its churches, the richest; its squares, the most magnificent in Europe. Its great church of St. Isaak is a wonder of marble, gold, and jewels. It cost $35,000,000, or about one hundred and fifty of the new Trinity. The picture gallery is one of the greatest of the world, with some pictures one cannot see anywhere else. The whole country about the city is full of magnificent palaces, with splendid grounds and fountains, where one goes in the afternoon, and hears bands play in the evening, and takes a quiet sail on the Neva back to St. Petersburg, with the moon shining on the golden domes. What do you think of that?

Grand as St. Petersburg is, it is only the vestibule to Moscow. You come here by rail, a long, dreary ride of twenty hours, with poor sleeping cars, for which you pay fifteen dollars. This Russia is the most expensive country I have ever traveled in. But when you get here, you are in the midst of picturesqueness such as you can see nowhere else. Think of three hundred domes and spires, all different, all gold or silver, blue or green, with golden stars, crosses, and crescents, and blazing under the intense sun that beats down on this plain. Yesterday afternoon, I drove out to a hill near the city, the hill from which Napoleon first saw it, and the view, as it lay glittering in the afternoon sun, was like fairyland. Then you step inside a church or palace, and it is all brilliant with gold; barbarous in taste, but very gorgeous. The streets are full of splendor and squalidness, all mixed together. First the grand coach and splendid horses of a nobleman, and then the wretched procession of convicts, chained together, men and women, starting off on their long journey to Siberia. Everything has the look of semi-civilization, exceedingly interesting, though not attractive; but a country with some vast future before it, certainly.

I hope you are all well, but I have not heard yet, nor shall I for a couple of weeks. I have been very unfortunate, but your letters at the last must reach me at Copenhagen. The last tidings I had were dated only a week after I sailed. It has detracted much from the pleasure of my journey, which otherwise has been very delightful. The weather here is exquisite. I see no Americans and few English. I have been with an Englishman, but leave him to-morrow to go to the Great Fair at Nijni-Novgorod, where we have only the company of a French interpreter. Thence, in the last part of the week, I begin to turn my feet westward; next Sunday, I shall probably write to you from somewhere outside of Russia. Love to all.

Yours affectionately,

PHILLIPS.

HÔTEL DU NORD, BERLIN,
August 25, 1872.

DEAR WILLIAM, — I remember very well writing a letter to you from this very hotel seven years ago. It was about the beginning of my first trip to Europe. There have been several changes since then, and I hope for the better. I reached here only this morning, and find Berlin the same bright, cheerful-looking, great city I remember it. It has grown and improved immensely. Everywhere you feel that you are in the midst of a very great, strong, self-assured Empire. Prussia is certainly the biggest thing in Europe to-day. But Russia is not to be sneezed at, either.

I was at Moscow when I wrote last. From there I went on a trip to Nijni-Novgorod, on the Volga, where the great annual Fair is being held. It is about twelve hours from Moscow, and quite in the centre of Russia, so that the journey there and back gives one a chance to see much of the country. Vast numbers of people gather every year from the east and west, and set up a whole city of temporary shops for three months, on a low, sandy point of land, at the meeting of the Volga and the Oka. The crowd is most curious and picturesque. Persians, Tartars, Armenians, Chinese, Caucasians, Jews, and Europeans of every sort; with all their various goods — teas, skins, fruits, carpets, great miles of iron from Siberia, and wheat from the Black Sea, — every language and dress you can picture. All this goes on for three months, and then they shut up shop and go home, and the place is deserted until the next year.

The Fair was in full blast this week, and I saw it to good advantage. Then I came back to Moscow, spent another day, and saw the wonders of the Kremlin again. Then to St. Petersburg and to Warsaw, where I had a day, and a very pleasant one. It is a bright, live city, with fine buildings and beautiful palaces and gardens. I liked what I saw of the Poles very much indeed. Yesterday I left Warsaw at three, and reached here this morning at five. I went to church this morning and heard a very poor sermon. I hope you had a better one in Trinity. Now I am going to Lubeck and thence to Copenhagen. I sail from Hamburg two weeks from next Wednesday. . . . I shall be glad to be at home and at work again, though very sorry to break off this pleasant life. . . .

Is it really true that Greeley stands a good chance for the Presidency?

My kind love to Mary, Agnes, and all at home. Thanks for the letters which you have written.

Yours always, PHILLIPS.

HAMBURG, September 1, 1872.

DEAR FATHER, — I feel as if I owed you and mother about a dozen letters to-day, for since last Sunday I have been wonderfully blessed in the way of hearing from you. At Copenhagen I received eighteen letters, the accumulation of the summer, and now I understand all about you and your doings up to August 16. You must have had a frightful summer, with the heat and the thunder-storms. I am sorry for the discomfort you must have suffered, but glad of the philosophy with which you seem to have borne it.

I passed a day in Berlin, and then went to Lubeck, where I stayed another day. It is a picturesque old place, the most old-fashioned town in northern Europe, and I had a good time there. Then a pleasant sail of fifteen hours carried me to Copenhagen, where I spent three days. It is full of interest. The Museum of Northern Antiquities is something quite unique. I had a letter from Mr. Winthrop to the Director, Professor W——, but found that he had gone away to the Archæological Congress at Brussels, but the letter secured me a reception by one of his assistants, who went carefully with me through the museum. I found also in Copenhagen a gentleman with whom I crossed in the Hammonia two years ago, who was very hospitable, and so I enjoyed the place very much. I bought one or two pieces of old carved furniture, which will be at home by and by. One day I went to Elsinore, and saw the ships in the Straits, and walked on the platform where Hamlet met the ghost. The great Exhibition is open at Copenhagen, and I saw the King, all the royal people, and the Princess of Wales. Last night I came thence by rail and boat to this great town. Among my letters was one from Fred, who wanted me to meet him in Paris, and I think I shall do so. I have thought of going back to Berlin for the great review next Saturday, but I shall give that up, a noble sacrifice to fraternal affection. I shall go by way of the Rhine, and next Sunday Frederick and I will be at the Hôtel du Louvre, Paris. Two weeks from to-day we shall be on the Thuringia. . . .

Your affectionate son, PHILLIPS.

FROM LONDON TO VENICE.

1874.

ALBEMARLE HOTEL, LONDON,
Sunday morning, July 19, 1874.

DEAR WILLIAM, — This Sunday morning, your atmosphere must be a great deal clearer than the smoky London air in which I am looking out, through which I can just tell that it is a very pleasant day. I hope you will have a good Sunday. . . .

Your letter, which came day before yesterday, was the first that reached me, and was a most welcome beginning to the new spell of correspondence. It seems curious to start it off again for the fourth time. This trip, so far, has been a little different from the others. I have seen something more of people and received more hospitality than when I have been in England before. Everybody has been most cordial and civil. . . . What I have seen have been mostly clerical circles, but in some ways clergymen and laymen are more mixed up and have more common interests here than in America. For instance, all are excited now about the Public Worship Bill. They talk of it at dinner, and write of it in the newspapers in a way that much surprises us, who ordinarily leave such things to our Bishop and the people who go to the General Convention. It seems now as if the Bill would become a law, and it is hard to believe that it can do much good.

I have seen a good deal of London over again with

Arthur. There are many things in it that never tire, and the great city seems to grow more and more enormous every time we come. Last Monday we went all over Westminster Abbey with Dean Stanley, who knows it as well as I know the Technological Hall. It was a very interesting morning, and I wished you were there. I preached there the evening before to such a crowd, and under such a roof, and among such columns and monuments as one does not often see. On Tuesday I went to the annual dinner of the singing people of the Abbey, in the Jerusalem Chamber, where we did all kinds of queer old English customs, sang, and made speeches till ever so late. I was the only one of the preachers of the year present, and had to speak for them all. Think of speaking for Bishops and Archbishops! . . .

On Friday, Arthur and I went to a dinner at Mr. Freemantle's, who was in America last year. Arthur sat next to Lady Augusta Stanley, the Dean's wife. He (Arthur) has been off for four days on a cathedral trip, and I have been visiting in the country. To-day I am to preach in St. Philip's Regent Street, for Mr. Leathes, whom I saw in America last year. To-morrow morning we leave for France by New Haven and Dieppe, and begin at once on Normandy. How I wish you were here. Shall we not come together some day? Write me punctually, and I will always answer. Affectionately, PHILL.

MORLAIX, FRANCE, July 28, 1874.

DEAR MOTHER, — Arthur says this is a "dutiful scene." He is sitting on one side of a wretched little table, in this quaint old hotel, writing to John, and I am just beginning this note to you upon the other side. I dare say our letters will be very much alike, for there is nothing to tell, except where we have been and what we have seen; that is rich enough. A week ago yesterday we crossed from New Haven to Dieppe, and had a very beautiful voyage. The sea was calm and bright; the coast that we left and the coast to which we came, both were beautiful. Then we went up to Rouen, and spent a lovely day among its old Gothic architecture. There is nothing more beautiful in Europe. Then we struck off into the country, and for a week we have been wandering around among old Norman towns, each odder and more picturesque than any that have gone before. Pont-Audemer, Lisieux, Caen, Bayeux, St. Lo, Coutances, Granville, Avranches, Pontorson, Dol-Rennes, Morlaix, these are mere names to you, as they were a week ago to us, but now they are all places to remember,— old towns, each with its churches six or eight hundred years old, some with magnificent cathedrals, and all with curious houses tumbling out over the streets, and carved from top to bottom with the queerest figures in their oak timbers, apostles, prophets, martyrs, dragons, donkeys, trees, soldiers, and great wreaths of flowers. The streets themselves are full of interesting people, doing the oddest things. Women with high, white caps, men with wooden shoes clattering along the pavements, children playing strange games, and donkeys laboring along with loads three times as big as themselves.

All the places are full of history. Here William the Conqueror was born, and here he was buried; here the Huguenots once burned the church, and there the Royalists withstood the Republicans in the French Revolution. All this makes Boston seem far away, and the sense of vacation very complete. To-day we passed from Normandy to Brittany, a rougher, ruder country, and a wilder people. Last Sunday we spent at Granville, a curious French watering-place upon the coast, and after a service in the old cathedral, we bathed and swam from the great beach. Arthur is well, and seems to enjoy it all. To-night we received letters up to July 9. Here are some nice old people and "Little Wanderers" from Brittany. Are n't they pretty? Love to all. Write often.

PHILLIPS.

Tours, Tuesday Evening, August 4, 1874.

DEAR WILLIAM, — Here I have just received your second letter, full of pleasant talk, and telling every kind of interesting thing about Andover, Mary, and all the other people. I was glad to get it. For a week we have wandered on through Brittany, looked at old castles and cathedrals, and talked together about you all, but have heard nothing since last Tuesday evening. Arthur receives no end of newspaper cuttings, telling about the great Chicago fire, but my only home letter is yours, and I am satisfied. I wonder if you have followed us upon the map? We have rounded the promontory of Finisterre, out on the northern side almost to Brest, as far as St. Pol de Léon and Lesneven; then down to Quimper, and by Auray and Carac to Angers, where we spent last Sunday. To-day, our trip has been to Poitiers, and here we are to-night at Tours. It has been almost exactly the journey which I laid out at my table in the Kempton, and has proved about the best that could be made. I have been amazed at the richness of the old architecture of the country. In little out of the way villages, reached only by rickety country wagons, we have found glorious and immense churches of the rarest beauty, — churches that took centuries to build, and stand to-day perfect in their splendor, with wonderful glass in their windows, and columns and capitals that take your breath away for beauty. The people of Brittany are rough enough, and some of the inns at which we spent the night were dirty and forlorn; but the people were always kind and civil, and did their best to make us comfortable. They show clearly enough that they are of the old Celtic stock, true cousins of the Irishmen we know so well. We had some drives, and we met laborers by the score, who might easily have been turning up the bog in Ireland, or driving a dirt cart among the ruins of Fort Hill. They are a very devout folk, even to superstition, and altogether interesting and filthy.

Now we are out of Brittany, and making our way from town to town along the splendid valley of the Loire. There is a cathedral here in Tours (with twin towers) that staggers you with its splendor, as you come suddenly out of a little dark, crooked street and stand in front of it. Yesterday, Le Mans had another, and to-day Poitiers was wonderfully rich. All the while your letters come in most welcome, and are better than cathedrals. Now you must be just about going up to Andover and cooling yourself after a hot day. My blessing to you always, and to Mary and the bairns. Do not forget to write. Yours always,

P.

VENICE, Friday Evening, August 21, 1874.

DEAR WILLIAM, — I fully expected, when we arrived here this afternoon, to find a letter from you, and perhaps from some of the other good folks at home, but they had not come, so this goes not as answer to anything in particular, but only to tell you generally how we fare. We have reached the Adriatic. After two days in Milan, we rode to-day across the beautiful plain of northern Italy, and came in over the Lagune to this wonderful city. It is nine years since I was here, but the city, which has stood for more than nine hundred years, has not changed much since I saw it last. St. Mark's is just where I left it in the great square, and the gondoliers are singing and rowing in the canal under my windows, just as of old. It has been a varied enough trip that we have taken, London, Brittany, Paris, Switzerland, and Italy. It has been delightful. We have been rather too much hurried; I think we shall stay here for a week, and see the strange old city thoroughly. Arthur is enjoying it very much.

The hotel here is full of English and American people. At the table to-day everybody, except one, talked English; but there is nobody we ever saw before, and we still make each other's company. I wonder if you have had a pleasant summer? In spite of all the delight of this sort of life, it will not be bad to get back again, settle down, and talk it over in West Cedar Street or Berkeley Street.

. . . The news from home seems quiet, except that I see there is more trouble at the South.

Four weeks from to-day I shall be on the ocean, and six weeks from to-day I will spend the evening with you if you will ask me. My kindest love to Mary, the babies, and all at home.

        Yours most affectionately,   P.

Sunday, August 23, 1874.

DEAR FATHER, — This has been Sunday in Venice. This morning, we set out like good boys to go to church, but when our gondola reached the palace on the Grand Canal where service is wont to be held, we found a man upon the steps to say there was no service because the chaplain had gone into the country. It sounded very much like what might be said upon the steps of Technological Hall; so Arthur and I made a round of the great churches, and looked at the pictures in them until dinner time. If we did not go to church, we went to churches. This evening, the moon is splendid on the water, and we took a gondola again, and rowed round about the beautiful old place for an hour. That has been our Sunday. We are lying by at Venice for refreshment, and nothing could be more delightful. The weather is exquisite, cool, clear, and cloudless. The pictures are glorious, and you do not walk anywhere, because you cannot, but are rowed wherever you want to go in the most luxurious style.

We came here over the Alps and by Milan. There we spent two days, about one of which I wrote last night, a letter which you will see by and by in the "Standard of the Cross." We shall stay here till Thursday or Friday, and then start through the Tyrol, slowly, by way of Munich and the Rhine, to Paris. Three weeks from Thursday we sail. On the 8th of September we mean to reach Paris. Think of us there.

I wonder what you are doing; how I wish you were here to see the Ducal Palace with us to-morrow. It would be great fun, too, to see the gondolas go out. I have seen nothing of the Winthrops, but have had a letter from Mrs. Winthrop, who is in Germany. My love to all. P.

MAYENCE, September 4, 1874.

DEAR WILLIAM, — Let me see. The last time I wrote to you I was in the top story of a hotel at Venice, looking down upon the Grand Canal. Tonight, I am in the top story of a hotel at Mayence, looking down upon the Rhine. From Italy to Germany! The change is complete enough, but the two evening views out of the windows are not so unlike. We have come up through the Tyrol, over the great Ampezzo Pass that I have long wanted to see, and which we saw pretty well. There was more or less of rain to keep the magnificent Dolomites from showing their most splendid heads, but on the whole the three days were a success, and brought us by Innsbruck to Munich, where we spent Sunday and Monday. I have been there several times before, but it is a bright, cheery city, full of art treasures, which I do not care how often I see. Then we went to Ratisbon, and to Nuremberg, which was quaint and lovely. They were celebrating Sedan, and the gray old town was gay with colored banners and flowers. Then there was a queer Fourth-of-Julyish procession in the afternoon, and the boys sang the " Wacht am Rhein" about the streets all the evening. After that we went to Heidelberg, and saw the grand old castle, the noblest thing of its sort in Europe. To-day, we came up to Worms and saw the cathedral, and thought of Luther at the Diet, and this afternoon we journeyed on to this place; to-morrow, go down the Rhine to Cologne, where we shall spend Sunday.

So our faces are set homeward, and ten days after

you get this you will get us, if the Siberia goes well. We have not seen any one we know since we left Venice, but all around us the papers tell of multitudes of our countrymen having their good time. I wonder whether they all enjoy it as much as I do. Sometimes, especially when I read home papers (and I thank you for those you sent me last), I grow conscience-stricken and restless, and want to be at work; then I make up my mind to work all the harder when I reach home, and thus dismiss the anxiety and go on my easy way.

I hear that father and mother will stay another year in Hancock Street. . . . I should think it is the best plan, and we will still climb the hill to see them. I shall be glad enough to see you as we draw up at East Boston. My brotherly love to M.

    Affectionately,   PHILLIPS.

ENGLAND AND THE CONTINENT.

1877.

LONDON, July 4, 1877.

DEAR FATHER, — Hurrah for the Fourth of July! William has gone for a day or two by himself on a trip to see cathedrals, and I have no doubt is enjoying everything between here and Durham. I think he will be back to-night, and then we shall keep together for the rest of the time. Since we arrived and came to London, we have been very busy. William has been doing the sights, and I have been about with him most of the time. Last Saturday we went down to Salisbury and spent a delightful Sunday in that quiet, little cathedral town. In the afternoon we drove out to Stonehenge, which is, I think, the best thing to see in England. It is so old that it would puzzle the Historical Society itself.

I left William there and came back to London early Monday morning to go and lunch with some parsons. Indeed, I have been parsoning a good deal of the time. We are to dine with Dean Stanley on Saturday evening, and I am to preach for him in the Abbey on Sunday morning. This evening I am to dine with Mr. Pierrepont, the American minister. I suppose General Grant will be there. What a time he has been having here.

. . . To-day I have been at Convocation, or sort of General Convention of the Diocese of Canterbury, though they are wholly clergymen, no laymen. To-day they have been discussing confession, and ended in a vote by a large majority on the Protestant side.

Friday night we have an order for the House of Lords and House of Commons. So you see we are having a good, busy time. Monday morning we leave for the Continent and then our real traveling begins. I hope that you are getting better and better all the time. Do not forget that you and mother are to come and spend two weeks with me at 175 Marlboro' Street. My kindest love to her and the aunts.

Affectionately,   P.

OLD BIBLE HOTEL, AMSTERDAM,
Sunday, July 15, 1877.

DEAR MOTHER, — I want you to understand that you must answer this letter yourself, with your own hand. I think it must be ten years since you have written me a regular letter, hardly since I was in Amsterdam before, so remember!

They call this hotel the Old Bible Hotel because the first Dutch Bible was printed in this house some two hundred years ago, and now we are lodged here, yesterday and to-day. This morning we went to a Dutch church about six hundred years old and heard some awful singing and a very earnest sermon, of which we did not understand a word. This afternoon we went into the country to a place called Zaandam, and saw all sorts of queer sights among the country people. On the whole, our first week on the Continent has gone first-rate, and we shall spend this week entirely in Holland, bringing up at Cologne on Saturday night. We are both well and are having a good time. In England all went nicely. I saw a good many people in London, and they were pleasant and civil. General Grant was the great sensation. I dined with him on the 4th of July at the American minister's. He did not say much, but was simple and dignified. We saw a great deal of Dean Stanley, who is very pleasant.

I am so glad to hear how well father is, and that the summer goes so happily with you all. Our time is one third up, and it will not be long before we are talking of home again. A letter from James tells me that I am a Doctor of Divinity at Harvard. I am very sensible of the honor, but I hope people will not begin to call me by the title. My best love to father and the aunts, and I am forever

Your affectionate son, PHILLIPS.

LUCERNE, Sunday, August 12, 1877.

DEAR MARY,[1] — Now I will tell you all about it. I dare say William has written you since we arrived at Liverpool, but perhaps he has not told you anything about where we have been, or what we have been doing. I must go back to the steamer, where there were a great many pleasant people. We sailed along as quietly as if we were paddling on this quiet lake of Lucerne, the sea bag hardly wiggle-waggled on the wall. Everybody came to dinner, and the tables were dreadfully crowded. On the whole, it was n't much of a voyage, quiet, dull, and respectable. We probably shall get something livelier going back, when the September sea will throw up its heels and make some sort of rumpus.

Then we came to England, where, if it had not been for General Grant, we should have been of some consequence, but they were all taken up with him, and looked at us as if they wondered what we had come for.

[1] A sister-in-law.

And we went about among them as if we had as good a right as they had, because our great-great-great-grandfathers came from there. Their country looked beautiful, and London never seemed fuller of people, and was pretty hot. It is terrible to think how many times we have been sizzling with heat and shivering with cold since we left New York. I feel like one of the pieces of meat which we have had served up at our many dining-places, which have evidently been heated over and then cooled down again a dozen times for different travelers who came. However, it is a pretty healthy process, and we are getting as tough as some of the pieces of meat. Well, that is what we did in London.

Then we crossed over to the Continent and so came to the Belgians and Hollanders. The country up there was damp and interesting. It was curious to see how hard they have worked to save it from the sea, and you wonder why they wanted to save it. The men looked wooden-headed and the women golden-headed, not as to their hair, but they wear gold blinders, like very swell horses, which make them look very funny, and compel you to go on the other side of the street when you meet a first-rate à la girl. But they were a dear old people, and I can hear their wooden shoes clattering about the Amsterdam pavements now. I have no doubt they will go on growing up (those of them who don't fall into the canals and get drowned in early youth), generation after generation, for ages to come, and thinking they have got the best country in the world.

Then came the Rhine, and a little glimpse of Germany, and Gothic architecture, and all that sort of thing, our romantic period. It was all pretty, and

William kept up a lively life, sight-seeing all day. . . . Then came the green Tyrol, running up to the White Alps and sending us over from the snow-storm on the Stelvio to swelter in Verona. We put on overcoats and wondered whether we had really thirsted for a drop of water only two days before. Then came Venice, as fascinating and dreamy as it always is, beautiful hot Florence, bright Milan, then the hills again, and now we are in Switzerland. That is all. There is a lake outside this fourth-story window that is prettier than anything in Pomfret, and to-morrow we are going over where those clouds are lying, to see the beauties of the Bernese mountains. I expect to see the Jungfrau wink at William to-morrow evening. He is as well as a healthy cricket. Thank you for letting him come, and I'll return him safe. My love to the babies, if they have not forgotten me, and I am just as usual, Your affectionate P.

STRASBURG, August 26, 1877.

DEAR ARTHUR,[1] — You were a blessed good boy to write me from Bar Harbor. I only received your note last night when I came here, and here's a word of answer, though we are so near coming home that it hardly seems worth while to write. We have had a lovely summer, much of it on our old ground. First, London and the Dean (I did not see Stopford Brooke or Freemantle); then the Rhine, Venice, and Milan (but the gallery there was closed, and we did not see the Luinis); then Zermatt and Chamounix. All these brought back our pleasant days. We roamed about and lunched at Bauer's, which stood just as we left it opposite St. Moses. It seems as if we had been

[1] His brother, Rev. Arthur Brooks, D. D.

there only a week before, in fact just run up to Conegliano and back again.

And you have been in the old haunts in Mt. Desert. You were cooler than we were in Venice, certainly. I have seen no parsons from America, though I heard of Tyng being about in Switzerland. The minister at Geneva wrote and wanted me to lay the corner stone of his new church, but I wrote him I could not, and he asked General Grant, which no doubt pleased him a great deal better. . . .

There has been a terrible summer in America, has n't there? Matters must be in an unsettled state and delay the return of prosperity sadly. Over here, it really seems as if Russia had got a much harder job than anybody dreamed, and one perhaps too hard for her to accomplish. Nothing but Gladstone, and the popular feeling which he excited and expressed, has kept England neutral.

I wonder if you are back in New York and at work again. Look out for the Scythia on Tuesday, the 18th, when we arrive under the care of Captain Hains. I shall feel by and by as if I could not cross the ocean except with him. Give my best love to Lizzie, and tell her I count on her and you to be my first visitors in the new house. We will have lots to talk about. To-morrow we start from Paris, and a week from next Saturday, ho for New York!

Always affectionately, P.

IN PARIS, ENGLAND, SCOTLAND, AND IRELAND,

1880.

HÔTEL DU LOUVRE, PARIS, July 7, 1880.

DEAR WILLIAM, — You know this place. The Louvre is just opposite, the Palais Royal is just behind, and you and I were here in 1877. You see we have not been quite able to keep to our plan of not going out of the United Kingdom. I have to be in London, or rather at Windsor, next Sunday, to make a few remarks to the Queen, so we ran over here for the week between. It looks just as it used to. The Venus of Milo is over there in the round hall, with the red curtains behind her, and the Titians, Murillos, and Raphaels are upstairs. The cabs go whirling over the asphalt, just as they used to when you and I were in them. It is very jolly and pretty, and I wish that you were here. Everything in London was very good. The Dean was all civility. He gave us his dinner party, and Farrar and others were there; and we went to the great Bradlaugh debate in the House of Commons, and stayed until it broke up at two o'clock in the morning. We went also to Lambeth, and saw the Archbishop, but did not lunch with him. The pictures in Trafalgar Square were just as fine as ever, and I bought some Waukenphasts, and preached in the Abbey on the 4th of July evening. Farrar preached in the morning, and beat me on Yankee

Doodle! Tell Mary I shall write her from the Highlands. My love to her, the babies, and all Nahant.

Affectionately, P.

STEAMSHIP COLUMBA, July 29, 1880.

DEAR WILLIAM, — I am on a steamboat between Oban and Glasgow on the coast of Scotland. John is up on deck somewhere, and the scenery outside has grown a little tame, so I take this chance to tell you that we are well, and the Scotch trip, which is drawing near its end, has been a great success, just as the Dutch, the Tyrolese, and the Swiss trip were three years ago.

We left London on the 12th of July; the day after I wrote a beautiful letter to Mary from Windsor Castle, and went to Edinburgh, where we saw many pretty sights, and quite a number of interesting people. Dean Stanley had furnished us with introductions, and everybody was very civil. We stayed there three days, and then went to St. Andrews, where we saw the great ruined cathedral, and some more agreeable people connected with the university there. We spent a queer night at an old castle, where some of Dean Stanley's relations live, and all was very nice and funny. Then we struck north, and have been wandering about the Highlands and the Island of Skye for the last ten days. First-rate weather, lots of queer adventures, and all sorts of ridiculous stopping-places, with superb scenery everywhere, made it a delightful journey. Now our faces are turned homeward. A day upon the Lowland lakes, a day in Glasgow, a week among the English lakes, a Sunday, August 8, at Chester, three days in Ireland, the Germanic at Queenstown on the 13th, New York some time on Saturday, the

21st; then Nahant, Boston, the new house, and sermons. . . .

I received Mary's letter last week, and consider it an answer to the epistle from Windsor. Tell her I thank her for it. Good-by. Affectionately, P.

WELLS, August 5, 1880.

MY DEAR MARY, — Thank you for your letter, which was very good to get. We are too near home (for we sail a week from to-morrow) for me to write you a great long answer, but it just occurs to me that I may reach Boston at some untimely hour, and want to get into my house, while you and William are comfortably sleeping at Nahant. So will you ask him, about the time we are expected, to leave the house keys at the Brunswick, directed to me, and I can get them there. I will thank you when I see you.

We have had a beautiful time. It has always rained except just where we were, and everybody has seemed to go out of his, her, or its way to make us happy. Now we are getting a few days down here among the southern towns. We have just come back from Glastonbury, which was very pretty, and I am writing to you in a queer little mahogany coffee-room. John is beside me, writing an immense letter to his wife, which is a thing that all my traveling companions have done in their several turns. At the other end of the table, an old gentleman with a bald head is studying a railway time-table, and his wife, who is very ugly, is asleep in an armchair in the southeast corner. At the northeast corner of the room, a man is eating his supper of fried sole and boiled eggs. The old gentleman has just called for a glass of "brown brandy and soda water," and he seems to think it will taste good. There is a row in the hall because an omnibus has just arrived from the station with some more guests, and the landlady is running about like an over-busy hen. That is about all that seems to be going on to-night in Wells. The old gentleman, who seems to be the liveliest member of the party, has got his drink, and is ordering a boiled sole for his breakfast at half past eight to-morrow morning. Now Wells is perfectly quiet. Not a sound. . . .

Ever yours affectionately (if you don't forget about the keys), P.

A YEAR IN EUROPE AND INDIA.

1882-1883.

STEAMSHIP SERVIA, June 28, 1882.

DEAR JOHNNY,[1]— We have had a wonderful passage, and here we are just getting ready to see Fastnet light this afternoon. Does n't that bring back two years ago, and all the long dreary day between Queenstown and Liverpool? I hope that we shall have a more cheerful experience to-morrow. Dr. John Hall is aboard, and Dr. Lorimer, and Lawrence Barrett, and T. B. Aldrich, and four hundred and fifty more; and we have had a bright, sunny, happy time. McVickar and James and I and Richardson and John Ropes make up a sort of party who sit together at the cabin table, and smoke together in one corner of the deck, and talk about whatever chooses to turn up.

And so the year of wandering has begun. It is not easy yet to realize that it is more than a mere summer's journey, but every now and then it comes over me that the gap is to be so great that the future, if there is any, will certainly be something different in some way from the past. I don't regret that, for pleasant as all these past years have been, they don't look very satisfactory as one reviews them; and although I am inclined to put a higher value on their results than anybody else would be likely to do, they have not certainly accomplished much. I should like to think that the years that remain, when I get home, would be

[1] His brother, Rev. John C. Brooks.

more useful. There is surely coming, and it has partly come, a better Christian Day than any that we or our fathers for many generations have seen. One would like to feel before he dies that he had made some little bit of contribution to it.

Well, well, all that is far away; and here come the stewards rattling the plates and getting ready for an immediate lunch, — soup and cold meat and prunes and baked apples; that is the next step in this small floating world, and the future of Christianity does not interest any of them at this moment.

I wonder what is going on at home. Your Marion home must be almost done. I hope with all my heart you and yours may be very happy there *in secula seculorum*. Think of me sometimes, and when you think, write. My love to Hattie and the babies.

Ever affectionately, P.

STEAMSHIP SERVIA, June 28, 1882.

DEAR WILLIAM, — We reached Queenstown last night, and I wish you were here this morning. I would tell you what a pleasant voyage we had, since you left us a week ago this morning; what a splendid great ship this is, and how McVickar and I have rattled round in our little stateroom. I preached last Sunday, and we had an entertainment last night for the Liverpool Seamen's Home. I presided, and Lawrence Barrett read "Horatius," and girls and boys sang songs. "William," our old steward of the Scythia, is on this boat, and waits on James. The Captain never speaks to anybody; we have four hundred and fifty passengers, are awfully over-crowded, and have to dine in two batches. It is all delightful and confused, and as funny as an ocean voyage always is.

But you are not here, so I will not try to tell you all this, but we have really had a most remarkable voyage.

I think we are likely next week to turn our steps southward and spend the summer in southern France and northern Italy, with perhaps a run into northern Spain. Richardson will probably join us there, and architecture be the main interest of the tour. But art, life, and scenery shall not be forgotten. You shall hear all about it.

Did Gertie get the list of passengers I sent her? I thought she would see a good many names that she knew, and would be interested in knowing who my companions were. James has just passed by, pacing the deck with jocund tread, and sends his love.

It was good of you and Mary to come and see us off. I think you are both very good to me all the time, and to think of your goodness will be one of my greatest joys this long year. P.

HOTEL BELLEVUE, BRUSSELS, July 9, 1882.

MY DEAR WILLIAM, — Do you remember pretty Brussels? And this comfortable hotel and St. Gudule and the nice time we had here five years ago? Well, here we are again, James and McVickar and I, and I will tell you how we got here. We landed after a most wonderful passage from the Servia on Thursday evening, the 29th of June. The next morning we left Liverpool, and James and I spent the night at the Peacock Inn at Rowsley, where we went to see Chatsworth and Haddon Hall. It was the most delightful English afternoon. Saturday morning we took a train for Lincoln, and saw the big cathedral, which you know. That was good, too, and James seemed to enjoy it very much. In the afternoon we drove to

Boston, where we saw the Vicar, who insisted that we should remain for Sunday. We declined his invitation to the vicarage and stayed at the Peacock Inn.

It is a very neat and pretty town, as dull as death, with nothing but the St. Botolph Church to give it distinction. On Sunday morning James read the Lessons in the big church and I preached. It was a pleasant sort of experience. John's visit of two years ago was constantly referred to, and seems to have become historic in the town. The Vicar is a very pleasant old gentleman and hospitable as he can be.

From there we went to Peterborough, and on Monday saw Ely and a good deal of Cambridge, and finally brought up at London on Monday night. We went to one or two hotels about Trafalgar Square, but they were crowded, and at last we brought up at the old door of the Westminster Palace Hotel, where they took us in, and it was like a bit of the old times.

Here we stayed three days. One night we went to the House of Commons. Of course I went into the Abbey and saw the Dean's grave, and I called at the old deanery, but the new Dean was out. Farrar came to see me and asked me to preach. I saw Lady Frances Baillie, and we had much talk about Dean Stanley. Then we went out to see Burne Jones the artist, and again to see William Morris the poet, at his factory at Merton Abbey, where he makes his beautiful things. These, with some sights of London, took up our time. McVickar, who had been to see his sister, joined us again in London, and here we also met Richardson, and arranged to go with him to southern France and Spain. Think of us there when you get this.

On Friday, James, McVickar, and I crossed from Dover to Ostend, and yesterday we went to Louvain, where McVickar had to see about some bells for Holy Trinity. There is a bright and busy ten days since we landed. How are you all? I tried to picture you at Andover this Sunday afternoon, with the aunts taking care of you. Oh, how I wish you and Mary were here, and could go down with us to hear the Vesper music at St. Gudule. It is all very pleasant and will last for six weeks more, and then for Germany, and something rather more like work. It is hard to realize that a year and more must come before I see you all. God keep you. My best love to Mary and the children. Affectionately, P.

HÔTEL DE L'EMPIRE, PARIS, July 14, 1882.

MY DEAR GERTIE, — I was very much pleased to get your letter, and think it was very nice indeed in you to write. It was the first letter I received, and I read it as I was sitting in the vestibule of the House of Commons in London, waiting for the doors to open, to let us go in and hear the great men make their speeches. Since then we have traveled on and on, and now are in great Paris. It is all excitement here, because this is the great Fête Day, just like the 4th of July in Boston. Years and years ago, the old prison of the Bastile was taken, and the prisoners were released on the 14th of July. Susie will tell you all about it. The streets to-day are full of flying flags, and there are bands of music going all about town, and hosts of soldiers marching. This evening, the city is going to be illuminated, and there will be fireworks everywhere. And it is all as pretty as pretty can be. Don't you wish that you were here? Some day you and I will come. The funny thing is that the people here speak French. The little children about the streets speak it, just as well as you speak English. The boys and girls are very queer. The common little boys wear blue blouses, and the little girls wear small white night-caps all the time. It is bright, and sunshiny, and delightful.

I am glad you have had such a nice time in New York, and that you saw Central Park and the Elevated Railroad. Now I am glad you are having such a good time at Andover. Go and see the beautiful pig, and write me a letter and tell me how he looks. Get your map and find Bayonne, down in the southwest corner of France. We shall be somewhere about there when you get this letter.

Good-by, and don't forget your affectionate uncle
PHILLIPS.

NÎMES, FRANCE, July 23, 1882.

DEAR WILLIAM, — I am afraid that a little letter which I wrote from Paris must do duty, and fill the gap between my last to you and this. After we left Paris, we traveled somewhat rapidly through France until we reached this place. What we saw specially was a group of churches in Auvergne, in and about Clermont, in which Richardson is especially interested, and which indeed give the key to a great deal that is in Trinity. They are very curious, and I am glad to have seen them. Besides, we saw one or two funny little French watering-places and some fine scenery, finer than anything which I had supposed there was in France. We are spending a quiet Sunday here, and next week shall very possibly start for Spain, where we may spend a few weeks, but our plans are uncertain. Richardson and his young friend Jacques are still with us.

I have heard little from home, but am thankful to know that all goes well. There were a few lines on the outside of a forwarded letter, which reached me here, in which you told me that Arthur and Lizzie sailed on the 11th. They must be now in Europe. I hope they will let me know their whereabouts, and that I may see them before they go home. It seems very strange that we should all be in Europe, and not know anything about each other's ways. Allen writes me about the church, which seems to be getting on well.

I wish you were here, but do write me all about everything. My love to all. P.

GENOA, July 30, 1882.

DEAR WILLIAM, — . . . You do not know what a lovely Sunday this is here. The sea breeze is blowing, the palaces are shining, the people are chattering, the sky is a delicious blue, and you, if you were only here, would add another picture to your gallery which would be worth keeping all your life. Since last Sunday we have strolled through southern France, seen Provence with its wealth of old Roman remains, and sailed, with the loveliest passage, across from Marseilles to this delightful town. To-morrow, we start by steamer for Leghorn, Pisa, and Florence. Northern Italy will have the next three weeks, — until James leaves us for home, and the whole party goes to pieces. We have had some hot weather, but nothing oppressive, — nothing like what I fear you have had at home.

We are evidently going to have a troubled year in Europe, and just at present it cannot be nice to go to India. It seems most doubtful what will be the end, especially if, as now seems likely, the religious question gets mixed up with it, and a Mohammedan sacred war is proclaimed. England is sure to come out strong. Her action in Egypt must certainly be for the advantage of civilization and the world. . . .

FLORENCE, August 6, 1882.

DEAR WILLIAM, — How do you all do this week? Dear me, how the weeks go by, and the hot summer slips away! Since last Sunday we have had a pretty sail from Genoa to Leghorn, a bright day in Pisa, a nice three days in Florence, and a visit to Sienna and Orvieto. Just think of Orvieto, where we slept Friday night, within two hours and a half of Rome itself!

Do you remember Florence? There is a cathedral here, a Baptistery, a Campanile, and there are Donatellos, Andrea del Sartos, and Lucca della Robbias; and they all look just the same as they did five years ago. It is not quite so hot as when we were here last, but it is the same bright, happy-looking place, and the same man sells lemonade under the shadow of the loggia. To-morrow morning we are off for Bologna, Ravenna, and then Venice. Think of us on Sunday the 20th, at Milan, and Sunday the 27th, at Paris. Our party has held together beautifully, and there has been lots of fun. I shall meet Arthur and Lizzie for a while after the 1st of September. I heard from John yesterday, who seems delighted with Marion and his house. . . .

My next prospect is Germany, and I am counting much on it.

VENICE, August 13, 1882.

DEAR GERTIE, — When the little children in Venice want to take a bath, they just go down to the front steps of the house and jump off, and swim about in the street. Yesterday I saw a nurse standing on the front steps, holding one end of a string, and the other end was tied to a little fellow who was swimming up the street. When he went too far, the nurse pulled in the string, and got her baby home again. Then I met another youngster, swimming in the street, whose mother had tied him to a post by the side of the door, so that when he tried to swim away to see another boy, who was tied to another door post up the street, he could n't, and they had to sing out to one another over the water.

Is not this a queer city? You are always in danger of running over some of the people and drowning them, for you go about in a boat, instead of a carriage, and use an oar, instead of a horse. But it is ever so pretty, and the people, especially the children, are very bright, and gay, and handsome. When you are sitting in your room at night, you hear some music under your window, and look out, and there is a boat with a man with a fiddle, and a woman with a voice, and they are serenading you. To be sure, they want some money when they are done, for everybody begs here, but they do it very prettily and are full of fun.

Tell Susie I did not see the Queen this time. She was out of town. But ever so many noblemen and princes have sent to know how Toody was, and how she looked, and I have sent them all her love.

There must be lots of pleasant things to do at Andover, and I think you must have had a beautiful summer there. Pretty soon, now, you will go back to

Boston. Do go into my house when you get there, and see if the doll and her baby are well and happy (but do not carry them off); and make the music box play a tune, and remember your affectionate uncle
PHILLIPS.

CHIOGGIA, August 16, 1882.

DEAR MARY, — Did you ever come to Chioggia? If you ever did, you are not likely to have forgotten it, for it is the queerest, dearest little place in the world. Perhaps some time when you have been at Venice, you have taken the steamboat early in the morning, and run down here and spent the day, which is what Mr. McVickar and I have done to-day. We left James just dressed and ready for his breakfast, meaning to have a beautiful day in Venice; he preferred that to Chioggia, and we shall meet again to-night when we get back to dinner. You have no idea how well he is, and how he wanders around in gondolas like a Doge, and how good it has been to have him here all these weeks. But about Chioggia.

It is an old, old island, two hours from Venice, where the people fish for a living, and hardly anybody who once gets born on the island ever goes away. The harbor now is full of fishing-boats, with sails of red, blue, and green, with pious pictures all over them, and picturesque fishermen dropping queer nets over the sides. The old piazza in front of the tavern where we have been eating our collazione is full of men unsnarling their nets and spreading them out to dry. Picturesque children are begging around the door; and a little brown rascal, with nothing on but a pair of bathing trousers, is standing on his head for a cent. The garçon has just got mad and thrown one of the café chairs into the midst of them and scattered the clamorous multitude, who are laughing at him from a safe distance.

Up the street there is a jolly old church, and two funny little old lions are carved on the bridge, which crosses the canal just opposite. It is as pretty as a picture,— prettier than most. I hope you saw it the last time you were in Venice. If not, you must be sure to come here next time. The only trouble is that you have to stay six hours, when three is quite enough ; but this gives me the chance for which I have been looking, to thank you for your letter, which was very good indeed to get. It came from Mt. Desert, which is not altogether just like Venice, but is something made out of land and water, at any rate.

I like to think of you all at Andover, where I am sure you have had a good, happy summer. I hope when you get back to dear old Boston, you will be good enough to miss me dreadfully. I expect to be full of miserableness when you get this, week after next, which will be the time when our pleasant summer party is breaking up and I shall be beginning my solitary winter. Think of me then, and how good it always used to be to get back in the autumn and start the winter life again. I wonder if those times will ever come back again just so. God knows !

Let me hear often. Most affectionately, P.

HOTEL CONTINENTAL, MILAN, August 20, 1882.

DEAR WILLIAM, — They have a new hotel at Milan, so we are not staying where you and I put up five years ago. I have thought very much about our visit here. Indeed, the whole of the last three weeks has reminded me of much that we did together in that pleasant and memorable summer. Florence, Bologna, Venice, Verona, we have been to all of them, throwing in some new places, some of which I had never seen before. I think that I enjoyed the re-seeing of old places almost, if not quite, as much as the discovery of new ones. The deepening and filling out of old impressions is very delightful.

Here our summer party begins to go to pieces. Mr. Richardson and Mr. Jacques start to-morrow morning for Marseilles and Spain. James, McVickar, and I go northward by Maggiore and the Simplon to Brieg, Martigny, Chamounix, Geneva, and Paris. Our journey together has been very delightful. Richardson is full of intelligence and cultivation in his own art, and Jacques is a pleasant fellow, who has made us all like him very much. We shall miss them both exceedingly. Almost no other Americans have come in our way. I saw Mr. Augustus Lowell and his family in Venice; and Daniel Dougherty of Philadelphia (whom you and I went once to hear lecture, — do you remember?) turned up in the cathedral the other day.

I thank you for your good letters, and for an "Advertiser" which I received yesterday. I hope that you will give a newspaper a chance of reaching me now and then. . . .   P.

HÔTEL DE L'EMPIRE, PARIS, August 28, 1882.

DEAR WILLIAM, — I have just been to the station to see James and McVickar off for England, whence James sails on Wednesday for America. You probably will see him before you get this letter. He will tell you about our last week, how we made a run through Switzerland, had a splendid day on the Simplon, crossed the Tête Noire, just as you and I did five years ago, found clouds and rain at Chamounix, so that we saw nothing there. We just stopped for dinner at Geneva and came on to Paris, which we reached early Friday morning. After three pleasant days together in Paris, they have gone this morning, and I am all alone.

It has been a delightful summer, and now I feel as if my work began. A week from to-day I hope to reach Berlin, where I shall stay for some time. I am very anxious to study, and the prospect of unlimited time for reading opens most attractively. I do not feel as if it were a waste of time, or mere self-indulgence, for all my thought about the work which I have done for the last twenty years, while it is very pleasant to remember, makes it seem very superficial and incomplete. I do not know that I can make what remains any better, but I am very glad indeed of the opportunity to try.

On my way to Germany I shall probably meet Arthur and Lizzie, who are to be in Belgium some time this week. . . . I shall be glad to get sight of them, but it will be very brief, hardly more than a hand-shake with each other, I am afraid. We have seen almost no Americans this summer, until we reached Paris. Yesterday, the little American church was quite full of them. . . . The Winthrops were at Chamounix, and we spent an evening with them. Mr. Winthrop seemed to be enjoying his travels.

Of course, everybody is anxiously watching the progress of affairs in Egypt. We know no more about it than you do in America. But the general impression is that it cannot be a long affair, though the English are evidently finding Arabi's people stronger and braver than they had expected. But any day they may collapse.

Paris is cold and rainy, not at all the bright and sunny thing which you saw when you were here. . . .

      Always affectionately,   P.

                      HANOVER, September 4, 1882.

DEAR WILLIAM, — The great event of the last week was the meeting of the waters. Two Brooks boys, Arthur and I, came together in the ancient city of Cologne. It was Thursday evening when it happened; Arthur had started that morning from Mayence and come down the Rhine, the way you know, and I had started from Paris, at an awful hour, and come all the way through by rail, and we met in the hall of the Hôtel d'Hollande at about eight o'clock P. M. We had a long talk that evening, and the next morning we went through the sights of Cologne once more. Then we took rail to Aix la Chapelle, and I saw that again in this new company. I had been there once before this year with James and McVickar.

Then we went to Maestricht, where we spent the night and saw a queer cave. Then we came to Brussels, with various experiences on the way, and once more I found myself in that very familiar town. There we spent a very quiet, pleasant Sunday, went to church, and talked to each other a great deal. Late last night, we bade each other a long, long farewell. This morning, I was called at half past four, and have come to-day (passing through Cologne again) as far as here. . . .

I have started my journey three or four times already. Now to-day it really has begun. I have said good-by to my last relative, and there is nobody else whom I have any engagement to meet until I land in New York a year hence. I am quite alone. To-morrow, I am going to Hildesheim and Magdeburg, and the next day to Berlin. There I shall get your letter, which I have missed this week, and which will be very welcome indeed. I have thanked you most heartily for all your letters, and have got to counting upon them as regularly as the week comes round. So do not ever dare to omit. . . . Everybody now is expecting an advance in Egypt, and news of a battle, anyway. France is getting very restless. There are stormy times coming in Europe.

I hope you are all well, and happy as kings and queens, or happier. My love to everybody. P.

HÔTEL DU NORD, BERLIN,
September 10, 1882.

MY DEAR GERTIE, — This is Sunday morning. It is just after breakfast, about a quarter before nine o'clock. In a shop window on this street, I see a great big clock every time I go out. It has seven faces, and each face tells what time it is in some one of the great cities of the world. The one in the middle tells what time it is in Berlin, and all around that are the other great cities; it has not got North Andover, for that is too small; it is not one of the great cities of the world; but it has New York. Yesterday, as I passed it about one o'clock, I saw that it was about five in New York, so I know now that it cannot be quite three in North Andover. You will not go to church for a good while yet, so will have time enough to read my letter twice before you go.

I came here last Wednesday, and am going to stay

for some time. In fact, I feel as if I lived in Berlin. I send you a picture of the house, with a line drawn around my two windows. The children at the door are not you and Agnes. I wish they were.

The children in Paris all wore blouses, and the children in Venice did not wear much of anything. Here they all wear satchels. I never saw such children for going to school. The streets are full of them, going or coming, all the time. They are queer little white-headed blue-eyed things, many of them very pretty indeed, but they grow up into dreadful-looking men and women. They wear their satchels strapped on their backs like soldiers' knapsacks, and when you see a schoolful of three hundred letting out, it is very funny.

Only two houses up the street lives the Emperor. He and his wife are out of town now, or no doubt they would send some word to Toody.

Affectionately your uncle PHILLIPS.

HÔTEL DU NORD, BERLIN,
Sunday, September 17, 1882.

DEAR WILLIAM, — To-day I am going to write and tell you what I have been doing in Berlin. I have been here for ten days, and have fallen into the most regular way of living, just as if I had been a Berliner instead of a Bostonian, and had lived all my youth in the Unter den Linden instead of in Rowe Street. Do you want to know how it goes? I get up in the morning and breakfast at eight o'clock; then I go to my room, which is very bright and pleasant, where I have a lot of books and a good table, at which I am writing now. Here I stay until eleven or twelve, reading and studying, mostly German; then

I go out, see a sight or two, and make calls until it is two o'clock. Then I go to Dr. Seidel, my teacher, and take a lesson, reading German with him for two hours. Then it is dinner-time, for everybody in Berlin dines very early. They have North Andover fashions here. Four o'clock is the table d'hôte time at our hotel, and that is rather late. After dinner I get about two hours more of reading in my room, and when it is dark I go out and call on somebody, or find some interesting public place until bedtime. Is not that a quiet, regular life?

The people here to whom I had letters have been kind and civil, so far as they were in town; but Berlin ways are very like Boston ways, and the people whom one would like to see are largely at North Andover or Nahant. The family of which I have seen most is Baron von Bunsen's. He is a son of the old Bunsen of whom one hears so much in the last generation, is a very cultivated, intelligent gentleman, a member of the German Parliament, and an excellent scholar. He has a charming family, and a delightful house in the new part of Berlin, which is very beautiful. He has given me a good deal of time, going to museums, etc., and I have been several times at his house. Tuesday I am to dine there and go with them to see Schiller's "William Tell."

The theatre here is such a different thing from what it is with us. It is like a sort of lecture. It begins at half past six and is out before ten. Ladies come unattended. Some of them sit and knit. The whole thing is as quiet as a sewing-circle, and quite free from any of the air of dissipation that belongs to theatre-going in America. Of course there are the other kind of theatres, but I speak of the best sort, and those which Government maintains. One night I went to see "Hamlet" in German. The acting was poor, but the audience was interesting.

Besides the Bunsens I have seen a good deal of Dr. Abbott, who has been settled here for forty years, and knows Berlin through and through. Last night I dined with him at the Zoölogical Garden, and saw a pretty picture of Berlin life. To-morrow I am going out to dine at Wansee (which seems to be a sort of Berlin Brookline) with Baron von der Heydt, who is going to have some of the Court preachers to meet me. A good many other people have called on me, and talked about German things and people; so that I see all I want to see of folks, and the days are only too short. Unfortunately, the university is closed, and the professors are all off on vacations, so that I miss many men whom I should like to see. Indeed, I fear the universities all through Germany meet so late, that if I go to India the first of December I shall be able to see very little of the professors and to hear hardly any lectures. But I am counting much on India. Yesterday I met Lord Amthill, the British minister here, and he offered to give me letters to the Earl of Ripon, who is Governor-General of India, and to other people there, which will insure me the chance to see whatever is going on. What a tremendous victory Wolseley has gained this week! Now Arabi will not block my way.

Do you remember the little statuettes from Tanagra which are in our Art Museum? There are a great many here and I am much interested in them. Yesterday I found some capital reproductions of them, and bought three, which are to be sent you by mail. Well, my paper is full, and though I could go on a week about Berlin, I stop. I am just going down to preach at a little American chapel which is here. I shall stay about a week longer, and then travel through Germany. . . . P.

WITTENBERG, Sunday, September 24, 1882.

MY DEAR AGNES, — I was glad to get your letter, which reached me a few days ago in Berlin. I think you were very good indeed to write me, and it was a nice letter. . . .

Did you ever hear of Wittenberg? You will find it on the map, not very far from Berlin. It used to be a very famous place when Martin Luther lived here, and was preaching his sermons in the church whose clock I just now heard strike a quarter of one, and was writing his books in the room whose picture is at the top of this sheet of paper. I am sure you know all about Luther. If not, ask Toody, she knows most everything. In the picture, you can see Luther's table, the seat in the window where he and his wife used to sit and talk, the big stove which he had built to warm his cold room, and the bust of himself, which was taken just after he died, and hung up here. With the exception of that, everything remains just exactly as he left it, over three hundred years ago, before your papa, mamma, or aunt Susan were born.

It is a queer old town. Just now, when it was twelve o'clock, I heard some music, and looked out and found that a band of music was playing psalm tunes away up in the air in the tower of the old parish church. My window looks out on the market-place, where there are two statues, one of Luther, and one of Melanchthon, who was a great friend of his. Gertie will tell you about him. And the houses are the funniest shape, and have curious mottoes carved or painted over their front door. I came here from Berlin yesterday, and am going to travel about in Germany for a few weeks, and then go back to Berlin again. Berlin is very nice. I wish I could tell you about a visit which I made, Friday, to one of the great public schools, where I saw a thousand boys and a thousand girls, and the way they spelt the hard words in German would have frightened you to death.

Tell Susie that I thank her for her beautiful little letter, and hope she will write me another. You must write to me again. Give my best love to everybody, and do not forget your affectionate uncle   P.

FRANKFURTERHOF, Sunday, October 1, 1882.

DEAR WILLIAM, — . . . I arrived here late last night, after spending the whole week on a journey from Berlin. It was a sort of Luther journey, for I went to Eisleben, where he was born and died; Mansfeld, where he was brought up; Erfurt, where he went to school; Wittenberg, where he was professor; Eisenach and the Wartburg, where he was a prisoner; Gotha, Weimar, Halle, where he preached; and Marburg, where he had his great disputation with Zwingli. Here in Frankfort there is a house of his, just opposite the Dom, which, by the way, they have finished repairing and have re-opened. I went to service there this morning, before I went to the little English chapel where you and I went five years ago.

Besides these Luther visits, I had a pleasant day at Halle, with Professor Conrad, professor of political economy, to whom I had a note of introduction, who was very civil, showing me all over the university and telling me all that I wanted to know about it and the students. There, too, it is vacation. None of the universities begin until the middle of October, and many of them not until the first of November, so that I shall not get much of them. I am now on my way to Heidelberg, where I hope to stay some time, probably two or three weeks, so think of me as there when you get this. I enjoyed Berlin exceedingly, and found the people most courteous and obliging. Indeed, I made some friends there, especially the Bunsens, whom I was very sorry to leave. I may possibly get back there, but it is not likely. India draws near. I received a letter from the Peninsular and Oriental Steamship Company last week, saying they had reserved a berth for me on the steamer which leaves Venice the first day of December.

All this about myself. I wonder how it is with you all. Are you drowned out? And is General Butler going to be Governor of Massachusetts? I have had no letters this week, but shall get them at Heidelberg. Autumn is here and you are all getting back. I wish I could look in on Boston for a day. . . .

Ever affectionately, P.

HEIDELBERG, October 8, 1882.

DEAR WILLIAM, — I suppose that Bishop Williams is preaching to-day at Trinity, so you are all considerably better off than if your own dear pastor were at home. . . .

It has been a very pleasant week for me, but not an eventful one. On Monday I went to Giessen and saw the university and one or two of the professors. It is one of the smaller universities, but a very interesting one. Then I went to Worms, which I had seen before, but at which I wanted to get another look that I might see some things relating to Luther. From there I came to beautiful Heidelberg, and have been here since Tuesday night. You saw Heidelberg, and know something of how beautiful it is. Just now the hill on which the castle stands is one mass of splendid color; almost as bright as anything that one sees in our American woods are the trees in this valley of the Neckar. I have my German teacher here and the use of a library, where I go every day, so I am far from being idle. Here probably I shall stay through this week, and then begin slowly to work back to Berlin, where I want to get a week or two more before I start for the south.

Egypt looks now as if one might find his way through, but there are great difficulties to be overcome before the question of its government is settled, and all Europe is such a tinder-box that a general war may be lighted at any moment. Just at present it does not seem as if any of the great powers wanted much to fight. Certainly Germany does not. The general feeling among her people seems to be a sort of dull disappointment with the results of the last war. It has not brought the country either the wealth or the freedom that they hoped. Germany is poor, and Bismarck's watchful and jealous eye is on everything. The people are proud of their splendid army, but they feel the drain of it tremendously. . . .

There will be no war this winter, and I shall go to India as quietly as possible in December. You must be just about getting up in Boston. Good-morning to you all!

      Most affectionately, P.

WURTZBURG, October 15, 1882.

MY DEAR GERTIE, — I owe you a letter; indeed, I am afraid that I owe you more than one, but we won't be very particular about that. You shall write as often as you can, and so will I, and then we will call it square.

You ought to have a great deal more to say than I, because Boston is a great deal livelier place than Wurtzburg, and besides you have lived in Boston all your life, and know lots of people there whom I should like to hear about (including Susie), while I have been here only since yesterday, and know but one person; and you would not care to hear about him, for he is only a stupid old professor. But you would like to go down the queer old streets and see the funny houses; and you would have liked to see the big church crowded with people, that I saw this afternoon, and heard them sing as if they would shake all the carved and painted saints down off the walls. I wish that once before I die I could hear the people sing like that in Trinity Church in Boston. But I never shall. It was a great day in the church here to-day, because it was the thousandth anniversary of the death of the man who built the first church here long before you were born, and so they had a great procession, and went down into the crypt under the church, where he is buried, and sung a Te Deum. I wish you had been there with me.

Then there is a tremendous great palace where the bishops used to live. . . . Nobody lives there now, because bishops are not such great people as they used to be; but you can go through it all, and see the splendid rooms, and there is the loveliest old garden behind it, with fountains and statues and beautiful old trees, where the people go and walk about on pleasant afternoons, and a band plays. If you and I ever spend an afternoon in Wurtzburg, we will go there.

I wonder if you have been at Trinity to-day, and who preached, and whether you know the text, and whether Sunday-school has begun.

I am on my way from Heidelberg to Berlin. After I have stayed there for a week or two, I shall go to Dresden and Prague and Vienna and Venice, and I have got a ticket to sail in the Poonah from Venice for Bombay on the first day of December. It is not as pretty a name as the Servia, and the ship is only about half as big; but she is a very good vessel, and I have no doubt she will get out there safely before Christmas. I wish you would come to Venice and see me off, as you did to New York. Good-night and pleasant dreams. Give my love to everybody and don't forget

Your affectionate uncle   PHILLIPS.

HÔTEL DU NORD, BERLIN, October 22, 1882.

DEAR WILLIAM, — Just think of its being four months ago yesterday since you saw the Servia sail. More than a quarter of my long vacation gone. Why, I shall be walking in on you before you know it! And when I hear the report of the first Sunday of October at Trinity, and all about Bishop Beckwith's long and eloquent sermon, it seems as if I were within speaking distance of you all the time.

I reached here yesterday, after one of the pleasantest journeys I have ever made. Now it seems like getting home, to come to this familiar Berlin again. The folks seem to recognize me upon the streets, and all the swell guards about the royal palace looked as if they wanted to salute me, but were not quite sure that it was right. I spent three days this last week at Leipsic. It is a very curious town, full of business, I believe, but apparently given up to music and education. The hosts of students on the streets, and the multitudes of concerts everywhere, seem to shut out everything else. I actually went to two concerts myself, one of them a high Wagner affair, with the most select and high-toned musical audience. I thought I should be glad to see what it was like, and I was surprised to find that I rather liked it. I saw one or two professors, who were very civil, and showed me all there was to see. It is rather a depressing place, I think, to one who is conscious of knowing nothing in particular, and having only a general smattering of a lot of things. Everybody there is a specialist. One man is giving himself up to Arabic, another to Sanskrit, another to cuneiform inscriptions, and another to a particular sort of bug. So every man has some subject, on which he talks you out of your depth in half a minute. It must be a delightful thing to think that you know anything, however small, through and through. If I were twenty-five years younger, and not minister of Trinity Church, I should go to Leipsic and stay there till I knew something, so that no scholar in the world could puzzle me. Then I would come home and go into general life with that one little corner of omniscience always kept to fall back upon when I was reminded in some one of the ways (in which I am constantly reminded) of what an ignoramus I am. But it is no use now. And I must go on with my basket of broken victuals to the end.

So you are back in Boston, and the summer was a

great success. I am very glad of it. Who knows but some day the old Andover house may be our summer home, as a fixed thing, with a pretty little establishment that will make summer as domestic and regular a time as winter. It would certainly not be bad. I am glad the children were pleased with the book. I thought they might like it. . . .

Affectionately, P.

HÔTEL DU NORD, BERLIN, October 29, 1882.

DEAR WILLIAM, — How the weeks go, don't they? It seems impossible that seven days have slipped by since I wrote you last Sunday. But they have, and they have been very pleasant ones here. Delightful weather, — a sort of Indian summer, such as we used to look for in Boston, and never quite knew whether we had it or not. I can hear father and aunt Susan at the old table in Rowe Street, debating about it now.

Berlin is quite different on my return from what it was when I left it. The people are back, the streets are crowded, and everything is in full blast. The university lectures began last Monday, and there are no end of them all the time. It is the freest sort of institution. The doors of every lecture-room stand wide open, and any stranger may go in. This week I have been like a college student, going to hear what the great men have to say about theology and other things. I have German enough now to follow a lecture quite satisfactorily, and you do not know how I enjoy it. Of course I have not taken up any systematic course of attendance. My time is too short for that. I only roam round and pick up what I can and fill it out with reading from the books of the same men, a good many of which I have. There are four thousand other students here in Berlin, so that one can go and come in the great university quite as he pleases, and be entirely unnoticed.

A good many people who were away when I was here before have come back, so that I have as much social life as I want. The Bunsens have gone to England, but Dr. Abbott is here. I go there when I feel like it, and always meet pleasant people. Then there is a certain Dr. Kapp, who used to live in New York, and is now a member of Parliament here, who has been very civil; Professor Hermann Grimm, who wrote the Life of Michael Angelo and other things, and one of the university provosts, Dr. Gneist, who styles himself on his card " *Oberverwaltungsgerichts-rath*," — that's his title.

It is very pleasant to see how quietly and simply these scholars live, and what cordial, earnest folks they are. I have also seen something of the ministers, but I do not think I like them so much as the scholars. German religion seems to be eaten up with controversy, and is hampered everywhere by its connection with the state. There is a certain Pastor Stöcke here, at whose house I have been, who is the political character of the town. . . . He and the rest are doing very good work among the poor.

They have just been having an election for members of the Reichstag, or Parliament, which has been very interesting to follow in the papers and in the talk of the people, though one saw nothing to indicate election day in the streets.

This week I leave here for good, and go to Dresden, where I shall get a week for art. The beautiful gallery there I have never thoroughly seen. I shall have my books too, and do some studying. Then Vienna, where there are splendid pictures also, then Venice and India.

My heart stood still for a minute the other day when I opened the paper which you sent me and saw "Trinity Church on Fire." When I found that they had put it out and that it was only going to cost the Corporation $50, I sang a small Te Deum, and concluded to go on with my journey. Thank you for all your letters. They always tell me just what I want to know, and cheer me immensely. . . .

. . . Think of me on Thanksgiving Day in Venice. I shall think of you and wish that we were all in Clarendon Street. My love to M—— and the children.

Affectionately, P.

HÔTEL DU NORD, BERLIN, October 30, 1882.

JOHNNY DEAR, — I don't want to break up my life in Berlin, as I shall in a few days, without writing to you from what has become very like home to me. How I wish you were here this morning. First, we would have a quiet after-breakfast smoke and talk, then we would put on our hats and stroll across the street to the university, where there are some forty lecture-rooms, a professor hard at work in each of them, and the whole thing open to anybody who chooses to drop in. We could hear Dillman firing away at the Old Testament, Weiss exegesing on St. Luke's Gospel, Pfleiderer discoursing on the Philosophy of Religion, or Steinmeyer haranguing on Church History. Hengstenberg is dead, and so is Baumgarten-Crusius, your friend. There are plenty more of them left, and if we grew tired of Berlin to-day, why we could run down to Leipsic to-morrow, where the theology is rather richer than it is here, and where we could hear Luthardt and Delitzsch. We should not understand all that these men said, but a great deal of it would be clear enough, and there would be lots to think and talk about when we came out. Then after an hour or two of this we would go into the Thiergarten, the most fascinating park in Europe, and perfectly delightful on these Indian summer days. There we would wander about and talk some more. We would come home to a queer dinner at four o'clock, and, if you liked, at half past six we could go to the theatre and see a play of Schiller, or, if you preferred, go to see some pleasant people, who are abundant and always hospitable in this cheerful, busy town. Then we'd come home and smoke and talk some more ever so late. You must come quickly, or we cannot do this, because I am starting Wednesday, — bound for Dresden, Vienna, and Venice, whence I sail on the 1st of December.

It has all been very delightful and wholly different from any experience which I have ever had before in Europe. I shall remember Berlin and many of the people in it with delight. There are hosts of American students here, but they hide themselves in German families as much as possible, and one sees little of them. There is much work being done, and the thoroughness of their real scholars makes me feel awfully superficial and ashamed.

I am delighted to hear how very successful your house and your summer have been. I hope that they have put you in splendid condition for the winter. . . . Another year I shall be there again, and meanwhile you will tell me all about it, won't you? I think the beauty of being here for a while is that it makes the things at home which really are worth caring for seem all the more precious.

Now I am going out to hear a lecture, then I shall go into the Gallery for an hour, then take a German lesson, and get a little more of this good place before I leave it. Think of me often, and be sure I think of you. . . . My love to Hattie and the babies.

Ever affectionately, P.

HÔTEL BELLEVUE, DRESDEN,
November 5, 1882.

DEAR WILLIAM, — The scene is changed, and this is Dresden, instead of Berlin. I left that big town for good on Thursday, and shall not see it again; but I have had a first-rate time there, and shall remember it most pleasantly. Dresden is prettier than Berlin, and the Sistine Madonna is over there in the Museum, so I am enjoying a few days here very much indeed. I get a good deal of time for reading my German, and am just beginning to get up the books on India, which now seems to be drawing very near.

I have no friends here, except one or two families, to whom my Berlin friends introduced me, but that does not so much matter for a few days. Robert Cushing and his family are staying in this hotel. Henry Potter, his wife and three children, are living in town. I dined with them last night. This morning I preached at the American church, and this evening I have promised to preach for the Scotch Presbyterians, so it is rather more like Sunday than any first day of the week that I have passed for a good while. I shall leave here probably Wednesday, and after stopping a few days in Prague, shall go to Vienna, where I hope to make a considerable stay.

Think of me there when you get this letter. Of course you have seen the terrible accounts of the floods on the southern side of the Tyrolese mountains. Among their smaller mischiefs, they make the access to Venice very uncertain, so that I am not quite sure how I shall get at my steamer. I shall get there somehow, probably by rail from Vienna to Trieste, and thence by sea to Venice.

Your last letter brought things at home up to the 16th of October. Perry had just preached in Trinity. Does it not seem strange to think how long ago it was that he used to be with Dr. Vinton at St. Paul's, and that we are the same fellows as the boys who used to listen to him there? The minister of the American church, for whom I preached to-day, is a Mr. Caskey, who succeeded Arthur in Williamsport. What a time we would have before the Madonna to-morrow, if you were only here; the concerts and operas in Dresden are tremendous. No matter; some day when I get back we will go to the Art Museum and the Music Hall together, and make believe that it is pretty little Dresden. . . .

PRAGUE, November 12, 1882.

. . . You never saw Prague, did you? You must some day. It is immensely curious and picturesque. It is Austrian, and Austria is poor stuff by the side of Germany. Austria really seems to be no nation at all, made up as it is of a heap of people and languages, which have no association with each other. Germany has ideas, and a great notion of her future, and of having a mission in the world. All that makes her interesting. Austria has nothing of the kind, and her petty tyranny is endless. These riots in Vienna are signs of what a suppressed and discontented life her people lead. But still she is worth seeing, and for two weeks I shall be on her soil. Thanksgiving Day I spend in Venice, and the next day the Poonah sails, so think of me as you eat your turkey, dining at Danielis, and direct your letters after you get this, until further notice, to the care of Messrs. Lang, Moir & Co., Bombay.

Will you do an errand for me? Will you go into Williams's and get two copies of my "Influence of Jesus" and send them to some Berlin friends, to whom I have promised them?

. . . .

Grand Hotel, Vienna, November 19, 1882.
Very private!!

Dear Gertie, — This letter is an awful secret between you and me. If you tell anybody about it, I will not speak to you all this winter. And this is what it is about. You know Christmas is coming, and I am afraid that I shall not get home by that time, and so I want you to go and get the Christmas presents for the children. The grown people will not get any from me this year. But I do not want the children to go without, so you must find out, in the most secret way, just what Agnes and Toodie would most like to have, and get it and put it in their stockings on Christmas Eve. Then you must ask yourself what you want, but without letting yourself know about it, and get it too, and put it in your own stocking, and be very much surprised when you find it there. And then you must sit down and think about Josephine De Wolf and the other baby at Springfield whose name I do not know, and consider what they would like, and have it sent to them in time to reach them on Christmas Eve. Will you do all this for me? You can spend five dollars for each child, and if you show your father this letter, he will give you the money out of some of mine which he has got. That rather breaks the secret, but you will want to consult your father and mother about what to get, especially for the Springfield children; so you may tell them about it, but do not dare to let any of the children know of it until Christmas time. Then you can tell me in your Christmas letter just how you have managed about it all. . . .

This has taken up almost all my letter, and so I cannot tell you much about Vienna. Well, there is not a great deal to tell. It is an immense great city with very splendid houses and beautiful pictures and fine shops and handsome people. But I do not think the Austrians are nearly as nice as the ugly, honest Germans. Do you?

Perhaps you will get this on Thanksgiving Day. If you do, you must shake the turkey's paw for me, and tell him that I am very sorry I could not come this year, but I shall be there next year certain! Give my love to all the children. I had a beautiful letter from aunt Susan the other day, which I am going to answer as soon as it stops raining. Tell her so, if you see her. Be a good girl, and do not study too hard, and keep our secret.

Your affectionate uncle   PHILLIPS.

GRAND HOTEL, VIENNA, November 22, 1882.

DEAR AUNT SUSAN, — No letter since I left home has given me more pleasure than yours which I received a week ago. It took me back into North Andover, and made me feel as if we were all in the little parlor, and the Austrian town which I could see out of the window were all a dream. You were very good indeed to keep your promise, and I hope I shall hear from you more than once again before I drive up to the side yard door next autumn.

. . . We had a small snowstorm here yesterday, and to-day the hills around Vienna are all white with snow. I wish you could escape the winter, as I mean to do, by running down into countries where the only trouble about winter weather is the heat. The second week in December, when you get this, and when the whole of North Andover is shivering with cold, we shall be running down the Red Sea and trying to get into the shade of anything to keep ourselves cool, and looking over the side of the Poonah to see if we can see any of Pharaoh's chariot-wheels.

It is eighteen years since I was in Vienna, on my first European journey. Then I was on my way to Palestine. One difference between that year abroad and this I feel all the time. Then the old home in Chauncy Street was still there, and father and mother were both waiting to hear what one was doing, and one of my pleasures was to write to them and to think how I would tell them all about it when I got back. I miss all that part of the interest of travel very much now. Sometimes it is hard to realize that they are not still there, and that I am not to write to them. At this distance all that has come since I was here before seems like a dream.

I hope by Christmas that the window in their memory will be in the little church. William writes me that it is getting on, and I shall be glad to know that it is fairly in its place. I hope it will be there for years to keep people reminded of them. You must tell me how you like it when it is up. It seems as if we came pretty near losing Trinity Church lately by fire. It would have been a pretty hard thing to have to go to work and build it all up again. As it is, they seem to be having trouble with it in the way of repairs. I hope your new church will tempt no incendiaries and meet no accidents.

If I were in Boston I would come up to Andover this afternoon. But as I am in Vienna, I can only send this letter to tell you I am thinking of you. My best love to aunt Sarah and aunt Caroline.

Your affectionate nephew PHILLIPS.

VENICE, November 26, 1882.

DEAR WILLIAM, — It is a rainy Sunday in Venice, which, as you may imagine, is not a very cheerful thing. The gondolas are dripping at the quay outside, and San Giorgio looks dull and dreary through the mists. . . . Now that I have come home, and have got a fire in my room, spread out my German books, and lighted my pipe, everything is cheerful inside, however dreary the outside may be. I have just come here to get a few quiet days of Venice, before the Poonah sails. She is here, lying in the harbor; and I have been on board and looked her over. She is a beautiful, great vessel, with a big, broad deck and a bright, pleasant cabin, looking as if she might be a capital home for three weeks. . . .

My stateroom is on deck, with air all around it, and I have it to myself, so I am counting very much upon my voyage. How I wish you were going to take it with me! What delightful days and nights we would have down the Red Sea and across the Indian Ocean! The officers of the ship say that at this season the ther-

mometer does not go above seventy, even in the Red
Sea, and that there is never any chance of bad
weather in December between Suez and Bombay. It
seems to be the very perfection of ship life. . . .

I had a very good time in Vienna, where I stayed
about a week. I do not think I like the city much,
certainly not as well as Berlin. But then I knew
none of the people, which made a difference. The
Brimmers were there part of the time, and it was
pleasant to see them. Also Judge Endicott and his
family, who were at the hotel all the time I was there.
I am very sorry Mr. Brimmer could not go to India.
. . . I shall go alone now, unless possibly a young
collegian of this last class at Cambridge, a friend of
Arthur's, Evert Wendell, should go on the same
steamer. I saw him in Berlin, and he wants to go and
has sent to ask his father's leave.

. . . The Venetians are going to have a great fête
and concert to-night and to-morrow in the piazza, for
the benefit of the sufferers by the floods. A month
ago the whole ground floor of this hotel was three feet
under water. I wish you would go to India with
me. . . .

STEAMSHIP POONAH, LYING AT BRINDISI,
Sunday, December 3, 1882.

DEAR WILLIAM, — . . . The Poonah is an old ship,
rather noisy, not at all fast, and not very clean. But
she is well arranged, and in good weather must be
very pleasant. The sail from Venice to Brindisi
has been cold, rough, and rainy. The Adriatic has
behaved badly. We could not touch at Ancona,
which is on the programme, because of the rough
weather. This Sunday morning is bright, but cold

and windy; not a bit of suggestion of the tropics yet. In a day or two we shall get it, and I only hope we shall not get too much. The people on the Poonah, so far, are not very interesting, but they are only a few. The best are supposed to come on board here at Brindisi, having come by rail from London, so I hope when we sail to-morrow morning, we shall find ourselves in the midst of that delightful society which the voyage to India has always been said to furnish. Young Wendell is on board, having turned up at the last moment in Venice. He makes bright, pleasant company, and we shall probably be together through India.

Thanksgiving Day passed quietly in Venice. I did not preach, or even go to church, except to pay a farewell visit to St. Mark's. I dined with the Walleys. They are staying in Venice, keeping house in an apartment, and asked me to dine with them. We had a turkey, and did the best we could to keep Thanksgiving, and it went off well. . . .

Think of the Poonah, when you get this, as paddling across the Indian Ocean, and wave your hat in that direction. I shall see it and wave mine back. A happy Christmas to you all. Now I am going on shore to see Brindisi.

STEAMSHIP POONAH, IN THE SUEZ CANAL,
December 9, 1882.

DEAR JOHNNY, — You do not know what a queer-looking thing this big ditch is, with the long stretches of sand reaching out on either side, and the curious effects of light everywhere in the distance, and the superb blue sky, and our great steamer slowly plodding along at about six miles an hour towards the Red Sea.

And inside the steamer it is just as queer, a host of wild-looking ruffians for sailors, and a lot of Englishmen. It is all very pleasant and foreign. I have been up on deck all the morning, looking at the strange figures who occasionally appear on the banks, watching the steamboats which pass us every now and then, and talking with the Englishmen who are mentioned above. I have got a little tired of it all, so I thought I would come down into the cabin and send you a greeting which I will mail to-night at Suez, and which you will get almost, if not quite, in time to wish you a Merry Christmas!

What are you doing? Every now and then there comes some glimpse of the old life going on at home. Sermons and convocations and clubs, and the winter season with its work gradually thickening around you. . . .

I wonder who will be up to the mark of honestly admiring A. V. G. Allen's remarkable paper in the "Princeton Review," and seeing how the change which he has described so ably is every whit as important and significant as the reformation of three hundred years ago. Surely the club and the church ought to be proud of the man who wrote the article.

Have you got some good carols for Christmas, and a good text for your Christmas sermon? I feel almost like writing one myself and asking some Hindoo in Bombay to lend me his mosque in which to preach it.

I hope you went to the December club, and that it was a success. I shall hear all about it in India and will tell Chunder Sen. We are getting to Ismailia, and I must go up on deck and see. Good-by. A Merry Christmas and God bless you to you and Hattie and the children.   Ever affectionately,   P.

SUEZ, Sunday Morning, December 10, 1882.

DEAR WILLIAM, — We are just tying up to the wharf in Suez, and nobody seems to know how long we are to stay before we start on our voyage down the Red Sea. I will write my Sunday letter at once, and tell you that I have come thus far in happiness, health, and safety, and in the Poonah. I sent Gertie a postal card the other day from Alexandria, which I hope she will excuse. I am not in the habit of sending postal cards, but there was no other way. We were only there for a very short time and all the time we had was spent on shore. It was curious to see the results of the war so close at hand. The great square of Alexandria is all in ruins, and looks like Liberty Square in Boston after the great fire. The forts which brought on the bombardment are all banged to pieces, and the guns are standing on their heads. There must have been some wonderful firing on the Englishmen's part.

Then we sailed over to Port Said, the steamer rolling about badly in the long swell. There was plenty of room at the dinner-table on Thursday. Port Said looks as I remember seeing Lawrence look when father took us there from grandmother's, one day when we were boys. It is an extemporized town of shanties and cheap buildings, with everything to sell, which it is supposed that uncomfortable and extravagant travelers will buy. Only the population does not look like Lawrence people. They are brown Egyptians and Nubians as black as coals, and a few British soldiers with white pith helmets and red coats.

The sail down the canal has been delightful. The air was fresh and bright as spring, yet had the warmth of summer in it. The atmosphere was delightful, and though we sometimes ran between high banks of sand, which hid everything, most of the time the view was made up of long stretches of desert, reaching away to distant hills, with effect of light and color on them, all which were beautiful. This morning I saw out of my stateroom window a glorious sunrise, just such as the children of Israel must have seen on their famous trip from Egypt into Palestine some years ago. We passed yesterday Ismailia, where the British headquarters were this autumn, and saw the way they started to Tel El Kebir. And there we heard of the verdict in Arabi's case, about which nobody seemed to care.

Now we really start upon our voyage. Up to this point has been mere preparation. Here the passengers for Australia and Calcutta leave us, and we take on board the passengers for Bombay, who have come all the way by sea from London. We shall be quite a new company. We have lost two or three days by having to go through the canal, and shall not be in Bombay certainly before the 22d, perhaps not till later. I like the ship, the people, the life on board, and all is going beautifully. Merry Christmas to you all. . . .

ON THE POONAH, December 15, 1882.

DEAR WILLIAM, — I write my Sunday letter this week on Friday, because to-night we are to arrive at Aden, and there can mail our epistles. There will not be another chance until we come to Bombay. All this week we have been running down the Red Sea. The weather has been sultry and oppressive; not particularly hot by the thermometer, but such weather as makes one want to get in a draft and do nothing. In the great cabin, the punkas are hung up, long cloth fans, which are fastened to a rod that runs along the ceiling over the dining-table; every meal-time they are kept swinging by a long cord, which runs through the skylight, and is attached at the other end to a small Mohammedan on deck, who pulls, and pulls, and pulls. We could hardly live without it. This morning we were passing Mocha, where the coffee comes from, and this afternoon we shall go through Bab-el-Mandel. When we are once out into the Indian Ocean, the special sultriness of the Red Sea will be over, and we shall have a week of charming sailing.

The ship is very comfortable, but she is old and slow. She is four days behind her time, and we shall not be at Bombay before Saturday, the 23d, more than three weeks from the time we left Venice. But it has been very pleasant. There is a miscellaneous and interesting company on board. Here is the general who led the cavalry charge at Tel El Kebir, and is coming back from England after being decorated by the Queen. Here is Lord Charles Beresford, who ran his boat up under the guns at Alexandria at the time of the bombardment, and did wonders of bravery. Here is a young Cambridge parson, going out to a missionary brotherhood at Delhi. Here are merchants of Calcutta and Madras, whom one pumps continually for information about India, — Englishmen, all of them. At Bombay we shall break up, and I suppose I shall stay there about a week, and then travel by Delhi, Jeypore, Agra, Lucknow, Allahabad, and Benares to Calcutta, taking about a month, bringing us to Calcutta about the 1st of February. A week there, a week's trip to the mountains, and a two weeks' journey to Madras and its neighborhood, will bring us to Ceylon about the 1st of March; after a week there we sail again, direct for Aden and Suez. So there is our winter. And you can tell about where we are at any time. . . .

There is a long gap in letters. The last was yours, which reached me just as I went on board at Venice. The next will not come until the steamer after ours reaches Bombay, but I am sure you are all well and happy, and getting ready for Christmas in the old cheerful fashion. I shall think of you all that day, as I sit sweltering in church at Bombay.

Ever affectionately, P.

BOMBAY, Sunday, December 24, 1882.

DEAR WILLIAM, — In India at last! And you do not know how queer and beautiful it is. I will tell you about it. On Friday night, at eleven o'clock, the slow old Poonah dropped her anchor in the harbor opposite the Apollo Bandar, which is the landing-place of Bombay. That night we slept on board, but by six the next morning we were in a boat and being rowed to shore, where we had a jolly good breakfast at Watson's Hotel. While we were eating it, two gentlemen sent in their cards. One was Mr. George A. Kittredge, who is the head of the Tramway System here. The other gentleman was Mr. Charles Lowell, who is a son of the Rev. Dr. Lowell, who used to be at St. Mark's School. These two gentlemen insisted on taking charge of us during our stay in Bombay. Lowell is in the banking business here. We were immediately carried to his bungalow, and here I write to you.

Fancy an enormous house, rambling into a series of immense rooms, all on one floor, piazzas twenty feet deep, immense chambers (in the middle of which stand the beds), doors and windows wide open, the grounds filled with palms, bananas, and all sorts of tropical trees, the song of birds, the chirp of insects everywhere, and a dazzling sun blazing down on the Indian Ocean in front. A dozen or more dusky Hindoo servants, barefooted, dressed in white, with bright sashes around their waists and bright turbans on their heads, are moving about everywhere, as still as cats, and with no end of devotion to their little duties. One of them seems to have nothing to do but to look after me; he has worked over my limited wardrobe till he knows every shirt and collar better than I do myself. He is now brushing my hat for the twelfth time this morning. The life is luxurious. Quantities of delightful fruit, cool lounging-places, luxurious chairs, a sumptuous breakfast (or "tiffin," as we call it here), and dinner table, and no end of kind attention. I am writing in my room on the day before Christmas as if it were a rather hot August morning at home.

Yesterday, we drove about the town and began our sight of Indian wonders: Hindoo temples, with their squatting ugly idols; Mahommedan mosques; bazaars thronged with every Eastern race; splendid English buildings where the country is ruled; a noble university; Parsee merchants in their shops; great tanks with the devotees bathing in them; officers' bungalows, with the handsome English fellows lounging about; wedding processions, with the bride of six years old riding on the richly decorated horse behind the bridegroom of ten, surrounded by their friends, and with a tumult of horrible music; markets overrunning with strange and delicious fruits; wretched-looking saints chattering gibberish and begging alms, — there is no end to the interest and curiosity of it all! And this is dead winter in the tropics. I have out all my thinnest clothes, and go about with an umbrella to keep off the sun. This morning, we started at half past six for a walk through the sacred part of the native town, and now at ten it is too hot to walk any more till sundown. But there are carriages enough, and by and by we go to church. I was invited to preach at the cathedral, but declined.

We shall be in and about Bombay for about a week. You must not think that we shall suffer from the heat. This is the hottest place that we shall visit. As soon as we leave here we shall be in the hills, and by and by shall see the thermometer at zero. How I shall think of you to-morrow! It is holidays here, and our friends have nothing to do but to look after us. Banks close for four days! Good-by, my love to you all always.

BOMBAY, Tuesday, December 26.

Do you care to know how we spent Christmas? I will tell you. We arose in the cool of the morning at six o'clock. After we had a cup of tea, some fruit and bread and butter, the open carriage was at the door, and we put on our pith helmets to keep off the sun, and drove away. First we went to the Jain hospital for animals. The Jains are a curious sect of Hindoos, and one of their ideas is the sacredness of animal life. So they have this great hospital, where they gather all the sick and wounded animals they can find, and cure them if they can, or keep them till they die. The broken-legged cows, sick pigeons, mangy dogs, and melancholy monkeys are very curious. We stayed there a while, and then drove to the Parsee burial-place. The Parsees are Persian sun-worshipers, who have been settled here for centuries, and are among the most intelligent and enterprising citizens. Their pleasant way of disposing of their dead is to leave a body on a high tower, where vultures devoted to that business come, and in about an hour consume all its flesh, leaving the bones, which, after four weeks of drying in the sun, are tumbled into a common pit, where they all crumble together into dust. You see the towers with the vultures waiting on top for the next arrival, but no one is allowed to enter.

Then we came home and had our breakfast, after which we drove into the town, whence I sent a telegram of "Merry Christmas" to you at eleven o'clock. We went to the service at the Cathedral, which was very good. . . . Then I drove out to the Government House, where the Governor, Sir James Fergusson, had invited me to lunch. Very pleasant people were there, and the whole thing was interesting. The drive out and in, about four miles each way, was through the strangest population, and in the midst of the queerest sights. After my return (I went there alone) we wandered about the native bazaars and saw their curious trades. At eight o'clock, Mr. Kittredge gave us a sumptuous dinner at the Byculla Club, where with turkey, plum pudding, and mince-pies, we made the best which we knew how of that end of Christmas Day. After that, about ten o'clock, we wandered out into a native fair, where we saw their odd performances until late into the night, when we drove home along the cool seashore, and went to bed tired but happy, after the funniest Christmas Day we ever passed.

We go off now for a short trip to Karli and Poonah to see some curious old Buddhist temples. When we get back from there, we start for a long journey to Ahmadabad, Jeypore, Delhi, Lahore, Agra, Lucknow,

Cawnpore, Allahabad, Benares, and Calcutta. This will take three weeks or a month.

I hope you had a happy Christmas. And now a happy New Year to you! Hurrah for 1883! I hope you will have a splendid watch-meeting and think of me. . . .

BOMBAY, January 2, 1883.

DEAR WILLIAM, — A happy New Year to you! May 1883 be the happiest of any yet! I see no reason why it should not be. We shall not frisk about quite as much as we did thirty years ago, when we were boys. For all that, there are soberer joys even for such old chaps as you and I, and if the birds fly somewhat more sluggishly than of old, why perhaps it will be all the easier to get the salt on their tails. So a happy New Year to you! The new year broke on me as I was driving in a tonga from Deogaon to Nandgaon. A tonga is a queer sort of dogcart, drawn by two sharp little ponies with a yoke over their necks, as if they were oxen; — you see we have been spending a good part of the last week in going up to the hills to see the wonderful Buddhist and Braminical caves and temples. Sunday we spent in a bungalow on the top of a hot hill, out of which two thousand years ago these wonderful people hewed these marvelous affairs.

Think of a structure bigger than Trinity Church, with spires, columns, and domes a hundred feet high, which is not a structure at all, but is carved out of solid rock and hewn into chambers, corridors, courtyards, and shrines; covered, in almost every inch of its surface inside and out, with sculptures, some very big and stately, some as fine as jewels, and all full of the most interesting religious and historical meaning.

Think of that, old fellow! That is the most splendid of the caves, but there are thirty-five of them, all more or less wonderful, and some almost as fine as this. We spent Sunday there, and Sunday night about ten o'clock (for you do everything you can by night to avoid the heat) we took our tongas and drove six hours down from Ellora, where the caves are, to the railway. On the way, just as we were stopping to change ponies, and some half-naked Hindoos were howling to each other over their arrangement, and the Southern Cross was blazing in the sky, and the moon struggling up, 1883 came tripping in. I thought of you at home, and wondered whether you were having a watch-meeting and what you thought of the New Year; then I remembered it was only three o'clock in Boston, and that you were just going to afternoon church. So I tumbled back into the tonga again and we jolted on.

You see I am getting somewhat at the country. It is interesting far beyond anything I expected. Our friends, Kittredge and Lowell, have been more kind and devoted than you can imagine. No one in a week could have seen more, or seen it better, than we. This afternoon we leave Bombay and launch out for ourselves. We have a capital fellow for a traveling servant, a dusky gentleman with a turban and a petticoat, a low-caste Hindoo named Huri. When you get this, about the 1st of February, we shall have passed through northern India and shall be in Calcutta. In a day or two we shall get out of excessive heat, and not be troubled with it again until we leave Calcutta for southern India. I am splendidly well. My young traveling companion is very pleasant. I love you all very much, and hope you will remember

PHILLIPS.

BANKAPUR, Tuesday, January 3, 1883.

DEAR LIZZIE,[1] — Since I wrote you, we have come over from Benares, and to-day have been making a delightful excursion to Buddh-gaya, where, as Sir Edwin Arnold tells us so prettily, Gautama sat six years under a bo-tree, and thought and thought, until at last the Dukha-Satya was opened to him, and Buddhism began. In these days, when a large part of Boston prefers to consider itself Buddhist rather than Christian, I consider this pilgrimage to be the duty of a minister who preaches to Bostonians, and so this morning before sunrise we started for Gaya and the red Barabar Hills.

We had slept in the railway station, which is not an uncommon proceeding in the out of the way parts of India, where there is no pretense of a hotel, and where you do not know anybody to whose bungalow you can drive up, as you can to that of almost any man to whom you ever bowed in the street. They are a most hospitable folk, only when you go to stay with them you are expected to bring your own bedding and your own servant, which saves them lots of trouble. Think of my appearing at your door some afternoon with a mattress and Katie. We had to drive ten miles in a rattling gharry, and as we went the sun rose just as it did on Buddha, in the same landscape in the fifth book of the " Light of Asia," which (as you see) I have been reading with the greatest interest. We had to walk the last two miles, because the ponies, who must have been Mohammedans, would not go any farther. It was a glorious morning, and by and by we suddenly turned into an indescribable ravine. One tumbled mass of shrines and monuments, hundreds on hundreds of them, set up for the

[1] A sister in law.

last two thousand years by pilgrims. In the midst, two hundred feet high, a queer fantastic temple (which has been rebuilt again and again) which has in it the original Buddha figure of Asoka's time; a superb great altar statue, calm as eternity, and on the outside covered with gold-leaf, the seat on which the Master sat those six long years. The bo-tree has departed long ago, and the temples were not there when he was squatting and meditating, but the landscape was the same, and though this is one of the places where thousands of pilgrims come from both the Buddhist and the Brahmin worlds, the monuments which they set up are not as interesting as the red hills on one side, and the open plain on the other, which Sakya must have seen when he forgot for a moment to gaze at the soles of his own feet and looked upon the outer world.

It is a delightful country, this India, and now the climate is delightful. The Indian winter is like the best of our Indian summer, and such mornings and midnights you never saw. We had two weeks in Delhi, because my companion, Evert Wendell, must needs pick up the small-pox. It is rather good to know one town of a great country so well as I know that, and it is on the whole, I suppose, the most interesting town in India. I think I know every one of its superb old tombs by heart. Wendell could not have chosen a better place, if he was bound to do such a ridiculous thing at all.

I wished you a happy New Year when the old year left us in the midst of a night drive among the hills. I hope you felt my wish around the globe, or through it, which ever way wishes go. May everything go beautifully with you. May you get all you want and nothing which you do not want. It will be bad for you, but it will be pleasant. May the new church be better even than you expect. May you get any number of dry concerts and delightful books. May I come and see you flourishing gloriously through it all next September. I am not sure just what you want, but, whatever it is, may you get it abundantly. Give my best love to Arthur, and write me all about what you are doing. Affectionately, P.

JEYPORE, January 7, 1883.

MY DEAR GERTIE, — I wish you had been here with me yesterday. We would have had a beautiful time. You would have had to get up at five o'clock, for at six the carriage was at the door, and we had already had our breakfast. But in this country you do everything you can very early, so as to escape the hot sun. It is very hot in the middle of the day, but quite cold now at night and in the mornings and evenings. Well, as we drove into the town (for the bungalow where we are staying is just outside), the sun rose and the streets were full of light.

The town is all painted pink, which makes it the queerest-looking place you ever saw, and on the outsides of the pink houses there are pictures drawn, some of them very solemn and some very funny, which makes it very pleasant to drive up the street. We drove through the street, which was crowded with camels and elephants and donkeys, and women wrapped up like bundles, and men chattering like monkeys, and monkeys themselves, and naked little children rolling in the dust, and playing queer Jeypore games. All the little girls, when they get to be about your age, hang jewels in their noses, and the women all have their noses looking beautiful in this way. I have got a nose jewel for you, which I shall put in when I get home, and also a little button for the side of Susie's nose, such as the smaller children wear. Think how the girls at school will admire you.

Well, we drove out the other side of the queer pink town, and went on toward the old town, which they deserted a hundred years ago, when they built this. The priest told the rajah, or king, that they ought not to live more than a thousand years in one place, and so, as the old town was about a thousand years old, the king left it; and there it stands about five miles off, with only a few beggars and a lot of monkeys for inhabitants of its splendid palaces and temples. As we drove along toward it, the fields were full of peacocks and all sorts of bright-winged birds, and out of the ponds and streams the crocodiles stuck up their lazy heads and looked at us.

The hills around are full of tigers and hyenas, but they do not come down to the town, though I saw a cage of them there which had been captured only about a month and were very fierce. Poor things! When we came to the entrance of the old town, there was a splendid great elephant waiting for us, which the rajah had sent. He sent the carriage, too. The elephant had his head and trunk beautifully painted, and looked almost as big as Jumbo. He knelt down, and we climbed up by a ladder and sat upon his back, and then he toiled up the hill. I am afraid he thought Americans must be very heavy, and I do not know whether he could have carried you. Behind us, as we went up the hill, came a man leading a little black goat, and when I asked what it was for, they said it was for sacrifice. It seems a horrid old goddess has a temple on the hill, and years ago they used to sacrifice men to her, to make her happy and kind. But a merciful rajah stopped that, and made them sacrifice goats instead, and now they give the horrid old goddess a goat every morning, and she likes it just as well.

When we got into the old town, it was a perfect wilderness of beautiful things, — lakes, temples, palaces, porticos, all sorts of things in marble and fine stones, with sacred long-tailed monkeys running over all. But I must tell you all about the goddess, and the way they cut off the poor goat's little black head, and all the rest that I saw, when I get home. Don't you wish you had gone with me?

Give my love to your father and mother and Agnes and Susie. I am dying to know about your Christmas and the presents. Do not forget your affectionate uncle PHILLIPS.

CAMBRIDGE MISSION, DELHI, January 10, 1883.

DEAR JOHNNY, — A happy New Year to you and H—— and both the babies. I received a beautiful letter from you in Bombay, which deserves a better answer than I am afraid it will get from me before dinner is ready. It was full of the spirit of home work, and of all those pleasant things to which I shall be glad enough to get back by and by, pleasant as it is meanwhile to be wandering in these queer places.

Do you see where I am writing? On the voyage from Aden to Bombay I met a young Church of England missionary, with whom I had a good deal of talk, and who asked me, when I came to Delhi, to put up with him. So here we are. Three young fellows, all graduates of Cambridge, scholars and gentlemen, live here together, and give themselves to missionary work. They have some first-rate schools, and are just starting a high-class college. They preach in the bazaars, and have their mission stations out in the country, where they constantly go. I have grown to respect them thoroughly. Serious, devoted, self-sacrificing fellows they are, rather high churchmen, but thoughtful and scholarly, and with all the best broad church books upon their shelves. They are jolly, pleasant companions as possible, and yesterday I saw a cricket match between their school and the Government school here, in which one of these parsons played a first-rate bat. Under their guidance I have seen very thoroughly this wonderful old city, the great seat of the Mogul Empire, excessively rich in the best Mohammedan architecture.

How I wish you would ask me something about the Aryans, Davidians, about Brahmins, or Buddhists, or Parsees, or Mussulmans, or Jains. I could tell you all about them, but perhaps you do not care so much as one gets to care here, where the snarly old history becomes a little bit untangled, and you get immensely interested in the past of this enormous people. One goes about picking up all sorts of bits and piecing them together. To-day it is a Cambridge missionary. Yesterday it was a traveling Calcutta Brahmin. Last week it was a Parsee merchant, with whom I got a scrap of talk, and all the time there are wonderful sights, — Buddhist caves, Jain temples, woods full of monkeys and peacocks, rides on elephants, visits to the English governors, and, first of all, three or four charming days at the Bombay bungalow of Charles Lowell.

I wish you were here, and we could talk it all over, and to-morrow night start together for Amritsir and Lahore. But you are not, and I am afraid you do not feel very much interest in the Punjaub and the Sikhs just at present. You will whenever you come here. Meanwhile you must be getting your sermon ready for the second Sunday after Epiphany. I am sure that it will be a good one and wish that I could hear it. And by the time you get this, Lent will be close upon you, and all those hard questions about Confirmation and Lent service will be crowding you. . . . God bless you, Johnny. Love to all.

DELHI, January 14, 1883.

DEAR WILLIAM, — I write you a rather unexpected letter to-day, for the last week has been different from what I looked for. Last Sunday I wrote to G—— from Jeypore. On Sunday night we left that place and came to Delhi, reaching here on Monday at noon. We intended to stay till Thursday, and then go to Lahore. But this is what happened: Wendell had not been feeling very well, and when we arrived, it seemed best that we should see a doctor. The doctor at once told him that he had the Indian fever, and must go to bed. In two days the fever was broken, then it came out that behind the fever he had the chicken-pox. Fortunately, he is in good hands. On the Poonah was a young missionary, an English clergyman, belonging to an establishment here known as the Cambridge Mission. He kindly insisted that when we came to Delhi we should stay with him, and so when Wendell was taken down it was at his house. Three of them (bachelors) keep house together, and the kindness of them all, under these very awkward circumstances, has been most wonderful. I was in their house three days, but when I found how things were looking, I insisted on going to a hotel close by, for I found one of the ministers was giving me his room, and going out every night to sleep. So I am at the United Service Hotel, Wendell lies at the Mission House, and I am constantly with him. . . .

Delhi is an immensely interesting place, and it is not a bad thing to see it thoroughly. It is the old centre of Mohammedan power in India. Here the Great Mogul ruled for years and years, and the great Mosque is one of the wonders of the Mussulman world. Here, too, was the centre of the great mutiny in 1857, and the town is full of interesting points connected with that history. And then the present life, both Hindoo and Mohammedan, is vastly interesting. The streets are endless pictures. This morning the Jumna was full of bathers in the sacred stream. The bazaars are crowded with the natives of all parts of India. The processions of marriages and burials meet you everywhere. The temples with their hideous gods are all along the streets, and the fakirs go clinking their begging-bowls everywhere.

At present there is particular excitement because the Lieutenant-Governor of the Punjaub is here with his whole suite. They entered the city yesterday morning, with a train of elephants and camels, and all the citizens in their best clothes turned out to see them. Now they are encamped on a broad field, just below the Mission, and they make a most picturesque array. For days whole hosts of wretched-looking folk have been sweeping the streets, dusting the temples, and cleaning up everything in anticipation of the coming of the Governor Sahib.

Later, Sunday Afternoon.

I preached this morning in the English Church, and had the usual English congregation. I am getting so used to English people in these days that a real American would seem a strange sort of creature. The English are faithful to their duties here, and their Indian Civil Service ought to be the pattern of the world. I wish that we had anything like it in America. The trouble about the whole thing is, that the Englishman does not really like the Indian and does not aim for any real liking from him; also the Englishman suffers so in this terrible Indian climate that he cannot live here permanently, and each officer is anxious to get through his service, and get his pension and be off to England. Such brave and devoted work as our missionary hosts are doing must tell, and the English rulers are gradually getting the Indians fit for more and more self-government. . . .

DELHI, January 21, 1883.

DEAR WILLIAM, — Here I am at Delhi for another Sunday. . . . The mission work is most nobly, sensibly and faithfully done here. . . . Yesterday afternoon, in the most desolate and degraded part of all the town, as I stood with a little crowd under a tree, with the hubbub of heathen life around us, with all sorts of faces, stupid and bright, hostile, eager, and scornful, I heard a native catechist preach the gospel in Urdu, of which I could not understand a word, and thought there could not be a better missionary picture. A group of Sikh soldiers came up, splendid-looking fellows, with fine faces, enormous turbans, and curled beards, who entered into lively discussion with the preacher, and for a time the debate ran very high. I could not make out which had the best of it, but the catechist seemed to understand himself very well.

The principal point of the Sikhs seemed to be that what God made every man, he meant that man to continue, so there could be no good reason for changing one's religion. But when the preacher asked them how the Sikh religion (which is only about two hundred years old) began, he rather had them.

Before Wendell's illness thoroughly declared its character, I went off for a three days' trip to Lahore and Amritsir, which was exceedingly interesting. They are in the Sikh country, which is a region quite by itself, with the finest set of men in India and a religion of its own. At Amritsir is their great place of worship, the Golden Temple, a superb structure, with the lower half of most beautiful mosaic and the upper half of golden plates, standing in the middle of an enormous artificial lake, called the Lake of Immortality. There is a beautiful white marble bridge connecting the island with the shore. I saw their picturesque worship one morning, just after sunrise. This was a very fine trip. . . .

The Lieutenant-Governor has been in camp here for two weeks, Sir Charles Atchison, to whom I had an introduction from Sir Richard Temple through Dr. Eliot. Friday morning, a stunning menial in red and yellow appeared on a camel at my door, with a note saying that he (the Lieutenant-Governor, not the menial) and Lady Atchison requested the pleasure of my company at dinner. The doctor said it was quite safe to go, and so I went. It was great fun. We had a swell dinner in a gorgeous tent, with about thirty persons, and no end of picturesque servants to wait on us. The Lieutenant-Governor was very pleasant, and when I left promised me some more letters to people in Calcutta. I took his daughter in to dinner, and had a nice talk with her. She is a sensible young Scotch lassie. Tell Dr. Eliot, if you see him, that both here and in Bombay I owe very much to his kind thoughtfulness.

I have been preaching again to-day, so that for three Sundays I have been on duty. Of course these are purely European congregations. A large part of the congregation is soldiers, of whom there is a considerable force stationed here. I wonder who preaches at Trinity? No letters have reached me for some time, but in a week I shall find some at Benares. Then I shall learn about your winter, and get the bearings of you almost up to Christmas time. When you get this I shall be about in Madras, perhaps even beyond, in Ceylon, with the Indian journey finished.

It is the most splendid weather possible now, like our best May or early June weather. In the mornings it is rather cold, and the natives go about with most of their bedclothes wrapped about their heads, though their legs are bare, and do not seem to mind the cold. By ten or eleven o'clock they are sitting in the sun, with almost everything off of them, and burning themselves a shade or two more brown. Their picturesqueness is endlessly interesting. But I do wonder what is going on at home. I know you are all well and that you wish I were with you. . . .

BENARES, January 28, 1883.

MY DEAR MARY, — . . . This is the sacredest place in India. There are five thousand Hindoo temples in Benares. . . . You stumble at every step on a temple with its hideous idol, and if you hear a gentleman muttering behind you in the street, he is not abusing you, but only saying prayers to Vishnu or Siva, who has a little shrine somewhere in the back yard of the next house. There is one sweet temple to their Monkey God, where they keep five hundred monkeys. I went to this temple yesterday morning, and the little wretches were running over everything, and would hardly let you go, wanting you to feed them. They are so sacred that if you hurt one of them, you would have an awful time. It reminded me of nothing so much as your drawing-room after dinner.

Then I went down to the Ganges, where hundreds and hundreds of people were bathing in the sacred river. Pilgrims from all over India had come to wash their sins away, and were scrubbing themselves, as thick as they could stand, for two miles along the bank of the stream. It is a beautiful religion, at least in this, that it keeps its disciples always washing themselves. . . .

By and by, we came to a place where, in a little hollow by the river's side, a pile of wood was burning; two men were waving a big piece of cloth to fan the flame, and gradually as it burned, you caught sight through it of a strange bundle lying in the midst of the wood and slowly catching fire. Then you knew that it was the funeral pile of some dead Hindoo, who had died happy in knowing that he would be burned beside the sacred river and that his ashes would be mingled with its waters.

Then came another curious and pathetic sight. Close by the side of this burning pile was another all prepared, but not yet lighted. Soon I saw a man leading a little naked boy some four years old into the water. He washed the little chap all over, then stood him up beside the pile of wood; a priest up above on a high altar said some prayers over him, and the man gave the little boy a blazing bunch of straw and showed him how to stick it into the midst of the wood until the whole caught fire. It was a widower showing his small son how to set his mother on fire. The little fellow seemed scared and cried, and when they let him go ran up to some other children, — probably cousins, — who put his clothes on for him, and then he squatted on his heels and quietly watched the flames.

While this was going on they had brought down the body of a child, perhaps seven or eight years old, and for it they built another pile of wood close to the water. Then they took the body into the stream and bathed it for a moment, then brought it out and laid it on the wood. The father of the child went into the water, and washed himself all over. After he came out the priest at the altar chanted a prayer for him. Then he went up to an old woman who sold straw, and bought a bundle, haggling some time over the price. This he lighted at the burning pile of the little boy's mother, and with it set his own child's pile in flames. They had covered the little body with a bright red cloth, and it was the prettiest funeral pile of all. By this time another body, a wasted and worn old man, had come, and they were already bathing him in the Ganges, while some men were gathering up the ashes of somebody who was burned earlier in the day and throwing them into the river, where they float to certain bliss. So it goes all the time, while a great crowd is gathered around, some laughing, some praying, some trafficking, some begging. While we looked on, an interesting-looking fakir came up with a live snake pleasantly curled around his neck, and begged an alms, while the boys behind kept pulling the tail of his hideous necklace to make him mad. Just down the slope beside the water, the mother was being burned by the little boy, and the child by her father.

This is not a cheerful letter, but on less serious occasions the Hindoos are a most amusing people. . . . They never sit, but squat all over the place. When you meet them they make believe take up some dust from the ground and put it on their heads. I wish you could see my servant Huri. He looks like a most sober, pious female of about forty-five. He wears petticoats and bloomers. Where he sleeps and what he eats, I have not the least idea. He gets $8 a month and finds himself, and is the most devoted and useful creature you ever saw, but as queer an old woman as ever lived. But good-by. I shall be glad enough to see you all again. . . .

The Hindoos are the most pathetic and amusing people. . . . This morning, after I had written this long letter, we went down again to the Ganges and watched the bathers and the burners for a long time. On the way we almost destroyed large numbers of the infant population, who crawl about the streets and run under the horses' feet and are just the color of the earth of which they are made, so that it is very hard to tell them from the inanimate clay. Almost none of them wear any clothes until they are six or seven years old; then their clothes soon get to be the same color as their skins and it does not help you much.

We passed a pleasant temple of the Goddess of Small-Pox, and looked in a moment just out of association. Her name is Sitla, and her temple is a horrid-looking place. On the way through the city there are all sorts of amusing sights. Here is a fellow squatted down in the dirt, blowing away on a squeaking flute, and as he blows there are a lot of snakes, cobras, and all sorts of dreadful-looking things swinging back and forth around him, and sticking their heads out of his baskets. Suddenly the musician starts up and begins a fantastic dance, and in a few minutes makes a dive at a chap in the crowd, and by sleight of hand seems to take a long snake (which he has concealed somewhere about him) out of the other fellow's turban. Then the crowd howl and jeer, and we throw the dirty musician a quarter of a cent.

All this it is pleasantest to see from the carriage; just as we are turning away, there is a cheerful noise of a band coming down the narrow street, and there appear a dozen men and boys playing on queer drums, cymbals, and trumpets. After them a crowd of women singing a wild and rather jolly air, then on horseback a small boy of twelve all dressed up in gilt paper and white cloth, and on another horse a little girl about the size of Tood, who is his bride. She is dressed like a most gorgeous doll, and has to be held on the horse by a man who walks behind. They have all been down to the Ganges to worship, and now are going home to the wedding feast, after which the bride will be taken to the boy's mother's house to be kept for him, and a hard time the little wretch will have. The wedding procession comes to grief every few minutes in the crowded street; sometimes a big swell on an elephant walks into the midst of the band, and for a few minutes you lose sight of the minstrels altogether, and only hear fragments of the music coming out of the neighboring houses, where they have taken refuge. Sometimes there come a group of people, wailing, crying, and singing a doleful hymn, as they carry a dead body to the Ganges, and for a while the funeral and marriage music get mixed; but they always come unsnarled, and the wedding picks itself up and goes its way. Then you stop a moment to see a juggler make a mango-tree grow in three minutes from a seed to a tall bush. Then you drop into the bazaars and see their pretty silks; then you stop and listen to a Gooroo preaching in a little nook between two houses; and so you wander on, until you see the Ganges flashing in the sun and thousands of black and brown backs popping in and out, as the men and women take their baths.

When they come out, they sit with their legs folded under them for a long time, look at nothing, and meditate; then they go to a gentleman who sits under a big umbrella with a lot of paint-boxes about him, and he puts a daub on their foreheads, whose color and pattern tell how long they have bathed and prayed, and how holy they are after it all.

I have been looking at Huri, who is squatted on the ground in the sun, just outside my door, as I am writing. He wears a gold and purple turban. The poor fellow was upset in a rickety cab last week, after he had left me at the station, and says his bones are bent, but he has been carefully examined, and we can find no harm. He always sleeps just outside my door at night. Last night I heard the jackals when I went to bed, and was quite surprised to find the whole of Huri in my room when I woke up this morning. I wish I could bring him home. . . .

CALCUTTA, February 3, 1883.

DEAR WILLIAM, — Lots of letters to-day, the best of them your Christmas letter, telling how you received my Bombay telegram, how you went to church and heard Bishop Clark, how you had lots of presents, and went to Salem in the afternoon. It was all delightful, and reading it as we drove along to-day in Dharamtolla Street (which means "the Way of Righteousness," and a funny, shabby old Hindoo Way of Righteousness it is), it seemed as if I saw you all at your home life. The palm-trees turned to elms, and the naked Indians to Boston men and women, with Boston great-coats buttoned up to their respectable Boston chins. It was all delightful! Do thank for me the whole Salem Round Robin.

Since I wrote that tremendous letter to Mary last Sunday, another week of India has passed. I have been down to Gaya, and seen where Buddha sat and contemplated for six years, and a marvelous strange place it is, with ten thousand Buddhas carved on every side. Then I came on here, and have been seeing interesting things and people for three days. Calcutta is not half as nice as Bombay, but there are people here whom I wanted very much to see. "Stately Bombay" and "Fair Calcutta" the Anglo-Indians are fond of saying.

I have just written an enormous letter to Arthur about Chunder Sen, to whom I made a long visit the other day. This afternoon I went to one of the schools supported by the Zenana Mission (of which you have sometimes heard from Trinity reading-desk), gave the prizes to a lot of little Hindoos, and made an address which was translated into Bengalee for my audience.

... I dined last night with the Whitneys, three Boston men who are out here in business.

Tell Gertie she has not sent me yet her Christmas report. At least I have not received it. What a succession of splendid preaching you are having! Oh, how I wish you were here to-night. God bless you all.

DARJEELING, INDIA, February 7, 1883.

DEAR MISS MORRILL, — Instead of writing you a letter which could be read at our Ash Wednesday meeting, I am writing to you on Ash Wednesday a letter which will hardly reach you before Easter. I explained to you before that I have been unable to see anything of the work of the Zenana Missionary in time to let you hear from me before the meeting. It is only now, after my visits to the places where our missionaries are at work, that I feel as if I had really something to say about their labors. From the time I entered India I heard much of the Zenana work. In Delhi, where I spent some time, English ladies are at work in this visitation and teaching of native women, and all persons who are interested in the religious and social condition of the people of India, whether clergymen or laymen, value their influence very highly. Of course, from the nature of the case it is not a work which can make much display of visible results, nor can a visitor like myself get any sight even of its processes. But he can talk with those who are engaged in it, hear their descriptions, and learn from those who see it constantly what are its effects. Also, besides the visitation of Zenanas, the same ladies are engaged in teaching school, which one can freely see, and of which he can form some judgment for himself.

The ladies of the American Union Mission whom I

have met are Miss Gardner, at Cawnpore, and Miss Marston, Miss Cook, and Mrs. Page, in Calcutta. I was sorry that Miss Ward was absent from Cawnpore, and Miss Lathrop from Allahabad at the times of my visit. They had both gone to Calcutta with reference to medical treatment for Miss Lathrop, and before I reached Calcutta they had returned to their respective posts. At Cawnpore the Mission House is a bright, pleasant bungalow, where the two American ladies live, together with a number of native teachers whom they have trained, and who go out every day to teach schools, which they have gathered either in the city or in some of the neighboring villages. There are fourteen such schools, I think, in or about Cawnpore. One of them is taught in the Mission House itself, and that I saw. The children were bright and intelligent, and (translated) answers showed that they knew what they were about.

I saw also what interested me very much, the school which is supported by the children of your class and Miss Lowell's and Miss Torrey's. I wish they could see it. It is described as the most difficult of all the schools, situated in a region of most benighted Mohammedanism, where the parents can hardly be induced to let the children come. Indeed, there were some fears lest the visit of a "Padre Sahib," or Mr. Minister, like me, might make trouble, and possibly break up the school. I hope that no disastrous results will follow from my well-meant and innocent appearance at the school-door. In the very heart of the crowded bazaars you turn from one dirty lane into another dirtier and narrower still, and then into the dirtiest and narrowest of all, which ends short at a native house of very poor sort, but making some small attempts at tidiness. The door admits at once to the only room, with an earth floor and a few benches, where you find a native woman who answers to the name of Dorcas, and around her about a dozen little, rough, sturdy, native girls, into whose dull heads she is trying to put the elements of Hindostanee learning. It is all homely enough, even wretchedly shabby and dreary, as the girls who support the school would think if they could see it, but if they saw the homes in which their strange little protégées live, and their parents, and knew the lives which are before them if they go untaught, and could see the condition of other schools (which began just as this is beginning), full of brightness, and happiness, and neatness, and intelligence, and religion, they would bid Dorcas go on with her work, and feel it a privilege to watch over the little school and nurse it to full life.

I was rather glad, on the whole, to find that our children had the hardest and most discouraging field in Cawnpore to work from. No one can talk with Miss Gardner and not be very much impressed with her good judgment and happy devotion to her work.

In Calcutta I have been several times at the Mission House and seen Miss Marston, Miss Cook, and their young native assistants, who live with them and make a most happy family. There, I could see nothing of the Zenana work, but they told me much about it, and from others, as well as from them, I heard such testimony as gives me the strongest assurance of its value. The only wonder is that the Baboos, or native gentlemen, so freely admit these ladies to their houses. In Bengal especially there is a strong desire for education, which even the secluded women feel, and either by their persuasion or by the husbands' own desire, the requisite permission is granted. Of course it is in every case clearly understood that the visitors mean to give Christian teaching. I have made special inquiry upon the point, and am assured that no such scandalous deception of the Baboo, as was described to us by the lady who addressed the Society last year in the chapel of Emmanuel Church, has ever been practiced or tolerated by our missionaries.

A good deal of talk with Miss Marston has impressed me with the good sense and intelligence of her methods, and I am more confident than ever that our church does better work nowhere than in the contribution which it makes to the Zenana Mission.

The schools which are under the care of these Calcutta ladies are very interesting. I have visited several of them, and heard their recitations both in English and Bengalee. The former was so good that I could have no doubt about the latter. And the children's faces told the story, which to any one who has watched for a month or two the ordinary look of Hindoo children's countenances was unmistakable.

Last Saturday afternoon I went to a prize festival of two of these schools, which I wish that the friends of the Mission could have seen. A generous Baboo had kindly offered the use of the courtyard of his house, which was prettily decorated for the occasion. He and a number of his friends came and looked on with the greatest interest. Even some of the ladies of his household were watching what went on from an upper gallery. Some hundred and fifty children were there, with that strange, pensive, half-sad look in their eyes which makes the faces of Hindoo children so pathetic. Some of them, however, had fun enough in them. Many of them were gorgeous in bright colors and trinkets. Most of them had fine rings in their ears, they all had rings in their noses, and the finest of them also had rings on their toes. Their little brown ankles tinkled with their anklets as they trotted up barefoot to get their dolls, and they answered Bible questions as I wish the children of Trinity school would answer them. They sang strange, sweet Bengalee words to tunes which all our children know, and after I had given them their prizes I made a little speech, which was translated to them, and I hope they understood, for I wanted them to know how much their American friends cared for these little friends of theirs.

I wish that I had time to tell you about Mrs. Page's Orphan Asylum. Most of these orphans are foundlings, and one could not look at them without thinking what their lives must have been, save for this home; if indeed without it, they could have had any life at all; many of them must have died in infancy. Now those who have been with Mrs. Page for years are as cheerful and cheery a lot of little Christian maidens as any school in America can show. Some of the teachers in the schools of which I have been speaking were brought up in this home. There are some seventy or eighty inmates now.

But I must not go on forever. You will see that my whole visit to this Zenana work and my acquaintance with the workers have deepened the faith in it which I have always rather blindly felt. I know it now, and I know that it is good. Those who have given their contributions year after year may rest assured that they have really helped the minds and souls of Hindoo women, shut up in the dreary monotony and frivolity of their Zenanas, and made possible for Hindoo children happy and useful lives, of which they had no chance except for such help. I congratulate you and the other ladies, who have had the privilege of helping on this work and keeping alive other people's interest in it. If anything that I can ever do or say can give it encouragement or strength, I shall be very glad.

Foreign missions lose something of their romance, but they gain vastly in reality and interest when one sees them here at work. I should be very glad to think that in all this long letter I had succeeded in giving you any idea of how it all looks when one sees it with his own eyes. Believe me ever

Most sincerely yours, PHILLIPS BROOKS.

CALCUTTA, February 11, 1883.

DEAR WILLIAM, — This week I have seen the Himalayas. Last Monday we left Calcutta at three o'clock by rail; at seven we crossed the Ganges on a steamboat, just as if it had been the Susquehanna. All night we slept in the train, and the next day were climbing up and up on a sort of steam tramway, which runs to Darjeeling, a summer station at the foot of the highest hills, but itself a thousand feet higher than the top of Mt. Washington. There the swells go in the hot months, but now it is almost deserted. We reached there on Tuesday evening in the midst of rain, found that the great mountains had not been seen for eight days, and everybody laughed at our hope of seeing them. We slept, and early the next morning looked out on nothing but clouds. But about eight o'clock the curtain began to fall, and before nine there was a most splendid view of the whole range. In the midst was the lordly Kinchinjinga, the second highest mountain in the world, over 28,000 feet high. Think of that! Certainly, they made the impression of height, such as no mountains ever gave me before.

By and by we rode about six miles to another hill called Senchul, where the tip of Mt. Everest, the highest mountain in the world, 29,002 feet, is visible. That was interesting, but the real glory of the day was Kinchinjinga. We gazed at him till the jealous clouds came again in the afternoon and covered him; then we roamed over the little town and went to a Buddhist village a couple of miles away. The people here are Thibetans by origin, and they keep associations with the tribes upon the other side of the great hills. A company of Thibetans, priests and Lamas, had come over to celebrate the New Year, which with them begins on the 9th of February. They had the strangest music and dances, and queer outdoor plays, and we were welcomed as distinguished strangers, and set in the place of honor, feasted with oranges, and begged for backsheesh.

The next morning there were the giant hills again, and we looked at Kinchinjinga (I want you to learn his name) till eleven o'clock, when we took the train again for Calcutta, and arrived there on Friday afternoon about five. It was a splendid journey, and one to be always remembered. On my return to Calcutta I found two invitations waiting: one was to dine at the Government House with the Viceroy on Thursday evening. Of course, I was too late for that, and was very sorry, for now I shall not see the great man and the viceregal court at all. The other was to an evening party on Friday, given by the Rajah Rajendra Narayan del Bahadur, "in honor of the late British victory in Egypt." Of course I went to this, and it was the biggest thing seen in India for years. It is said to have cost the old Rajah a lac of rupees, or $100,000. At any rate, it was very splendid and very queer, — acres of palace and palace grounds blazing with lights, a thousand guests, the natives in the most beautiful costumes of silk and gold; a Nautch dance going on all the time in one hall, a full circus, — horses, acrobats, clowns, and all, only after native fashion, — in a great covered courtyard, supper perpetual, and the great drawing-room blazing with family jewels. I stayed till one o'clock, and then came home as if from the Arabian Nights, and went to bed.

But I cannot tell you all I am doing or have done. This ·morning, for a change, I preached from Henry Martyn's old pulpit in the Mission Church. To-morrow morning, we sail on the P. & O. steamer Rohilla for Madras, a three days' voyage. Thence we travel by Tanjore, Trichinopoly, and Madura to Tuticorin. Then across by sea to Colombo, and after a week in Ceylon sail in the Verona (P. & O.) on the 7th of March (the day Daniel Webster made his speech) for Suez. From Suez by rail to Alexandria, seeing Cairo on the way, and the recent battlefield of Tel El Kebir. When you get this, about the 24th of March, I shall probably be in Alexandria, perhaps spend Easter there. Thence I somehow go to Spain, getting there about April 1.

Your New Year's letter reached me yesterday. A thousand thanks for it. Next year we will have such a watch-meeting as was never known. Now the year is more than half over. How fast it has gone, and henceforth we draw nearer and nearer to each other. When I get to England, it will almost seem at home.

Tell M., and A., and G., and S. that I love them all. G.'s Christmas report not yet received.

Affectionately, P.

MADRAS, February 18, 1883.

MY DEAR WILLIAM, — We had a beautiful sail down from Calcutta. For four days the Rohilla slid along over the most beautiful glassy sea, the sky was lovely at sunrise and sunset, the nights were the most gorgeous moonlight, and the sun at noon was hotter than Sancho. There were a good many pleasant people on board, two bishops, an archdeacon, and the usual queer lot of sailors who run the steamships in these Eastern seas. We arrived at Madras very early on Friday morning, and I have been charmed with the place ever since. It was glorious last night. I drove five miles into the country to dine at Mr. Sewall's. He is the archæological director of the district, and knows all about the Vishnu temples and the Buddhist Topes, of which the whole region is full. The road ran through long avenues of banyan-trees, which looked like ghosts with their long arms; little temples peeped through the trees, and picturesque groups of people were flitting about on foot, or in queer bullock carts, and it was all as unlike the Milldam as possible. We had a charming dinner with people who knew all about India, and drove home at eleven o'clock through the February summer night.

I sent from Calcutta a box which will reach you in due time; not for a long time, perhaps, for I left it there to be sent the first time there was a sailing vessel going direct to Boston. There is nothing particular in it. Only a few travel books, which I wanted to get out of the way, and a number of small traps, which have accumulated in my trunk. There is nothing really fine or artistic to buy in India. Art seems to have stopped here some two hundred years ago, so I have made no purchases, and these things in the box are mere trinkets and a few pieces of cloth and some photographs. . . .

There is something which I wish you would do some time, when it is not much bother. When I left I took some sermons with me in a great hurry. I did not make a very good selection, and do not like what I have brought; when I get to England I may preach some more. Would it be much trouble for you to go some afternoon into my study, and look in the back of my writing-table and find six or eight sermons, among the later ones, which you think would do, and send them to me at Barings', only marking them not to be forwarded, but kept for me there? You will know about the ones to send. There is one about Gamaliel, which I remember. Do not hurry about this, but if you think of it some afternoon, do it like a good fellow, won't you, and I will do as much for you when you come to India.

Strawberries are first-rate here, cocoanuts and plantains and oranges and guavas everywhere. It will be hard to leave these gentle Hindoos and their delightful land when the time comes, three weeks hence. The only compensation will be that I shall be coming nearer to you all.   Affectionately,   P.

TANJORE, INDIA, February 23, 1883.

DEAR AUNT SUSAN, — I hope you are all well, and I wish that I could drive up the side yard, this morning, and find you all there, going on in the good old-fashioned way. Instead of that, I am sitting here in the midst of heathenism, in the big room of an Indian bungalow, with a punkah swinging overhead to keep me cool, propelled by a rope which a naked heathen boy is pulling on the veranda outside, and with the sun blazing down on the palm-trees and bamboos as it never blazes, even in August, in the back garden. This morning, while it was still cool, I went to the great temple, and saw the worship of the great god Siva. The worshipers were a strange-looking set, some of them very gentle and handsome, others wild and fierce; but all groveling before the most hideous idol, and hiding their faces in the dust, while the big priest clothed the image with flowers, washed him, set his food and drink before him, and anointed him with dreadful-smelling oil.

It is strange to be right in the midst of pure, blank heathenism, after one has been hearing and talking about it all his life. And it is certainly as bad as it has been painted. I have seen a good deal of the missionaries here, and a good many of them are doing very noble work, but the hosts on hosts of heathen must be a pretty discouraging sight to them sometimes. However, I saw a dozen or more funeral piles burning the other day at Benares, and so there are that number less of unconverted heathen in the land.

We have had a splendid two months here, and now only two weeks remain before we shall sail from "Ceylon's Isle" for Europe, where it will seem as if I were almost in the midst of you again. But all the rest of my life I shall have pictures before my mind of these queer people riding on elephants (that they prod with a sharp iron stick behind the ear to make them go), squatting on their heels in the sunniest sunshine they can find, and religiously bathing in big tanks and tugging at the heavy cars on which they love to drag their horrible gods about the country; smiling, cheating, lying dreadfully, and making their country as picturesque as anything can be in all the world. It will be good to get back again, for after all one wants to be at work. William, Arthur, and John have written me from time to time, — William constantly, — and from them I have heard all the news. The best is that everything is going on without change, and that I shall find you all next September just as I left you last June. You will not doubt that I think of you a great deal. Give my best love to aunt S. and aunt C., and write to me when you can.

Ever most affectionately,

PHILLIPS BROOKS.

TRICHINOPOLY, February 25, 1883.

DEAR WILLIAM, — I am staying at the house of Mr. Sewall, the chief collector of this district, who has taken us in and given us his hospitality for a couple of days. We have reached southern India, and the hot weather is on us, so that except in early morning and late afternoon there is no possibility of moving about and seeing things. What people will do here two or three months hence I can hardly imagine. The sun's heat is tremendous, and even with perpetual punkahs swinging in every room where anything is being done, eating, or writing, or reading, or talking, or sleeping, life is hardly tolerable. Nevertheless, we have had a good sort of week. Last Sunday evening we went on board a canal-boat at Madras, a funny little tub of a thing, and were towed all night by coolies, running along the bank for about thirty miles, to a place called Mahabalihuram, where there are some wonderful pagodas or Hindoo temples, and some remarkable old sculptures on the rocks of enormous size.

It was a gorgeous moonlight night, and the sensation of being pulled along through this wild country by these naked figures, striding and tugging on the banks, was very curious. The next day we spent at the pagodas, which were built nobody knows when or by whom, and which have the whole Hindoo mythology marvelously carved in their rocky walls. Monday night we took the same way back, and it was hard to turn in and leave the strange picture which I saw, as I sat in the stern of the little craft.

We took our own servants, beds, and provisions with us, and stopped each evening and spread our table for dinner in the desert, by the side of the canal. After our return, we spent one more day in Madras, and then started southward toward Ceylon. · We stopped first at Chedambaram, where there is a stupendous temple, with heathenism in full blast, processions of Vishnu, Siva, and the other gods going about with drums, trumpets, and cymbals all the time. Then to Tanjore, where there is the most beautiful of the big pagodas, and where we spent a delightful day. Thence to this place, where yesterday we saw the richest temple of all, in which the jewels and gold clothing of two horrid little brass idols are worth ten lacs of rupees, $1,000,000. The collector had sent word that we were coming, and they had the jewels all spread out for us to see, while crowds of gaping natives stood outside the rope and watched the precious things as we examined them. A dozen officials had to show them, for the great chest has so many locks, and each official keeps a separate key. It cannot be unlocked without the presence of them all, a sort of combination-safety arrangement which I commend to the Boston bank directors.

I am sincerely blue at the prospect of leaving India in ten days more. I try to fix every picture in my memory, so that I may not lose it. But I hate to think that I shall never see it again. The people cheat, lie, worship false gods, and do all sorts of horridly wicked things, but they are evidently capable of a better life. Their land is full of monuments which show what they once were, and there is a courtesy, mild dignity, and perpetual picturesqueness about them which is fascinating.

This morning I went to an early service and saw the grave of Bishop Heber in the chancel. I was going to preach for the minister this evening, but he could not find a surplice of decent length, and it had to be given up.

On Friday I shall be at Colombo, and then shall get some letters from you all and learn what you are doing. I can imagine, but very often I wish that I could look through the thick world and see. At this moment you are sound asleep, preparing for the Sunday and the excitement of hearing some great man at Trinity. I hope it is n't very cold. Oh, that I could give you some of this heat! My love to everybody.

Always affectionately, P.

KANDY, March 4, 1883.

MY DEAR MARY, — Do you know I think this place is good enough and important enough from which to write you a letter. In the first place, it is the farthest point of my travels; from this time my face is turned homeward. In the second place, I

KANDY.

think it must be the most beautiful place in the
world. I do not see how there could be one more
beautiful. I wish you could have driven with me this
morning at sunrise, through the roads with hundreds
of different kinds of palm-trees, and to the Buddhist
temple, where they were offering fresh flowers to Buddha and banging away on drums in his honor enough
to kill you; then out to the gardens where cinnamon,
nutmeg, clove-trees, tea and coffee plants, pineapples,
mangoes, bamboos, banyans, India-rubber trees, and
a hundred other curious things are growing. Here
and there you meet an elephant or a peacock, and
the pleasant-faced natives smile at you out of their
pretty houses.

> Oh, this beautiful island of Ceylon!
> With the cocoanut-trees on the shore;
> It is shaped like a pear with the peel on,
> And Kandy lies in at the core.
>
> And Kandy is sweet (you ask Gertie!)
> Even when it is spelt with a K,
> And the people are cheerful and dirty,
> And dress in a comical way.
>
> Here comes a particular dandy,
> With two ear-rings and half of a shirt,
> He 's considered the swell of all Kandy,
> And the rest of him 's covered with dirt.
>
> And here comes the belle of the city,
> With rings on her delicate toes,
> And eyes that are painted and pretty,
> And a jewel that shakes in her nose.
>
> And the dear little girls and their brothers,
> And the babies so jolly and fat,
> Astride on the hips of their mothers,
> And as black as a gentleman's hat.

And the queer little heaps of old women,
And the shaven Buddhistical priests,
And the lake which the worshipers swim in,
And the wagons with curious beasts.

The tongue they talk mostly is Tamul,
Which sounds you can hardly tell how,
It is half like the scream of a camel,
And half like the grunt of a sow.

But it is too hot to make any more poetry. It is perfectly ridiculous how hot it is. I would not walk to that Buddhist temple opposite for anything. If I tried to, you would never see my familiar face in Clarendon Street any more. I am glad, with all the beauty of Ceylon, that there are only two days more of it. It is too near the equator. On Wednesday morning the Verona sails from Colombo, and will carry me to Suez, and the Indian trip is over. It has been one unmixed pleasure from beginning to end.

We have a new boy. Huri's language gave out at Calcutta. He did not know the queer tongues they talk in southern India, and he had to be sent back to Bombay. We parted with tears and rupees. Then came another boy, who had to be summarily dismissed. He was too stupid for anything. It made the journey far too laborious when we had to take care of him. Now we have a beautiful creature named Tellegoo, or something like that. He wears a bright yellow and green petticoat, which makes him look very gay, and a tortoise-shell comb in his hair. . . . Our association with him will be brief, for we leave him on the wharf when we sail, Wednesday, and there will be fewer rupees and no tears.

I went to church this morning, and the minister preached on the text, "Bake me a little cake first," and the point was, that before you bought any clothes or food, you must give something towards the endowment of the English church at Kandy. It was really a pretty sermon. . . .

There are the Buddhists howling again. It must be afternoon service. The priests go about without a bit of hair on their heads, and wrapped in dirty yellow sheets. . . .

P. & O. STEAMER VERONA, March 11, 1883.

DEAR WILLIAM, — I wrote last Sunday to M. from beautiful Kandy. That letter, I suppose, is somewhere on board this ship at this moment; but not to break my good habit of a weekly letter, I will send you this, to show how I felt when we were halfway from Colombo to Aden, and next Sunday I will send still another from wherever we are in the Red Sea. You will get them altogether, but you can read them in their order, and so get three consecutive weeks of my important biography at one time.

It seems so strange to be on the sea again and thinking about the Indian journey as a finished thing. The days from Venice to Bombay keep coming back, when I was full of wonder about it all. Now, I know at least a great deal about what I shall always think one of the most delightful and interesting lands in all the world. In some respects, the last bit of it was almost the best. The tropics had seemed to elude us before: Many a time in India it seemed as if the landscape were almost what one might have seen at home, but the minute that we touched Ceylon, everything was different. One cannot conceive of the gorgeousness of nature. Only the night before we left, we drove a few miles along the seashore, with such groves of enormous palms and cocoanuts on one side, and such color of sunset on the water on the other side, as no dream or picture ever began to suggest. And the whole four hours' ride from Colombo to Kandy is marvelous. The mountains are superb, and in the valleys there are depths of jungle which show what the earth is at only eight degrees from the equator. And then in Ceylon for the first time we saw Buddhism, that great religion which sprang up in India, and has completely disappeared in the land of its birth, but has spread elsewhere, till more than a quarter of the human race are Buddhists. We just caught sight of it when we were close to the Himalayas on the borders of Thibet, but in Ceylon we saw the strange system in its fullness.

Last Monday afternoon I drove out to the Buddhist college and saw the old high-priest teaching a class of students, who sat around him with their shaven heads and their yellow robes, getting ready to continue this atheistical religion for another generation. The old fellow looked up and asked us who we were. I gave him my card, which he spelled out with difficulty, then he asked me, "Do you know anything about me?" and seemed disappointed and disgusted when I was obliged to tell him that, much as we were interested in his religion, and glad as we were to see his college, we had never heard of him before in all our lives. He evidently did not understand how local his great reputation was. He dismissed his class and untwisted his legs, and got down and toddled away.

We have been four days on the Verona. The people are pleasant, the captain is cordial and agreeable, and the weather is cool, so the voyage is charming. The Archdeacon of Calcutta is on board, and preached this morning. He is a very jolly sort of person. I am to preach next Sunday. There are some private theatricals in prospect, so the future looks lively. Next Sunday you shall hear how the week has gone.

Long before you get this, the great house question will be settled, and you will have decided where your declining years are to be passed, whether in the house in G—— Street, which I know already, or in some new nest in M—— or B—— streets. Whichever it is, I have the deepest interest in it, and shall be very anxious to hear. Very many of my few remaining hours will be spent by the new fireside, and years hence, I shall come tottering up to the door to recall the old days when we were young and I went away to spend a winter in India. I cannot help wishing that the change, if there is to be one, might bring you nearer to the corner of C—— and N—— streets, instead of taking you farther away, as I fear it will. . . .

Spain is the next thing, and I am counting much upon it. I have some expectation of meeting the Brimmers there, but it is not at all certain. At present I am alone. Wendell left me at Suez to go to Cairo, and then to Palestine. He has been a very agreeable companion, intelligent, good-natured, always bright and obliging. I feel very much attached to him.

I had a letter at Suez from Canon Farrar, asking me to preach for him in the Abbey and also at St. Margaret's. I wrote him that I would do so, and England begins to seem as if it were not very far away. All of May and June I hope to be there. The Captain sends his love. Good-by.

STEAMSHIP VERONA,
Sunday, March 18, 1883.

MY DEAR GERTIE, — It seems to me that our correspondence has not been very lively lately. I don't think I had a letter from you all the time I was in India. I hoped I should, because I wanted to show it to the Rajahs, and other great people, and let them see what beautiful letters American children can write. But now I am out of India, and for the last ten days we have been sailing on and on, over the same course where we sailed last December. Last Tuesday we passed Aden, and stopped there about six hours. I went on shore, and took a drive through the town and up into the country. If you had been with me you would have seen the solemn-looking camels, stalking along with solemn-looking Arabs on their backs, looking as if they had been riding on and on that way ever since the days of Abraham. I think I met Isaac and Jacob on two skinny camels, just outside the gates of Aden. I asked them how Esau was, but Jacob looked mad and would n't answer, and hurried the old man on, so that I had no talk with them; but I feel quite sure it was they, for they looked just like the pictures in the Bible.

Since that we have been sailing up the Red Sea, and on Monday evening we shall be once more at Suez, and there I say good-by to my companion, who stops in Egypt, and goes thence to Palestine, while I hurry on to Malta and Gibraltar in the same steamer. She is a nice little steamer, with a whole lot of children on board, who fight all the while and cry the rest of the time. Every now and then one of them almost goes overboard, and then all the mothers set up a great howl, though I don't see why they should care very

much about such children as these are. I should
think it would be rather a relief to get rid of them.
Now, if it were you, or Agnes, or Tood, it would be
different!

There has just been service on deck, and I preached,
and the people all held on to something and listened.
I would a great deal rather preach in Trinity.

I hope you will have a pleasant Easter. Mine will
be spent, I trust, in Malta. Next year I hope you will
come and dine with me on Easter Day. Don't forget!
My love to Tood. Your affectionate uncle,

PHILLIPS.

ON THE P. & O. STEAMSHIP VERONA,
March 19, 1883.

LITTLE MISTRESS JOSEPHINE,
Tell me, have you ever seen
Children half as queer as these
Babies from across the seas?
See their funny little fists,
See the rings upon their wrists;
One has very little clothes,
One has jewels in her nose;
And they all have silver bangles
On their little heathen ankles.
In their ears are curious things,
Round their necks are beads and strings,
And they jingle as they walk,
And they talk outlandish talk;
One, you see, has hugged another,
Playing she's its little mother;
One who sits all lone and lorn,
Has her head all shaved and shorn.
Do you want to know their names?

One is called Jeefungee Hames,
One Buddhanda Arrich Bas,
One Teedundee Hanki Sas.

Many such as these I saw,
In the streets of old Jeypore;
They never seemed to cry or laugh,
But, sober as the photograph,
Squatted in the great bazaars,
While the Hindoos, their mammas,
Quarreled long about the price
Of their little mess of rice,
And then, when the fight was done,
Every mother, one by one,
Up her patient child would whip,
Set it straddling on her hip,
And trot off all crook'd and bent
To some hole, where, well content,
Hers and baby's days are spent.

Are n't you glad, then, little Queen,
That your name is Josephine?
That you live in Springfield, or
Not, at least, in old Jeypore?
That your Christian parents are
John and Hattie, Pa and Ma?
That you've an entire nose,
And no rings upon your toes?
In a word, that Hat and you
Do not have to be Hindoo?
But I thought you'd like to see
What these little heathen be,
And give welcome to these three
From your loving   UNCLE P.

STEAMSHIP VERONA, March 25, 1883.

DEAR JOHNNY, — I must send you an Easter greeting from this queer cabin, where, and on the deck above it, we have spent our Easter Day. I hoped that we should be at Malta for the great festival, but we were detained a long while in the Suez Canal, and shall not be at Malta till next Wednesday. On Saturday, I hope to land at Gibraltar.

. . . How I wish you were here to-night. We would sit late on deck, and you should tell me all about Springfield; and I would tell you all about India. This long return voyage is a splendid chance to think it over, and arrange in one's memory the recollections of the wondrous land. Besides the countless pictures which one saw every day, eleven great sights stand out which you must see when you go to India. They are these: —

First, the rock temples of Karli and Ellora. Think of buildings big as Christ Church, Springfield, not built, but hewn out of the solid rock, and covered inside and out with Hindoo sculptures of the richest sort.

Second, the deserted city of Ambir, a city of the old Moguls, with hardly a human inhabitant, and palaces and temples abandoned to the jackals and the monkeys.

Third, the Kuttub at Delhi, the most beautiful column in the world, covered with inscriptions; the most splendid monument of the Mohammedan power.

Fourth, the golden temple at Amritsir. Think of a vast artificial lake, in whose centre, reached by a lovely white marble bridge, is the holy place of the Sikhs, the lower half of most delicate marble mosaics, and the upper of sheets of beaten gold.

Fifth, the Taj at Agra, a dream of beauty: the tomb of an old Mogul empress, made of the finest marble, and inlaid in the most dainty way. The whole as large as the State House.

Sixth, the river shore of the Ganges at Benares. Mile after mile of palaces and temples, and in front of them the bathing-places of the living and the burning-places of the dead.

Seventh, Buddh-Gaya, where Buddha sat for six years under the bo-tree, till enlightenment came to him. A valley full of Buddhist temples is there now.

Eighth, the view of Kinchinjinga, from Darjeeling, the second highest mountain in the world. Think of a hill five times as high as Mt. Washington, blazing with snow in the sunshine.

Ninth, the seven pagodas near Madras, where whole stories of the Hindoo mythology are sculptured on the face of perpendicular rocks; and they are queer enough.

Tenth, the Sivite temple at Tanjore, one mass of brilliant color and sculpture, with its great pyramid, two hundred feet high.

Eleventh, the temple at Kandy, in Ceylon, where they keep Buddha's tooth. You see the strange Buddhist priests and their strange ways.

These are the greatest things in India, and there are ever so many more like them, only not quite so great or interesting. I am very glad I went, and I wish that everybody who cares about interesting things could go there, too. . . .

STEAMSHIP VERONA, March 25, 1883.

DEAR WILLIAM, — This is not much of a place for Easter Day. We have had the queerest sort of week. Last Monday night we reached Suez, and put about half our ship's company on shore to go to Alexandria, Brindisi, and Venice. Since then we have been dragging along through the Suez Canal. There were twenty-six steamships in single file; we were the eleventh. Every now and then, No. 1 or No. 6 would get aground, and then we all had to wait till it got loose, five or six hours, as the case might be. Every night, the whole twenty-six of us pulled up and tied fast to the bank, and waited for morning. So we crept along till yesterday (Saturday, Easter even), when we reached Port Said, where we stayed four hours, and then launched out into the broad Mediterranean. Now all is clear. The broad sea is rolling merrily around us, we have a lot of sail set, and are scudding on towards Malta. We shall get there on Wednesday; I hope to be put on shore at Gibraltar some time on Saturday, the 31st, and begin my Spanish experiences on April Fool's Day.

Meanwhile, here is Easter Day at sea. A missionary from New York, on his way home from China with a sick wife, has just read the morning service. He did not attempt any sermon, and the singing was uncommonly feeble. Only the religious passengers came down for service. Now there will be nothing more to show that it is Easter Day,— no children's service this afternoon, no flowers, no eggs, nothing but the monotonous plunging of the ship as she goes on towards Malta.

After all, it is rather good fun, this long voyage. I have had time to read big books on India, and the people are some of them pleasant, some of them amusing. They are mostly returning Anglo-Indians, with something the matter either with their lungs or with their livers. They are peevish and positive, not liking to be contradicted, and very set in their opinions. . . . It is all very nice. Then there are a few really bright, companionable people, and I have a beautiful pipe.

An Easter greeting to you all. . . . Thanks for a lot of good papers and letters, which I received at Suez. They were a great resource in the canal.

Ever affectionately, P.

GIBRALTAR, April 1, 1883.

MY DEAR GERTIE, — I am so sorry that you have been ill. If you had only come with me on the Servia, and not stayed at home to work so hard over your lessons, I do not believe you would have been ill at all. And this morning the long voyage from Ceylon would have been over. I wrote you a beautiful letter two weeks ago to-day from the Verona, which I hope you got. Ever since that, we have been sailing, and sailing, and sailing, till it seemed as if we were never going to stop. We did stop two or three times, but we always had to go aboard and start again. We stopped at Aden, and Suez, and Port Said, and last Wednesday at Malta. Malta was very nice. We stayed there six hours, and wandered about the streets while the Verona was getting coal. The town is beautifully white and clean, and the Verona, when we came back to her again, was very black and dirty. But they washed her all off while we were at dinner.

At Malta we saw the church where all the old knights of Malta are buried, and the armor which they used to wear, and then there is a queer old church, which the monks have the care of, and when a monk dies, they do not bury him underground, or burn him up with fire, which would be better, but they stand him up in a niche, in his monk's frock, and leave him; and there they are, a whole row of dry monks, dreadful-looking things, with their labels on them, to tell who they used to be when they were alive.

Well, Wednesday afternoon we left Malta and sailed on and on in the Verona. There did not much happen on the Verona all the way. The people were not very interesting. Only, Miss G—— got engaged to the fourth officer, and that interested us all very much indeed, and one morning Audley D—— and Lawrence K—— got into a great fight on deck, and Audley D—— hit Lawrence K—— in the eye and hurt him, and then the two mothers, Mrs. D—— and Mrs. K——, went at each other and scolded terribly. And that also interested us very much indeed.

This is about all I can think of that happened on board the Verona. I can't tell you much about Spain yet, for I have only been in it about an hour and half. The people talk Spanish, which is very awkward, but the sailing up to Gibraltar this morning was splendid. The narrow gate of the Mediterranean, with its two great rocks, one in Europe and one in Africa, was all ablaze with the morning sun, and through it, westward, lay America and Boston. I am going on Tuesday to Malaga and then to Granada. . . Give my love to everybody. Your affectionate,

UNCLE PHILLIPS.

GRANADA, UNDER THE WALLS OF THE ALHAMBRA,
April 8, 1883.

DEAR WILLIAM, — I am very glad to hear about the new house. I would rather see it this morning than the Alhambra, which is towering up above my windows! What number in M—— Street is it? Are you going to have ampelopsis growing on the front wall? Which is my room? . . . Do write me all about it, and tell me how it gets on and how it is going to look.

I have been a week in Spain. I landed at Gibraltar last Sunday morning, and immediately wrote a letter to G. to signal my arrival. I stayed there till Tuesday, and had a first-rate time. It was good to be on shore again, and, besides, on the Verona I had struck up quite a friendship with a certain Major Wing, who was coming home from India on sick-leave. He is a first-rate fellow. He landed at Malta, but he gave me a letter to the colonel who commands all the artillery at Gibraltar, and he was immensely civil. He took me all over the fortifications, introduced me at the Club, and made me almost live at his house, where were a very pleasant wife and children; so I saw Gibraltar at its best and have the brightest recollections of it.

Tuesday night I took the boat for Malaga. David Whitney and his family were on board, so that I feel myself really in the Boston atmosphere again. . . .

The Alhambra joins on remarkably to the remembrances of India. Here is the farthest west, as there is the farthest east, of the Mohammedan conquests, and Granada and Delhi have very much in common with each other. Granada is the more beautiful, at least in situation, for here is the Sierra Nevada (as pretty a range of snowy mountains as was ever seen) in view all the time, and the best parts of the Alhambra beat anything in the old city of the Moguls. Still I like to stand by India, and the substitution here of the English tourist (one of whom I heard at lunch declare that this is a very much overrated place) for the picturesque Hindoo or Mussulman makes a vast change.

I received some letters here, and among others two of yours, for which I am as always very grateful. They brought you down to March 19, just past Professor Allen's Sunday. There was another letter from Canon Farrar, fixing it that I am to preach at the Abbey on the 27th of May, and at St. Margaret's on either the 3d or 10th of June. If the latter, it will be Hospital Sunday, and so I want you to do me one more favor. Will you go to my sermons and get me several Hospital Sunday discourses (they are all inscribed on top over the text " Hospital Sunday ") and send them to me. . . . This week I expect to meet the Brimmers, next Sunday I shall probably be in Seville, the Sunday after in Madrid, and in London as soon as possible after the 1st of May. Good-by, love to them all. P.

MADRID, April 15, 1883.

DEAR WILLIAM, — Ever since I received your letter yesterday, I have been trying to realize that it is true that aunt S. and aunt C. are really gone. It seems almost impossible to picture the old house as it must be to-day. . . . I wish so much that I had been at home, and I hope I shall hear from you some time about the last of those two long, faithful lives. . . .

It seems as if this great change swept away from the world the last remnants of the background of our earliest life. Even after father and mother went, as long as aunt S. lived, there was somebody who had to do with us when we were babies. Now that generation has all passed away. How many old scenes it brings up. This is Sunday morning, right after breakfast, and it seems as if I could see a Sunday morning of the old times in Rowe Street, with the general bustle of mother and aunt S. getting off to Sunday-school, and father settling down to read to the bigger boys in the front parlor; and there are faint memories of much earlier days when the aunts must have been blooming young ladies, though they seemed to us then almost as old as they ever did in later times. I hope the last years of their lives have been happy, in spite of the suffering. They have been spared what was most to be dreaded, long, hopeless illness and helplessness. But I am so sorry to hear that aunt S—— had to suffer. . . . If there were ever lives totally unselfish, and finding all their pleasure in making other people happy, these were they. We know aunt S—— best, of course, but dear little aunt C——, with her quiet ways, had something very touching and beautiful about her. She seems to have slipped out of life as unobtrusively and with as little trouble as she lived.

When I left them, of course I knew it was very likely that I should not see them again. But all I had heard since made me feel as if they would be there when I came home. I had a nice letter from aunt Susan in the autumn, which must have been a good deal of an effort for her to write, and I wrote to her, from India, a letter which must have reached Andover after it was all over.

It cannot be long — one cannot ask that it should be long — before aunt S—— follows her sisters. Give her my love and sympathy. As it may be that she will go before I come home, the old house be left empty, and something have to be done about the property, I want to say that I should like to buy it, and I authorize you to buy it for me, if the chance offers. Or, if you and Arthur and John would not like that, I will join with any or all of you to buy and hold it. I do not know whether you liked it well enough last summer to think of making it a summer home, but I should like to hold it as a place where, for the whole or part of any summer, we could gather and have a delightful, easy time, among the most sacred associations which remain for us on earth. A few very simple improvements would make it a most charming place, so do not by any chance let it slip, and hold, by purchase or otherwise, to as much of the furniture as you can. One of these days, when I am a little older and feebler, I should like to retire to it and succeed Augustine Amory at the little church. Is not our window done there yet?

I am sorry for poor little G——. I hope she is better long before this. Tell her I would come home and see her if I really thought it would make her rheumatism better. If it does not get well quickly, tell her to get into the Servia and come over here, and we will lay her down in the Spanish sun, and melt it out of her. It is hard for the poor little thing to have to suffer so. Give her my love, and tell her I shall be back in about five months.

I am with the Brimmers and the Wisters of Philadelphia, a party of seven, which is quite a new traveling experience for me. I like it. I shall be almost in England when you get this. Good-by, P.

SALAMANCA, April 29, 1883.

DEAR WILLIAM, — And so aunt S—— too is gone, and the old house is empty! I only received your letter last evening, and all the night, as I rode here in the train, I was thinking how strange it was. These three who began their lives so near together, long ago, and who have kept so close to one another all the while, now going almost hand in hand into the other world. . . . How pathetic it used to be to see aunt S—— sitting there, full of pain, trying to do some little bit of good in her curious ways, with her queer little tracts, and her vague desire to exhort everybody to be good. I always thought she must have been one of the handsomest of the sisters when they were young. Surely, no end that we could have dreamed of for them could have been more perfect. But how we shall miss them!

. . . Such a dear old town as this is! I am here alone. Mr. Brimmer stayed at Madrid. I shall meet them again on Tuesday or Wednesday at Burgos. Nobody here speaks a word of anything but Spanish, and I have the funniest time to get along. This morning I spent two hours in the cathedral, with an old priest with whom I talked in Latin. One of the towers of the cathedral gave the suggestion, I think, of the tower of Trinity Church in Boston. You will find a cut of it in Fergusson's "Architecture" in my library. The whole town is a wilderness of architectural delight. Convents, churches, cloisters, colleges, and towers everywhere. How I wish you were here this afternoon. A good long letter from Arthur yesterday. Very bright and busy. Well, ours is the generation for the next twenty years, then we shall go as they have gone, and a new set of youngsters take our places. It is all right. . . .

BURGOS, May 2, 1883.

MY DEAR LIZZIE, — Your last letter gave me such a lively idea of what was going on in New York that Burgos, by contrast, seems a little dull. Nothing goes on in Burgos but the cathedral bells. My breakfast, for which I am waiting, does not seem to go on at all. But if I think of you all in New York, it will make my head spin as much as is good for it, in this quiet place, so I am going to answer your letter, in hopes to get another.

Wildes would have been so proud and delighted if he could have seen me this morning at 1.17, in fact, from that to 3.12. No trains in Spain ever connect with any others, so I was left over all that time at Venta di Baños, on my way from Leon here. And I sat in the railway restaurant at that dead hour of the night and read the report of the Eighth Church Congress, which had reached me just before I started on my journey. Think of it! ... Was ever such a tribute paid to the general secretary before? I was listening still to Dr. Shattuck's account of the early Ecclesiastical History of Boston, when the express train from Madrid came along, and I got in, and soon the cathedral of Burgos came in sight. It really is a very great cathedral, the first I have seen in Spain.

The glorious things I have seen in Spain have been, first, the approach to Gibraltar and the Pillars of Hercules; second, the Alhambra, with the Sierra Nevada behind it; and third, the pictures of Velasquez at Madrid. Those things are all superb, worth the journey here to see, if there were nothing else. There is a lot else scattered along the road, but those are the great things, and as to Gothic architecture, he who has seen Chartres, Rheims, Amiens, and Cologne (to say nothing of York and Durham) need not be impatient about seeing Seville, or Leon, or Toledo, or even Burgos; though Burgos is far the finest of them all, and must rank, though not very high, among the greatest cathedrals of the world.

There is something in their architecture that is like the people, a trace of something coarse, a lack of just the best refinement. The people whose great mediæval glory is the Inquisition, and whose great modern delight is the bull-fight, must have something brutal in their very constitution. Now the Moors were thorough gentlemen, not a touch in them of the sham which was always in the Hidalgo; so the Moorish architecture is exquisite in its refinement, and Velasquez was too great for the national coarseness to spoil him, though he has it, and Gibraltar belongs to England! So that Nature and the Moors and Velasquez have done the finest things in Spain.

. . . To-morrow I go to Paris, whence I started last August to join you in Cologne. It has been a long loop, and has inclosed a lot of pleasant things. Now the summer is almost here, and then comes — home. My friend Mr. Paine, of Boston, talked before I left of coming over to join me, about the first of July, and I think he will do so. Write me what you and Arthur are doing and planning. My love to him.

Affectionately, PHILLIPS.

WESTMINSTER PALACE HOTEL, LONDON,
Whit Sunday, May 13, 1883.

DEAR WILLIAM, — . . . I left the Brimmers at Biarritz and came over here from Paris last Tuesday. Mr. Brimmer has been the most charming company, and all the party have been very pleasant. I have seen a good many people since I arrived. Everybody is hospitable and kind. This morning I have been preaching for Canon Duckworth at St. Mark's in St. John's Wood.

Yesterday I went to the opening of the great Fisheries Exhibition, where they have everything you can imagine, from any land you ever (or never) saw, that has anything to do with catching fishes. The Prince and Princess of Wales were there, and the Prince made a speech. I saw him also the other day at the Stanley Memorial Committee. He is pleasant-looking and has easy manners. The new Dean is very cordial and friendly. I saw the new Archbishop the other day. He looks able and has a real ecclesiastical face.

I found at Barings' the two packages of sermons which you so kindly sent, and I was grateful to you in the midst of the row and hurly-burly of Bishopsgate Street. They were just what I wanted, except that I am not to preach on Hospital Sunday after all. Next Sunday morning I preach at the Chapel Royal, Savoy, one of the old historic churches of London. The following Sunday (27th) I preach at the Abbey in the evening, and the next Sunday, June 3d, I preach for Farrar in St. Margaret's.

I have a little plan in which I need your help. I want to send home some little thing for the church, and I thought I would get a piece of nice stained glass for the robing-room window, — the little window behind which we put on our surplices. It would brighten up a little that rather doleful room. Would you go to Chester and make him measure it very carefully, giving the exact size of the glass inside the frame, and also showing how much of the window is arranged to open. Please make him very careful about the exactness of the measures. Will you do this as soon as you can, so that I can see about it while I am in London?

I suppose by this time the Andover window must be in its place, and I hope it is quite satisfactory. I do not suppose that it can be made in any way a memorial of the aunts, as well as of father and mother. I almost wish we could put up somewhere a plain tablet with their names upon it, that they might be somehow remembered in connection with the church. They offered, I believe, at one time, a part of the old orchard as the site for it. I am anxious to hear what you think of my plans regarding the old house. The more I think of it, the more I want it.

Speaking of windows, I saw Mr. and Mrs. Fred Dexter in church to-night, and they tell me that the new window in Trinity is wholly satisfactory and very beautiful. At present I am very much troubled about the little triangle in front of Trinity. It looks as if it would be built on, and poor Trinity hidden away behind a tenement house. If you meet any fellow in the street who looks as if he would like to give sixty thousand dollars to keep it open, stop him for me and tell him we will put up a monument to him in Trinity when he dies. Good-by.

Affectionately, P.

WESTMINSTER PALACE HOTEL, LONDON,
Sunday, May 20, 1883.

DEAR WILLIAM, — I have been rich in letters this last week. First came M——'s, poetry. . . . Then Tood's letter, which shows how wonderfully the female mind is getting educated in America. To get these letters a few days after they were written makes me feel as if I were almost at home. On the strength of them, I went yesterday and engaged a passage from Liverpool for Boston on the Cephalonia, which sails the 12th of September. So that I ought to be in Clarendon Street on the 22d, and preach in Trinity on the 23d! Will you be glad to see me?

So you have sold your old house. We had some very good times there, and it will always be dear to you. I hope the new one which is building is going to see the happiest years of all. We are all good for twenty years more, and they shall be as happy as the accumulations of the past can make them. Now I am going off to preach at the Savoy Chapel.

Four P. M.

I have been and preached. There was a great crowd, and everything went off very well. . . . Then I took lunch with the Baroness Burdett-Coutts. I am going there to a dinner on Tuesday, to meet the new Archbishop. . . .

London is very pleasant now, full of interesting people. Friday I dined at Mr. Lowell's, with Professor Huxley. There were only four of us, so that we had the great skeptic all to ourselves, and he was very interesting. Next Saturday I am going to Farrar's to meet a lot of people. Among others, Matthew Arnold, whom I am very anxious to see. He is coming to America, I understand, this autumn.

I am glad John preached at Trinity. Tell the supplies to hurry up, for they will not have much more chance. I am coming home in the Cephalonia. Meanwhile, why cannot you run over and join Paine and me this summer? . . .

Affectionately, P.

WESTMINSTER PALACE HOTEL, LONDON,
May 27, 1883.

MY DEAR WILLIAM, — I am very late about my Sunday letter. The fact is, I am just home from the Abbey, where I have been preaching this evening. There was the same great throng of people that is always there, and the Abbey was as solemn and glorious as ever. I could not help putting into my sermon an allusion to our dear little Dean of old, which I think the people were glad to hear. Then we went into the deanery, just the way we used to do. I like the new Dean very much, and his love for Stanley is delightful. Mrs. Bradley and her daughters are also very pleasant. A young fellow, Hallam Tennyson, son of the Poet Laureate, was there. Does it not make "In Memoriam" seem very real to meet those two names together? He is a very nice fellow, and asked me to come down to the Isle of Wight and see his father, which I have a great mind to do. I preached for Canon Boyd Carpenter this morning, at Christ Church, Lancaster Gate, near Hyde Park. Next Sunday morning, I am to preach in old St. Margaret's for Farrar, which will be very interesting. He gave me a big dinner last night, with many clerical folk, the most interesting of whom was Lightfoot, the Bishop of Durham, one of the great scholars of the English Church. Matthew Arnold was to have been there, but at the last moment he was invited to dine with Prince Leopold, and it seems that means a command, and breaks every other engagement. . . . Farrar has asked me to lunch with him next Thursday, so I shall see him there.

I went on Tuesday to a tremendous dinner party at the Baroness Burdett-Coutts's, with swells as thick as huckleberries. Then, for variety, I went on Thursday night with K—— to an all-night meeting of the Salvation Army, what they, in their disagreeable lingo, call "All night with Jesus." They close the doors at eleven, and do not let anybody go out till half past four A. M. We made arrangements before going in that we should be let out at one A. M., and then we had to drive an hour in a hansom to get home. The meeting was noisy and unpleasant, but there was nothing very bad about it, and I am not sure that it might not do good to somebody.

One lovely day this week I went on a Cromwell pilgrimage to Huntington, where Oliver was born, and saw the register of his baptism, the house in which he was born, and the country in the midst of which he grew up. It was the sweetest of days, with the apple-trees in full blossom, and the hawthorn hedges just opening in white and pink. These and many other things have filled up my time very full, but it is very delightful.

I shall spend two more Sundays in London; then, on the 17th of June, I preach for Dean Plumptre at Wells, and probably on the 26th at Lincoln. I am going also to make a little visit to the Bishop of Rochester.

. . . The 23d of September will soon be here, and who knows but we may be all together in the old Andover house by the summer of 1884? I hope nothing will interfere with my plans there. I wish you were here for to-morrow. We would get up a 'scursion. . . .   Affectionately,   P.

WESTMINSTER PALACE HOTEL, LONDON,
June 3, 1883.

MY DEAR TOOD, — Your wicked papa has not sent me any letter this week, and so I am not going to write to him to-day, but I shall answer your beautiful letter, which traveled all the way to London, and was delivered here by a postman with a red coat, two or three weeks ago. He looked very proud when he came in, as if he knew that he had a beautiful letter in his bundle, and all the people in the street stood aside to make way for him, so that Tood's letter might not be delayed.

How quickly you have learned to read and write! I am very sorry for you, for they now will make you read and study a great many stupid books, and you will have to write letters all your days. When I get home, I am going to make you write my sermons for me, and I think of engaging you for my amanuensis at a salary of twenty cents a month, with which you can buy no end of gumdrops. If you do not know what an amanuensis is, ask Agnes, and tell her I will bring her a present if she can spell it right the first time.

Poor little Gertie! What a terrible time she has had. It must have been very good for her to have you to take care of her, and run her errands, and play with her, and write her letters. I suppose that is the reason why you hurried so and learned to write. It was a great pity that I never got her letter about the Christmas presents, but I am very glad that you liked the coupé. What do you want me to bring you home from London? Write me another letter and tell me, and tell Gertie I shall be very happy when I get another letter from her written with her own little fingers.

I want to see your new house, which I am sure will be very pretty. I wonder where you are going to be this summer? Now, I am going off to preach in a queer old church built almost a thousand years ago, before your father or mother was born. Give my love to them, and to Agnes, and to Gertie, and to the new doll. Your affectionate uncle PHILLIPS.

LONDON, June 10, 1883.

DEAR WILLIAM, — This past week has been happy in two letters from you. The week before I had none, as I remarked in my letter to Toody of last Sunday. That seems to have been only an accident of the mails, and not to mean any failure of brotherly kindness. For the riches of this week I am sincerely thankful, but it was sad news that your letter brought about the death of Miss Harmon. A long letter from Allen came at the same time, but I opened yours first and so learned it from you. She was a good, true woman, and the amount of help which she has given to the poor and comfort to the suffering is incalculable. I have been in the habit of trusting so much to her of that part of the work for which I have not the time and am not well fitted to do, that I shall miss her more than I can say. Her place can never be filled, and how we can manage to get along without her I do not see at once. It was a hard life, but I do not know where one could see a more useful one. . . . .

I have been preaching in St. Paul's to-day by invitation of the Bishop of London. It is Hospital Sunday; the Lord Mayor and Sheriffs came in state, and there was an enormous crowd there, but it is too awfully big, bald and barren, and needs color dreadfully.

I should rather have the Abbey, although it is good to get one chance at the great Cathedral. On Wednesday I am going to another great London sight. I am to dine with the Lord Mayor and the Lady Mayoress at the Mansion House, to meet the Archbishop and the Bishops, — a great city dinner with turtle soup and all that sort of thing. It will be good fun. Next Sunday I am going to spend at Wells with Plumptre, whom you remember, and who is now Dean of Wells. It is one of the prettiest cathedrals in England. John and I went there three years ago. On the 21st I am going down to the Isle of Wight to spend a day and a night at Tennyson's. I have been, and am going, to a great many dinners and receptions; everybody is very hospitable and kind, and it is very amusing.

In a few weeks I shall be ready to pull up and be off for the Continent again. I am going on Tuesday to stay with the Bishop of Rochester, and to-morrow I go with him to hear the discussion on the marriage with the deceased wife's sister in the House of Lords. That is the question which now is keeping England excited. I have an invitation from the University at Cambridge to come next spring in May, and preach three sermons before them. Do you think I could do it? Give my love to everybody.

Affectionately, P.

DEANERY, WELLS, June 17, 1883.

DEAR WILLIAM, — No letter from you the past week. I suppose there are two upon their way, and I shall get them both in a day or two. Meanwhile, I will not break my habit of a weekly letter, of which I am quite proud, for I have kept it up without a break all this year. Just think, it was a year next Wednesday that we were all huddled together on the Servia, and saw the last of one another in that tremendous crowd. It has been a delightful year, but one is not sorry to think that it is over, and only the last flourish of it left before one turns his face homeward.

Do you remember Dean Plumptre, and the day he preached at Trinity? He has grown older, and is now Dean of Wells, and I am staying with him ; in a few minutes I am going to preach for him, in one of the loveliest of the cathedrals. He is a true scholar and an interesting man. His wife was a sister of the great theological teacher, Frederick Maurice. . . . There is staying here a son of Maurice's, Colonel Maurice, who was in South Africa at Tel El Kebir, and who is writing his father's Life. He is a very charming person and makes my little visit much pleasanter than it could otherwise have been. Then close by lives Freeman, the historian, whose lectures at the Lowell Institute you and I went to hear. Colonel Maurice and I are going to his house to dinner this evening. . . . I dined the other day with another Lowell lecturer, Professor Bryce, whom we also went to hear together, and who is the pleasantest of men and hosts. Stopford Brooke was there, and other interesting people. One other evening last week I was at the Mansion House at the Lord Mayor's dinner to the Archbishops and Bishops. We had the city of London's famous turtle soup and ever so many curious customs. . . .

Only think, I am writing in a room which the Dean of Wells built in 1472, in which to entertain Henry VII. when he was coming back from the conquest of Perkin Warbeck. Does n't that sound old and bric-à-brac-ish ? . . .

FARRINGFORD, FRESHWATER,
ISLE OF WIGHT, June 22, 1883.

DEAR MARY, — Here is another place which seems interesting enough to be worthy of a few lines to you. Besides, it is the home of a brother, poet of yours, for Tennyson is sleeping somewhere downstairs, and that will interest you. So, as they do not have any breakfast until half past nine, and I am up and dressed at eight, here goes for a little letter.

I came down here yesterday, a long three hours' run from London, through a very pretty country, passing Winchester cathedral and other attractive things upon the way. At last we crossed the Channel in a little cockleshell of a steamboat, and landed at Yarmouth, where Hallam Tennyson was waiting for me with the carriage. Then a pretty drive over the Downs, with two or three small villages upon the way, brought us, in about three miles, to this house. Here the great poet lives. He is finer than his pictures, a man of good six feet and over, but stooping as he walks, for he is seventy-four years old, and we shall stoop if we ever live to that age. A big dome of a head, bald on the forehead and the top, and very fine to look at. His hair, where he is not bald, an iron-gray, with much whiter mustache and beard, a deep bright eye, a grand, eagle nose, a mouth which you cannot see, a black felt hat, and a loose tweed suit. These were what I noticed in the author of "In Memoriam."

The house is a delightful old rambling thing, whose geography one never learns, not elegant but very comfortable, covered with pictures inside and ivies outside, with superb ilexes and other trees about it, and lovely pieces of view over the Channel here and there.

He was just as good as he could be, and we all

went to a place behind the house, where the trees leave a large circle, with beautiful grass, and tables and chairs scattered about. Here we sat down and talked. Tennyson was inclined to be misanthropic, talked about Socialism, Atheism, and another great catastrophe like the French Revolution coming on the world. He declared that if he were a Yankee, he would be ashamed to keep the Alabama money, but he let himself be contradicted about his gloomy views, and by and by became more cheerful. We had tea out of doors, took a walk for various views, then, having come to know me pretty well, he wanted to know if I smoked, and we went up to the study, a big, bright, crowded room, where he writes his Idyls, and there we stayed till dinner time.

Dinner was very lively. Mrs. Tennyson is a dear old lady, a great invalid, as sweet and pathetic as a picture. Then there are staying here Mr. Lushington, a great Greek scholar, a Miss B., who knows everybody and tells funny stories, and another Miss B., her pretty niece, with the loveliest smile. After dinner, Tennyson and I went up to the study again, and I had him to myself for two or three hours. We smoked, and he talked of metaphysics, and poetry, and religion, his own life, and Hallam, and all the poems. It was very delightful, for he was gentle, and reverent, and tender, and hopeful. Then we went down to the drawing-room, where the rest were, and he read his poetry to us till the clock said twelve. "Locksley Hall," "Sir Galahad," pieces of "Maud," (which he specially likes to read), and some of his dialect poems. He said, by the way, in reading "Locksley Hall" that the verse beginning

"Love took up the glass of time," etc.,

was the best simile he ever made; and that and a certain line in the "Gardener's Daughter," were the ones on which he most piqued himself. Just after midnight we came up to bed. They had the prettiest way at dinner of getting up before the fruit came and going into the drawing-room, where there was a fresh table spread by the window, looking out on the lawn and Channel.

Well, so much about Tennyson. Thanks for your letter, which was very good to get. . . .

THE PRECENTORY, LINCOLN, June 23, 1883.

DEAR WILLIAM, — Is it not pretty hard, when I think I have a beautiful long letter from you, to open it and find nothing except some circulars? You might at least have written on the back of them. . . . I sent a photograph to G., the other day, which I hope she likes. Yesterday I came down here. Do you remember Lincoln? The cathedral is very gorgeous, and the old town is quaint. Last night, the Precentor, with whom I am staying, had a dinner-party of the clergy, with deans, sub-deans, and canons. The Bishop of Lincoln was there, Wordsworth, nephew of the poet, a man who ought to have lived five centuries ago. He said he thought the present House of Lords would not last more than five years longer, and ought not to, because they had passed a bill allowing a man to marry his deceased wife's sister! The Precentor, my host, is a nice old gentleman, and the place is very beautiful and full of association. . . . I preached this morning in the cathedral, close to the place where St. Hugo lies buried, and took tea this afternoon with the sub-dean, in the room where Paley, who used to be sub-dean here, wrote his "Natural Theology."

To-morrow, I go back to London. On Wednesday, Paine arrives from America, and my subsequent movements will be somewhat governed by him. Indeed, the 12th of September seems so near that it does not much matter what one does between. . . .

WESTMINSTER PALACE HOTEL, LONDON,
Sunday, July 1, 1883.

DEAR WILLIAM, — You are forty-nine years old to-morrow! Are you glad or sorry? Almost half a century, you see, and the only bother about it is that there is so much less remaining, for life has been very good, and one wishes there were more of it. I wish we were all going to live to be five hundred. But no matter! There are pleasant times still ahead, and we will make the most of them, so that when another forty-nine years are past, and you are ninety-eight, we shall agree that the second half has been even better than the first. I am all the more in a hurry to get home and begin the new period, now that you are forty-nine, seven times seven, which they say is the grand climacteric of life. But to-night I send you my heartiest God bless you, and congratulations upon all the past and hopes for all the future.

I am writing in Paine's room, for he has the luxury of a parlor, and I use it as if it were my own. He arrived on Wednesday, and I was glad enough to see him; since then we have talked over a thousand things. It is wonderfully like being at home again to hear so directly from you all. . . .

I preached for Dr. Vaughan at the Temple, this morning. It was a noble congregation, the church packed with lawyers, and the service very beautiful. The good doctor had a long surplice made especially for the occasion, and presented it to me as a memento, so the Temple surplice will stand in Trinity pulpit for many years. Last Sunday I wrote to you from Lincoln. I came back from there on Monday, and have had a very interesting week. There was a dinner at the Bishop of Carlisle's, with many interesting people, an evening in the House of Lords, where the bill for allowing marriage with the deceased wife's sister got defeated, a luncheon down at Dulwich, whither I went with the Bishop of Rochester and Dr. Boyd of St. Andrew's, who wrote the "Recreations of a Country Parson." At luncheon I sat between Robert Browning and Jean Ingelow, and had a delightful time. Then I went down to the Tower with a party of government people, Gladstone, and Foster, and Bright, and others. There was an evening party at Lady Stanley's, where I saw Browning again, and yesterday afternoon Newman Hall gave me a party. These and some other things have filled the week, and it has been most enjoyable. To-morrow, I am going down with Farrar to spend a night with a friend of his in the country, to meet Matthew Arnold, who lives somewhere there.

This afternoon, Paine and I drove out to Hampstead Heath and saw Holiday, who made his and Mr. Morrill's windows. The last time I saw him was when I went to order Paine's window, when you and I were in London together. How I wish you were here now! Paine is deeply interested in charity organizations, dispensaries, police stations, and all that sort of thing. We shall stay here probably three, certainly two weeks longer, and then be off for the great Continent. It has grown quite hot, and in a few weeks more we shall be glad to be away. There are a great many Americans here. . . . I watch every letter to hear what your plans are for the summer, and where you will be when I get home. Already the promise of autumn begins to appear. Allen has written to ask me to a dinner of the club on the 24th of September, and President Eliot wants me to take morning prayers at Cambridge during November. This is Commencement week. You have had Arthur and John with you, I suppose, and I hope that you talked about me. Good-by, my love to G——.

Your affectionate P.

WESTMINSTER PALACE HOTEL, July 8, 1883.

DEAR WILLIAM, —. . . I am having a first-rate time, but it is all the pleasanter because it is not going to last forever. The Cephalonia (No. 28 is our room) will sail on the 12th of September. I will tell you what I have been doing this week.

Monday, I went down to the country to stay with Mr. Leaf, a friend of Farrar's. It was a lovely place, with a glorious park, great trees, and a sumptuous house. There we passed an idle day, and in the evening had a big dinner, to which came Matthew Arnold and his daughter, who live close by. He was very amusing, and the next morning I went to breakfast with him, saw his wife, his house and study, and liked him very much. He has promised to stay with me when he comes to Boston.

On Tuesday, I came back to town, and we had a pleasant dinner party that night at the house of a Mr. Mills. After that was over, I went to one of Mrs. Gladstone's receptions, to which I was invited to see the Grand Old Man; he had to go to the House of Commons, and so I did not see him; but I am going there again next Tuesday. Wednesday was the 4th of July, which we celebrated by calling on the American minister. Thursday was speech day at Harrow School, and Paine and I went. I was there with John three years ago, and was glad to go again. The boys spoke well, and it was very bright and quite like Class Day. Then we had a luncheon, where Lord Dufferin and I made speeches. When I came back I went to dinner at Lady Frances Baillie's, the sister of Dean Stanley's wife. It was very pleasant. We had Grove, and Robert Browning, and the Bishop of Litchfield; and my companion was Mrs. Ritchie (Thackeray's daughter), who wrote "The Village on the Cliff" and all those nice novels, and who told me a great deal about her father. Friday, I went to Richmond and saw the prettiest view in England, and in the evening dined with the Precentor at the Abbey. After dinner, we went into the Abbey and strolled about in the dark, with wonderfully pretty effects in the great arches. Saturday, I went to a garden party at Fulham Palace, the Bishop of London's, where there were many clergymen, and in the evening ten miles out of town to Upper Tooting, where I dined with Mr. Macmillan, the publisher.

Have you read "John Inglesant"? Mr. Shorthouse, the man who wrote it, was the principal guest, and there were a great many agreeable people. This morning, we went to the Foundling Hospital and heard the children sing, so the week has gone with a good deal of sight-seeing to fill up the gaps. Everybody is hospitable and kind, and it would be pleasant to stay here a long time; but our departure now is definitely fixed for the 19th, when we shall go somewhere on the Continent. We do not yet know where, or I would tell you, but no doubt our uncertainty will solve itself in the course of the next week, and by next Sunday I can tell you something of our summer's route. All the time, while our weather here is delightful, you are sweltering in heat. This morning's paper says the heat in New York yesterday was terrible. I am awfully sorry for you. Do take a steamer and come over, you and the total family, and we will lie upon the grass in Hyde Park together till you all get cool. . . . God bless you all always. P.

WESTMINSTER PALACE HOTEL, LONDON,
July 10, 1883.

MY DEAR GERTIE, — . . . I wish you were here, for it is beautifully fresh and cool, and we would go off and see some kind of pretty things. I went down into the country the other day, and saw some people whom I met on the journey home from India. It was the prettiest place, and you would have enjoyed it ever so much.

They had the biggest strawberries you ever saw, and you would have enjoyed picking them a great deal more than I did. I wish strawberries grew on trees. They would be so much easier to pick. There was a nice little girl there who was a great friend of mine on the voyage. Her name is Nora, and she gave me her photograph. I think I will put it into this letter, so that you can see what an English child looks like, only you must keep it safe and give it to me when I get to Boston, for I told Nora Buchanan that I should keep it till I saw her again. Her father has a tea plantation up in the Himalaya Mountains, and her mother and she go there every winter. She has got a pony named Brownie, and a big dog and a little dog, and lots of pets.

When we get to living up in the old house at Andover, we will have some dogs too, and perhaps some day we will get a pony for you to ride on; or would you rather have a donkey with long ears, and a delightful little cart to drive in? What did you do on the 4th of July? The people here seemed to think that it was just like any other day; nobody was firing crackers, or blowing soap bubbles, and there were no American flags flying anywhere; but one day, two weeks ago, London was greatly excited, it being the Queen's Coronation Day, and I met the Lord Mayor in his coach, with a red cloak on and a big gold chain around his neck. I thank you so much for your little note, and for the picture of yourself, which is set up in my room. You must write to me again when you can, and I will see you in September. By that time you must be well and fat and rosy. Now goodby. My love to Agnes and Toodie.

Your loving uncle, P.

WESTMINSTER PALACE HOTEL, July 15, 1883.

DEAR WILLIAM, — . . . On Thursday next, the 19th, we leave England. We had to fix some certain day and hold to it, or we should have never got away. We go first through France into the Pyrenees, where we shall get a little journey, just enough to see what they are like, and then by interesting routes, more or less out of the way, into the Tyrol through Switzerland. Next Sunday, July 22, we probably shall spend at Bagnères de Luchon, pretty near the Spanish border. I am sorry to leave London, and never shall forget my two months here. It has been great fun, and the hospitality of everybody has been most abundant. The last week has been busy socially.

The pleasantest evening, perhaps, was Tuesday at Mr. Gladstone's, where I had a good sight of and talk with the great man, and gazed at a multitude of splendid folks with diamonds and titles. He is certainly the greatest man in England, and the look of him is quite worthy of his fame. Another evening I dined in the Jerusalem Chamber with the Dean and Chapter of the Abbey, and the members of their choir. That was very jolly, and recalled the time eight years ago when I went to the same dinner and sat by Stanley's side. This morning I am going to preach for Llewellyn Davis, whom you and I once went to hear in St. Paul's. He is a most interesting man and one of the best spirits in the English Church. This will be my last sermon in England. Mr. Macmillan has asked me to publish the sermons which I have preached here, under the title "Sermons Preached to English Congregations," and I have about made up my mind to do so. He is the publisher of my last volume. This one will have thirteen sermons, and be a pleasant memento of my English visit. I have declined the invitation to come and preach at Cambridge next spring, but they have intimated that it will be repeated some other year, and then I should like to come and make a university visit. I have seen nothing of the universities this time.

I want to see you all dreadfully. . . .   P.

LONDON, July 15, 1883.

MY DEAR HATTIE,[1] — It was most kind of you to take up the pen which your husband had so long dropped, and write me the pleasant letter which I got last week, and it seems that its quiet rebuke was felt, for John wrote the next day. Behold the noble

[1] A sister-in-law.

influence of a good wife! . . . Now I think of you as having the happiest of summers in your seashore home. As I listen Marionwards, I hear a rich, low sound of which I am not quite sure whether it is the moaning of the sea, as it beats on your back doorstep, or the theological discussions of B——, P——, and J—— under the haystack. Either sound would be delightful. To have them both together in your ears all day must be a little heaven below, and it must be all the pleasanter to you this year, because you can look back to such a bright, successful winter in Springfield, and look forward to another, which will no doubt be still better. I am so thankful to hear of the way in which every difficulty has disappeared. . . . I wish I could hope to run to Marion this autumn, and see you on your own rocks, with your young barbarians at play about you. But I shall be home too late, and dear me! I sometimes pleasantly shiver in the midst of this delightful idleness at the thought of how much there is to do next winter. It is like thinking of January in July. But, fortunately, less and less depends on us, and the younger clergy, who read Second Lessons at the Diocesan Convention, have the brunt of the battle.

Give my tenderest love to your young clergyman. Tell him I thank him heartily for his letter. Be sure that I thank you sincerely for yours. Kiss the babies for me, and remember that I am always,

Affectionately, P.

Pau, Sunday, July 22, 1883.

DEAR WILLIAM, — The curtain has fallen and risen again; the whole scene has changed. London, with all its fun, is far away, and here we are close to the

Pyrenees. It is delightfully cool and pleasant, and the view out of my window is wonderfully beautiful. I have time enough to look at it, for I am laid up with a lame leg. On the way from Chartres to Bordeaux I struck my leg in leaving the railway coach, and this morning I sent for a French doctor, who bade me lie still to-day. So here I am, writing, like M., on a book instead of a table. The queer little doctor assures me that it will be all right to-morrow morning, and then we shall push on up to Eaux Bonnes. It is only a bruise, I believe. Paine is as kind as kind can be, and does everything for me, and we are having a delightful time. Just now he has gone out to see the town, and I am trying to write in this miserable way upon my back.

 . . . We came through that night to Chartres, which Paine had never seen, and the next night to Bordeaux, and yesterday here. I have been buying a lot of books in London, and just before I left, Macmillan kindly undertook to have them packed and sent to your care. There will be one or two big boxes of them. Will you see to them when they arrive, and have them sent to my house? They are all for my own use, mostly theological books, and ought to pass as tools of trade. Of course, if they must pay duty, you will pay it for me. They have been bought so miscellaneously in many places, one here and another there, that I cannot say just what they have cost, but it is about $800 or $900. You must do what you think best about it, and I hope it will not give you a great deal of trouble. . . .

Yours affectionately, P.

BAGNÈRES DE LUCHON,
Sunday, July 29, 1883.

DEAR WILLIAM, —. . . We have had a splendid Pyrenean week. Great mountains with snowy sides, beautiful rich valleys, wild ravines, quaint villages, a handsome, happy people, and bright skies, — anybody ought to look back with pleasure on a whole week of these. It is not exactly like any other country which I know. Perhaps it is more like some parts of the Tyrol than anything else. It reminds me at times of some parts of the road up the valley of the Inn, which you and I drove up together once. There is a luxuriance about these valleys, of which I hardly ever saw the like. The way they overrun with water is delicious. You are never away from the sound of a brook or a waterfall. Streams run by the side of every road. There are fountains in every man's back yard, every bank has a small cascade tumbling over it, and all the rocks look as if Moses had been about here with his rod, striking out right and left. Last night the abundance of waters culminated in a drenching rain, and we reached here in the midst of floods. This morning all is bright as Paradise. It is a garden of a place, way up in the hills, and the Frenchmen have made a pretty summer resort of it. I am still a little lame, and am lying by to get well. The week's traveling has not given me much chance to repair my leg, and I hope my conversation has been better than my walk. Taking pity on my imprisonment, the band came this morning and played under my window, and the Frenchmen and Frenchwomen strolled up and down, and the sun shone, and it was like a sort of Class Day up in the Pyrenees on Sunday. It is as pretty as a picture.

There was a great deal grander place which we saw the other day at Gavarnie, where a wild valley pierces into the hills until it brings up against a tremendous wall of rock in a great amphitheatre, and has to stop because it can get no farther. It is like a splendid end of the world. You can only guess what lies on the other side of the rocks, heaven or hell. Really, it is Spain, which is a little of both. Out of the side of the high wall leaps a cascade, 1300 feet high, and tumbles down into a caldron of mist and foam. It is a wonderful place.

Last Wednesday morning we were at Lourdes, one of the strangest places in the world, and suggestive of all sorts of thoughts and questions. It was here that almost thirty years ago a little girl saw the Virgin Mary standing in a grotto, and a spring burst out which since that has been curing hosts of sick people, who have come from the ends of the earth. Now there is a gorgeous church there, crowds of worshipers, a hundred thousand pilgrims yearly, and a heap of disused crutches and camp stools, which the cured have left behind them. The street through the town is one long market of crosses, and pictures, and rosaries, and statuettes of Mary. The whole was wonderfully like the street which leads down to the Ganges at Benares, with its booths full of brass images of Vishnu, Siva, Ganesha, and Kali.

To-morrow we shall be off to Toulouse, and then by the Grande Chartreuse to Geneva, where we spend next Sunday. . . .

Ever affectionately, P.

HÔTEL DE LA PAIX, GENEVA,
August 5, 1883.

DEAR WILLIAM. — Yesterday I received your letter of July 23, which gave me the greatest anxiety about poor little G——. It is very hard indeed that she should have had a relapse, and lost something of the hard-won ground. I hate to think how she must have suffered this long winter and spring. My comfort is, that the news is two weeks old, and before this she must be in Sharon, which is to be the fountain of life to her. If I believed all the wonderful stories of what it does, I should send you a bottle of the miraculous water of Lourdes, and we would be grateful worshipers of the Virgin for all the good that it might do the dear little thing. I shall not do that, but I shall be very anxious until, next Sunday at Interlaken, I hear of your reaching Sharon and what are the results.

Do you remember this hotel, and the forenoon which we spent at Geneva? It is as bright as ever, and the lake this Sunday morning is shining like a monstrous jewel. Do you remember how we talked about the Grande Chartreuse and the possibility of getting there, but finally concluded that it was too remote and took the train for Basle and Strasburg instead? We came out of the Pyrenees by Toulouse and Nîmes, and spent last Friday night up at the Grande Chartreuse. Arthur and Lizzie went there last year. Whether they spent the night or not I do not know. The drive up to the wonderful old nest of the monks is very fine. Most splendid valleys, at first open and broad and bathed in sunshine, and then growing narrower and wilder, until they were nothing but woody gorges; and finally opening into the little plateau on which the monastery buildings stand and seem to fill the whole place from one mountain side to the other.

There are about forty fathers there, Carthusians, in their picturesque white cloaks and cowls. Solitude and silence is their rule. They spend the bulk of the time in their cells, where they are supposed to be meditating. I suspect that the old gentlemen go to sleep. There was a strange, ghostly service, which began at a quarter before eleven o'clock at night and lasted until two in the morning. The chapel was dim and misty, the white figures came gliding in and sat in a long row, and held dark lanterns up before their psalters and chanted away at their psalms like a long row of singing mummies. It made you want to run out in the yard and have a game of ball to break the spell. Instead of that, after watching it for half an hour, we crept back along a vast corridor to the cells which had been allotted us, each with its priedieu and its crucifix, and went to bed in the hardest, shortest, and lumpiest of beds. In the morning a good deal of the romance and awfulness was gone, but it was very fine and interesting, and the drive down into the valley on the other side at Chambéry was as pretty as a whole gallery of pictures. Thence we came by rail, and reached here Friday night.

Yesterday we drove out to Ferney and saw where Voltaire used to live; looked at the bed in which he used to sleep and at the church which he built. It has over its front door perhaps the strangest of all strange inscriptions which men have carved on churches, —

"DEO EREXIT VOLTAIRE."

Here we fall into the tide of travel again, and Americans abound. The Suters are all here. I shall preach to them in the American church this morning, and I shall find myself looking for you and your family two pews behind them. Richard Weld and his wife and sons are also here, and a lot of other Americans whom I never saw, but feel as if I had seen every day of my life. . . . Seven weeks from to-day I preach in Trinity. . . .

MÜRREN, August 12, 1883.

DEAR WILLIAM, — I went to church this morning in a little thing which the preacher declared to be the most splendidly situated church in Christendom, and I rather think he was right. Do you remember when we were at Interlaken and went over to Grindelwald, how after it stopped raining we climbed up to the Wengern-Alp and looked the Jungfrau in the face? On the other side of the Lauterbrunnen Valley, into which we descended that day, stands the great hill upon whose top is Mürren. We came here yesterday afternoon, and such a Sunday as this was hardly ever seen. From extreme right to extreme left was one unbroken range of the very highest of snowy peaks, and all day they have been superbly clear. I remember one Sunday, with a fellow up on the Gornergrat, which must have been about as fine. Finer Sundays than those two, nobody ever had anywhere.

There are a multitude of English and German people here, but so far as I have learned, R. T. Paine, Jr., and I are the only Americans. The preacher this morning was an old English friend, Dr. Butler, the master of Harrow School, and he is the only person whom I ever saw before. But that is all the better, for one has nothing to do but stare at the hills. I saw the first sunlight strike them at half past four this morning. Besides staring at them, I have been engaged to-day in reading my own sermons. Half the proof of the new volume reached me from Macmillan yesterday, and I have read the interesting discourses through to-day. I hope the public will not get so tired of them as I have.

To-morrow we go down again to Interlaken, then to Lucerne, over that Brunig Pass where you and I drove once in the dust, thence through the new St. Gotthard tunnel to lake Como, and then a journey by a back road through northern Italy, coming out in the Dolomites and working back to Paris by Munich. We shall be in Paris about the 5th of September, and six weeks from to-day I preach in Trinity.

. . . Tell G. I shall expect her to come and make me a visit just as soon as the old house gets to rights again. I will feed her up and get her well, show her all the pretty things I have bought, and give her a lot of the prettiest for her ownty-donty. How I wish you were all here this afternoon, with John, Arthur, and their families. Perhaps we can get up a great assembly at Andover next summer. I am hoping for a letter from you to-morrow at Interlaken. I am glad the Andover window is done and is so satisfactory. I am eager to see it. There goes an avalanche. . . .

MÜRREN, August 13, 1883.

MY DEAR LIZZIE, — I am not quite sure whether I owe you a letter, or you owe me one. I rather think our last letters crossed upon the road, and that always leaves a doubt. I imagine that a good many correspondences have died that way. But ours shall not. I will write to you anyhow, and show you that I am not mean. You have been at Mürren, have n't you? and can anything be finer than this Biger and Monch and Grosshorn and Breithorn and Mittaghorn? We have spent two whole days up here, reading novels and staring at the hills. Each morning at half past four we have seen the first sunlight strike the peaks, and all day the sky has been cloudless. Now we are going to turn our backs upon it and walk down to Lauterbrunnen. Every step now seems a step homeward, for six weeks from yesterday I am going to preach in Trinity again. It will seem strange to stand at that little desk once more. I shall crawl back before the people return to town, and when they come, full of the recollections of the splendors of last winter, they will find only me. But I shall enjoy it if they don't, and then the old life will begin again. There will be some changes, but it is good to know that I shall find you and Arthur just as I left you, only I want to see the new church and enjoy it, as I know I shall. . . .

. . . And where are you? Roaming along the shores of Grand Menan, or reveling like Sybarites in the luxurious life of "up the river." . . . You will come on to the General Convention and look at us, while we are sitting in the great assembly, will you not? And on the way there and back, I shall steal quiet evenings for logomachy and talk in the Madi-

son Avenue hermitage. How nice and familiar it all sounds, and it is almost here. Will you not meet us in Brussels, where we parted, and we will peel off sticky photographs for an evening, and then come home together. My love to Arthur.
Ever affectionately, P.

TRENTO, Sunday, August 19, 1883.

DEAR GERTIE, — I bought the prettiest thing you ever saw for you the other day. If you were to guess for three weeks, making two guesses every minute, you could not guess what it is. I shall not tell you, because I want you to be all surprised to pieces when you see it, and I am so impatient to give it to you that I can hardly wait. Only you must be in a great hurry and get well, because you see it is only five weeks from to-day that I shall expect to see you in the dear old study in Clarendon Street, where we have had such a lot of good times together before now. Just think of it! We'll set the music box a-going, and light all the gaslights in the house, and get my doll out of her cupboard, and dress Tood up in a red pocket handkerchief and stand her up on the study table, and make her give three cheers! And we'll have some gingerbread and lemonade.

I've got a lot of things for you besides the one which I bought for you the other day. You couldn't guess what it is if you were to guess forever, but this is the best of all, and when you see it you will jump the rheumatism right out of you. I hope you will be quite well by that time. What sort of a place is Sharon? Do not write to me about it, but tell me all about it when I see you. What a lot you will have to tell. You can tell me what was in that Christmas letter which the wicked mail-man never brought to me.

Good-by, dear little girl. Don't you wish you knew what it was that I bought for you the other day? Give my love to Agnes and Tood.

Your affectionate uncle, P.

TRENTO, August 19, 1883.

DEAR MARY, — I have come to another place which seems to justify a letter to you. Three hundred and twenty-eight years ago, a lot of clergymen climbed up here into the mountains and held the Council of Trent, and fixed forever the Church of Rome. Last night Paine and I arrived here in the train, and are holding our council now in the Hôtel de Trento. This morning we went to the old church in which the Council sat, and there we listened to a sermon which we did not understand, looked at a crowded congregation of people (as different from that which meets in Trinity as anybody can imagine), and wondered how the old church looked when the Bishops and Archbishops were sitting there in council three hundred and twenty-eight years ago.

Just in front of me was a poor old weather-beaten lady, who went fast asleep in the sermon time and woke up beautifully refreshed when it was over. I rather think the sleep did her more good than the sermon would have done, for she looked as if she had been overworked ever since she was a baby, and that was long ago. On the walls hung a picture of the Council, and after service we went off to the other church, where is the crucifix before which all the Tridentine Fathers, when their long work was over, said their prayers. How modern it makes our

General Convention of this autumn look, and yet it is the modern things that are of more interest to us than all the old ones; and more important to me to-day, a great deal, than the Council of Trent is poor little G.'s chamber at Sharon. I wonder whether, in the two weeks since she went there, the waters have done her good. I cannot tell you how anxious I am, or how, getting the news only once a week, I wait in suspense to hear what the blue envelopes will bring which the Barings send to meet us. If I were at home, I would take the train to Sharon and see what sort of a nurse I should make for the dear little woman. At least I could know how it fared with her, and perhaps you would not mind having me about, and if I were very much in the way I could go out and smoke my cigar behind the house. But it is not long now. Five weeks from to-day I shall be in the old place again. I will not think of anything else than that then you will be back from Sharon, with G. vastly better for it, and the new house as lively as a summer's day. And then what a winter we will have.

There goes the church-bell again! They are going to have another meeting in the Council church, but I shall stay at home and write my letters. To-morrow morning a carriage will start with us for a three days' drive through the glorious Dolomites, and next Sunday I shall hear at Wildbad-Gastein how you all are. . . .

TYROLER HOF, INNSBRUCK,
August 26, 1883.

DEAR WILLIAM, — . . . We ordered letters sent to Bad Gastein, but when we reached Innsbruck (you remember Innsbruck) we found there was to be to-day a Passion Play at Brixlegg, a little village only an hour from here, and we determined to stop over. We have spent the whole Sunday there, and it has been a wonderfully interesting day. Thirteen years ago I started for Ober-Ammergau, and the Franco-Prussian war stopped the play before I reached there. This Brixlegg play is Ober-Ammergau on a small scale and in rather a more primitive fashion. The whole story of Christ's Passion, from the Entry into Jerusalem to the Resurrection, is acted by the peasants in the most devout fashion, and with a power and feeling that are very wonderful. It occupies about five hours, with an intermission of an hour and a half in the midst. It is given in a rude barn-like building, set up for the purpose, with curious quaint scenery, and most effective tableaux. It is a good thing to see once, for it is a rare remnant of what was common in the Middle Ages, and furnishes a remarkable study of the character of the people to whom such a thing is a possibility. . . .

I will tell you all about this when I get home, if you want to hear. Innsbruck looks just as it did when you and I drove out of it five years ago on the way to the Stelvio. The big mountain still throws its shadow down the Theresien Strasse, and the wonderful bronze people stand around Maximilian's tomb in the Hof Kirche. But only think. The railway runs all the way to Imst, and the steam whistle has vulgarized the lovely valley. Are you not glad we went there first? Perhaps it has improved the Imst Hotel!

This last week I thought of you at the first sight of the Inn Valley, but up to that time we were in the Dolomites, where the associations were rather with Arthur, who traveled there with me in the early days, before you and I were fellow-travelers.

To-morrow we are off for Bad Gastein, and then come Ischl, Salzburg, and next Sunday, Munich; then, Paris and London. Two weeks from next Wednesday we set sail. So I shall send you only one more letter. But I shall hear from you, and I will thank you ever so much if you telegraph me just *one word* to the Cephalonia at Queenstown upon the 12th. Four weeks from tonight, perhaps we shall be smoking together in the rectory. . . .

INNSBRUCK, August 26, 1883.

DEAR GERTIE, — How I envy the little Tyrolese girls their health and strength to-day! I wanted to steal half of it, and send it home in a box to you. They never would have missed it, for they have a great deal more health than they know what to do with. Their cheeks are as red as the sunset, and they look as if they never heard of such a thing as rheumatism! But never mind, I am coming home soon now, and you will forget all about this ugly winter.

I have been seeing the people in a little village to-day act a part of the New Testament story. A lot of the children took part in it, and I send you a photograph of one of them, a little girl who walked in the procession which came with Jesus into Jerusalem on Palm Sunday. She was a cunning little thing, and carried her palm branch as you see, and cried, "Hosanna!" as she walked along. I wish you had been there to see her.

Was it not funny that I should hear about you on the street at Innsbruck? You see how famous you are and how people know about you all over the world. The person who knew about you here was Miss Wales, who came out of a shop last Friday afternoon just as we were going in. She looked just like a slice out of old Boston, and she had some letters from home about your visit to Sharon, or perhaps she saw it in the papers!

I wonder if you will be back when I get home, and I wonder if you will be glad to see me! I got you another present the other day, but you couldn't guess what that is either. Good-by! Get well! And give my love to Agnes and Tood. I think of you a great deal. Your affectionate uncle, P.

MUNICH, September 2, 1883.

DEAR GERTIE — When I came away, the first man that wrote me a letter only two days after the Servia had steamed out of New York Bay was *you*. And now that I am coming home, the last letter which I write from the Old World to any man in America shall be to *you*. For I want to tell you myself that I shall see you on September 22. I suppose you will not be quite able to run over to the wharf at East Boston when the Cephalonia gets in, but I shall come up to see you just as soon as the custom house people let me out of prison, after I have paid the duties upon all the heaps of presents I have got for you!

Wasn't it good that the baths at Sharon helped you so much? I was at a place the other day where the people take baths for rheumatism. It is called Bad Gastein, but it isn't bad at all; it is very good. It is away back in the hills, and there's a tremendous waterfall which runs right through the house, and keeps up such a racket that you can't get any sleep. But that does no great harm, because you have to take your bath so early that, if it were not for the waterfall in the next room, you would sleep over and never get your bath at all, and so some time you might have the rheumatism all your life. I didn't have any rheumatism, so I went and took a bath for yours, and I rather think that is what made you feel so much better. You thought it was the baths you were taking at Sharon, but it was really the bath I was taking at Bad Gastein!

I wonder how soon you will come and see me when I get back. Everybody here eats his breakfast, and luncheon, and dinner outdoors. I like it, and think I shall do so myself when I get home; so when you come to breakfast, we will have our table out on the grass plot in Newbury Street, and Katie shall bring us our beefsteak there. Will it not make the children stare as they go by to school? We'll toss the crumbs to them and the robins. But you must hurry and get well, or we cannot do all this. My love to Agnes and Tood. Your affectionate uncle, P.

HOTEL BAIERISCHER HOF, MUNICH,
September 2, 1883.

DEAR WILLIAM, — . . . This last day of home writing makes me feel queer. I wonder whether it is really true that three weeks from to-day I am to preach in Trinity. I wonder whether I shall really look so old and thin that people will not know me. I wonder whether those heathen are still chattering and chaffering in the Chandni-Chauk at Delhi. I wonder whether I have really got enough benefit out of all this pleasant year to make it worth while to have come. This last wonder is the hardest of all. Sometimes I think I have, and then again I do not know. At any rate I shall try, and if I find when I begin to preach that I am really as idiotic as I sometimes seem to myself, there are several little hidden nooks in Europe which I know, where I can go and hide my disgrace, and nobody will hear of me any more forever. But perhaps it will not come to that. . . .

Why cannot you make use of my house this autumn, until your own is thoroughly dry and safe? Pray do not think of going into it. You must not let G. run the slightest danger of a relapse. Nothing would give me greater pleasure than to find you all in Clarendon Street. On my return, on the 2d of October, I go to Philadelphia; shall practically be absent all that month, and you can have free swing. So pray do go there, and please me.

You remember this hotel and the bright, pretty city. . . . But what's the use of writing, when I shall be at home a week after you get this. *My last letter.* Hurrah! Hurrah! My final love; I am coming home.

Affectionately,   P.

ENGLAND AND EUROPE.

1885.

STEAMSHIP ETRURIA, May 15, 1885.

MY DEAR GERTIE, — This letter will show you that I have got safely over to Queenstown. The people are just finishing their breakfasts in the cabin, that is, the lazy ones who have come up late from their staterooms.

I had my breakfast two hours ago, and have been walking up and down the deck since then. There are a lot of people up there, among them a good many children. Some very nice-looking boys! Everybody seems to have had a pleasant voyage. There has been no storm, and most of the time the water has been as quiet as a bath tub. On Sunday it was a little rough. The Doctor read service, and we had no sermon, because the people wanted to get on deck again.

I received the letter which you all wrote to me. I found it on the table in the cabin, just after the steamer sailed. It was very good of you to write, and it made a very pleasant last good-by, after uncle Arthur had left me on deck, and I thought I should not see or hear from anybody I knew, at least for a whole week.

. . . I wish you were here! We would go to walk on the deck and see the people play shuffleboard, then we would find a quiet place behind the smokestack and sit down and smoke. I suppose you are getting ready to go up to North Andover. Do take good care of " Tom," and do not let the pony bully him. . . . When you get this, think of me in London having a beautiful time . . . Ever and ever

  Your affectionate uncle,   P.

       WESTMINSTER PALACE HOTEL, LONDON,
         May 21, 1885.

DEAR WILLIAM, — Here it is, begun all over again in the old fashion. The old hotel, the same dingy outlook from the windows, and the same chimes from the Abbey bells every quarter of an hour! We reached here yesterday afternoon at the end of our fourth day on shore. The voyage was very swift, pleasant, and uneventful. The Etruria is a superb ship, rather inclined to roll, when there seems to be no reason for it, but going through the water at a tremendous rate. . . . The only celebrity on board was Mr. Froude, who kept very much to his stateroom and was hardly seen. I am afraid the great historian was ill. We landed on Sunday morning at Liverpool, and I went to church, and saw and heard Bishop Ryle. Monday we spent in Chester, and went out to the Duke of Westminster's place, Eaton Hall, and also to Mr. Gladstone's Hawarden Castle. Neither of the great men was at home, but we looked at their houses. . . . Then we came on to Leamington, and saw Warwick Castle, Kenilworth, and Stratford-on-Avon, and then here.

  I saw Archdeacon Farrar yesterday afternoon, and found him well. I am to dine with him on Saturday to meet Browning and Lowell and Arnold, and the new Bishop of London, Dr. Temple. I saw my godson, who is staying with his grandfather, in the absence of his parents from London for a few days. He is a round, fat, English baby.

. . . .

Friday Morning, May 22.

Yesterday was a busy London day, and I did not finish my letter. Now it shall go to tell you that I am well and happy. Think of me on the 31st of May at Oxford; on the 7th of June at Harrow in the morning, and in Westminster Abbey in the evening; on the 14th of June at Cambridge. I will think of you all getting ready for North Andover, and by and by going there, and having, I hope, a lovely summer. Already I am beginning to think how good next summer will be when we are all there together, and " Tom " has grown to his maturity, and the old place has really come to look and feel as if it had begun a new life for our generation. . . .

I have not heard from you yet, though I got two letters forwarded by you and mailed the day we sailed. Not a bit of excitement here, apparently, about war or cholera, but both subjects quietly and very seriously talked about. Good-by, and my best love to all of you. May you be kept safe and happy.

Affectionately, P.

WESTMINSTER PALACE HOTEL, LONDON,
May 29, 1885.

DEAR GERTIE, — I received your note and Toodie's early this week, and to-night comes your father's to tell me that you were thinking of me as late as the 15th of May. I believe you are thinking of me still. Certainly I am thinking of you, and hoping you are all well and doing all sorts of delightful things. It does not seem as if it could be only three weeks this morning that I said good-by to you and took the train for New York. But it is, and I have been in London now more than a week. What have I done? Let me see. Last Sunday morning I preached at St. Margaret's in the forenoon; in the afternoon went to St. Paul's Cathedral, and heard Canon Scott Holland. . . . Monday we went to Windsor Castle, but it was rainy, and besides that it was "Bank Holiday," so there was a tremendous crowd, and we did not see very much. Tuesday I went down to the Bishop of Rochester's and spent the night, and it was very pleasant. He has a great big house and park, and everything very complete and pretty. It was a lovely day, the hawthorns were just blooming, and the grass and old trees were lovely. . . .

On Wednesday I went to a big dinner-party, and I had a very good time. Thursday I went down to the country and spent the day with some nice people who live in an old manor house, in a place called Chigwell. There is a school-house there where William Penn used to go to school, before he founded Pennsylvania, and there are many other interesting things. To-day we have had a long drive to Hampton Court, Richmond, and Kew, and seen no end of queer and delightful sights; and now to-night I am writing to you, so you see I am very busy. To-morrow I go to Oxford, where I spend three days, seeing the university and looking at all the great men. It has been cold and bleak, but now the weather is getting bright and warm, and the country is prettier than anything you ever saw, except North Andover.

I have not seen Nora Buchanan, but I saw her mother, the other day. Nora had gone to school, and

was very well. I wonder when you are going to North Andover. You must tell me when you write again, so that I can think of your getting settled and feel what a good time you are having. Remember that the corn-barn belongs to you, and you must be the mistress there. But do let S. and A. come in when they want to. Give them my love, and also to your father and mother. Do not forget that I am
    Your affectionate uncle, P.

          LONDON, June 5, 1885.

DEAR WILLIAM, — . . . Saturday I went to Oxford and stayed at the Vice-Chancellor's, Dr. Jowett's. Other people were staying there, and it was very bright and pleasant. On Sunday afternoon I preached the university sermon in St. Mary's Church. . . . The service was at two o'clock, an hour when I think nobody ever went to church before. Four men came to the Vice-Chancellor's house, and Dr. Jowett and I fell in behind them, and they escorted us along the street as far as the church. When we reached the church, another man took us in charge and brought us to the foot of the pulpit stairs, where the Vice-Chancellor and I solemnly bowed to one another, and he went up into his throne and I went up into the pulpit. Then I preached. . . . I spent the next two days in Oxford, and had a lovely time, going to all sorts of meetings, dining with the dons, seeing the men I wanted most to see, being rowed on the river, and all that. The weather was lovely; you cannot think how beautiful the place looked. . . .
    Your brother,   P.

WESTMINSTER PALACE HOTEL, LONDON,
June 12, 1885.

DEAR GERTIE, — . . . I have been running up and down this big world of London and seeing a lot of people, and every now and then going off into the country, which is wonderfully pretty now, with hawthorn and lilacs and laburnums all in bloom.

Last Sunday I went out to Harrow, where there is a great school, and there I preached to five hundred boys. How A. would like to go there, wouldn't she? In the afternoon I came back into town, and preached in Westminster Abbey to a host of people. The great place looked splendid, and it was fine to preach there. Yesterday I went twenty miles into the country, and preached at an ordination of forty new ministers. The fields were bright with daisies, and I wondered how North Andover was looking. You must be just packing up to go there now. Even with all the beauty of England, it makes me quite homesick when I think about it. You must tell me all about the removal there, and how you get settled, and how your corn-barn looks, and what new things you find to do in the old place; and you must have it all ready for me on September 12, when I mean to come up early in the morning and spend the whole solid week quietly there. That will be just three months from to-day. . . .

I go to Cambridge for next Sunday, and then to Oxford for Commemoration and my degree. Goodby; my best of love to all and you.

Affectionately, UNCLE P.

WESTMINSTER PALACE HOTEL, LONDON,
June 18, 1885.

MY DEAR TOOD, — You certainly deserve a letter, for your letters to me have been delightful and have made me very happy. I am sorry you have given up the poetry, because it was very interesting and amusing. Perhaps now that the strain of school is over, and you are among the sweet sights and sounds and smells of North Andover, you will drop into verse again. I shall be glad to hear you sing once more. Write me a poem about " Tom."

I am having a beautiful time, and I wish you all were here. If you were, I would get a big carriage this morning, and we would all go driving about London and out into Hyde Park, and perhaps far away into the country. We would see the rhododendrons, which are in full bloom now, and we would wish that the grass on the lawn in North Andover could be made to look half as soft and green as the grass on these beautiful English fields.

I have just come back from Oxford. You should have seen me yesterday walking about the streets in my Doctor's gown. It was a red gown with black sleeves, and is awfully pretty. It was only hired for the occasion, for it costs ever so much money, and I did not care to buy one. So you will never see how splendid I looked in it, for I shall never have it on again. . . .

Affectionately your UNCLE P.

WESTMINSTER PALACE HOTEL, LONDON,
June 19, 1885.

DEAR WILLIAM, — I hope you are well and happy, and I wish very much that I could see you all to-day.

You must be safe at Andover long before this, and I know how pretty it must be looking. I shall get a bit of it at the end of the season. It seems to be settled now that Archdeacon Farrar and his two friends will come with me on the Pavonia, September 2. I hope we shall arrive in Boston on Saturday, the 12th. Then we shall spend Sunday in Boston at the Brunswick. Monday I shall go with them as far as the White Mountains on their way to Canada, and then about Wednesday come back on the Boston & Maine Railroad to Andover. How I wish you could put off your vacation till then, and go with us to the mountains, and have a leisure week at Andover after our return. Think of it and try and do so. Tell M. how delightful it will be if she can join us for the mountains. We need stay there but a day or two, visiting merely Crawford's and the Glen.

I have had a busy and delightful week. Saturday afternoon I went to Cambridge, getting there just in time for the boat races, which were very picturesque and pretty. After that came a supper at Professor Jebb's, with lots of dons and professors. Sunday I spent at the Vice-Chancellor's, Dr. Ferrers' at the Lodge in Caius College. At two o'clock I preached the university sermon in Great St. Mary's to a big and imposing congregation. It was the Tolerance lecture which you heard in Cambridge, and it went off very well. Monday I roamed about among the beautiful colleges, lunched with an undergraduate, who had a pleasant party, and went to a big dinner party at the Jebbs'. Tuesday morning I went to Oxford, a slow four hours' ride, took lunch at Dr. Jowett's with some great university folks, and then went to the public theatre, where we had our D. D. degrees conferred on us with queer ceremonies. I send you some papers which tell about it. The next day, Wednesday, was the great Commemoration Day, with the conferring of the D. C. L. degrees, and a college luncheon and a brilliant garden party in the afternoon. Then I came back to London, and last night went to a dinner given in honor of the Precentor of the Abbey. Tonight I dine with Mr. Bryce, whom you remember at our Matthew Arnold dinner of last winter. So it goes all the time; but after two weeks more it will be over. On the 3d of July we go on to the Continent, and life will be quieter, or at least it will have a different sort of bustle.

. . . I have not been anywhere, except in London and at the universities, during all this visit. The papers tell us it is very hot with you. Here it is cool and pleasant. The crisis and change of government of course keeps everything excited. Gladstone goes out with honor, having saved the world a war. My kind love to all.

Ever affectionately, P.

WESTMINSTER PALACE HOTEL, LONDON,
June 25, 1885.

DEAR MARY,— . . . I love to think of you all at North Andover, and to look forward to the time when I shall be with you. The plan of which I wrote last week has fallen through. Archdeacon Farrar and his friends have made up their minds that they must sail direct for Canada, and so I shall come alone in the Pavonia, and the White Mountain trip will not take place. I shall come to North Andover on Monday morning, the 14th of September, and stay there quietly as long as I can. Archdeacon Farrar's party will not reach Boston until the first of November.

Everything here has been delightful. People have been very kind, and invitations flow in in far greater numbers than I can accept. It has been very interesting to be here during the political crisis and see the English people change their government. Right in the thick of it I met Mr. Gladstone at dinner at Mr. Bryce's, and he was full of spirits and as merry as a boy. Our new minister, Mr. Phelps, was there, and Senator Edmunds, and it was very interesting to see the English and American statesmen meet.

I was invited by Lord Aberdeen to go to his country place and spend Sunday with Mr. Gladstone, but I had promised to preach here and could not go. I was very sorry, for it would have been a capital chance to see the great man familiarly.

I am just back from Lincoln, where I have spent the day and preached this afternoon in the magnificent cathedral. On Saturday I go to Salisbury to stay with the Dean, and preach in that cathedral on Sunday. Monday I come back to town, and dine on Tuesday with the Archbishop of Canterbury at Lambeth Palace. Wednesday I start off to meet the Paines, who have been absent for two weeks in Scotland, and we shall travel together somewhere for a week; then back to London and off together to the Continent, about the time you get this note.

We have had hardly any heat, and to-day is as cold as March, but the country is looking glorious, and the town is as gay as Marlborough Street in February.

What are you all doing? And how does the old house look with its green grass and yellow hitching-post? Is Tom still alive after his hard winter's experience? How I wish I could look in on you to-night. It is most midnight here, but you are just about finishing supper and sitting down to logomachy. I have not seen the blessed game since we played it in Clarendon Street the night before I left. You must thank Agnes and Susie for their last letters. The New York trip must have been a great event. Yesterday I thought about Commencement and wished I was there. I hope Arthur was with you. Good-night. . . .

Ever and ever affectionately, P.

TINTERN, July 2, 1885.

DEAR WILLIAM, — A happy new year to you, and a great many more of them for years to come. You have had a good time for the last fifty-one years, and I am sure you have helped other people (such as I) to have a great many good times all along. Now you are just in the prime of life, with ever so many happy years before you, and I congratulate you on both past and future, and send you the heartiest, happy new year across the water.

One week more is gone, and now that I have heard from you at North Andover, I feel as if I had really got hold of your summer. The children's letters from there made it seem very real and near. . . . The pony seems to be a principal character in the household, and I am rejoiced that Tom has recovered from the trials and humiliations of the winter.

. . . I spent last Sunday at Salisbury, where I had a delightful day and preached in the cathedral, which is now thoroughly restored, and looks a great deal better than it did when you and I saw it filled with scaffolding. I stayed with the Dean, and saw some very pleasant people. Then I came back to London, and had two more days there, and on Wednesday came off for this little western tour. When you get this the Channel will have been crossed and the jabber of foreign tongues will be about us. The weather is delightful and all goes charmingly. . . .

BONN, July 11, 1885.

DEAR GERTIE, — It is a very lovely morning on the Rhine. I am afraid that it will be hot by and by, when the steamboat comes along and we start to go up the river; but at present, before breakfast, it is very lovely. There is a pretty village with trees and a church tower just across the river, and the little boats keep coming and going, and the children on the bank, in front of the hotel, are playing like kittens, and everything is as bright and sunshiny as if there was n't such a thing as trouble in the world. Speaking of kittens, I wonder if you have found the little thing that used to hide away in the barn, and that the boy could n't catch for a quarter of a dollar. But perhaps she has grown to be a big cat, and is n't worth the catching now, which is the way with a good many people. When you want them you cannot get them, and when you get them you don't want them.

A man has just come and set up a stand in the square under my window to sell cherries, and the children are looking at them hard, and no doubt wishing that they had two cents. I would give them two dollars apiece all around if I could talk German as well as they can. And so we all want something which we have not got. I wonder what you want. If it 's anything in Europe, write a letter and tell me the name of it instantly, and I will get it for you. . . .

We left London on Thursday morning, and I shall not see it again till the 1st of August, when I shall go there to get my playthings together before I sail in the Pavonia on the 3d. I have had a very beautiful time there, but now I am glad to be traveling again and on my way to the great mountains. I wish you were with me and were here this morning. I would give you some cherries.

I long to see the pony. Next year I think we must have one of our own, or would you like a donkey better, for which G. B. advertised? We must consult Tood about it. My best of love to you all and to "Tom." Goodby. Your uncle, P.

SALZBURG, July 15, 1885.

DEAR WILLIAM, — When I reached here yesterday, I found a group of delightful letters from North Andover, which had the flavor of the old place about them. I think about you now as settled there, with the Jack-o'-lanterns burning on the garden wall. . . .

I have left England after a most delightful visit. It was full of interesting occurrences, and I shall look back upon it with the greatest pleasure. Now we are on our way southward, and after a drive through the Tyrol, we shall probably bring up for a few days in Venice; then back to Switzerland, where we shall have about three weeks. Seven weeks from this afternoon I shall be afloat, headed for Queenstown and Boston. All goes beautifully. The weather is delightful, and the scenery, pictures, and cathedrals are the same splendid things that they have been for the last twenty years and many years before. Tell G. to keep as right as she can till the 11th of September, and after that I will look after her; and thank S. for her account of the corn-barn banquet, which made my mouth water very much indeed.

. . . The programme for the Church Congress in the

autumn, which you inclosed in your letter, really made one believe that there was to be a new campaign begun by and by, but it seems very far off now. Still, I think we will not carry out our little plan of retiring from active life this autumn. Let us wait another year. . . .

Ever affectionately, P.

HOTEL DANIELI, VENICE,
July 24, 1885.

MY DEAR MARY, — . . . How pretty it must be with you this afternoon; not half as hot as Venice, I am sure. But every now and then a breeze comes floating from the water, and there are gondolas skimming by, the beautiful St. Giorgio rises opposite out of the sea, and the bells are lazily ringing for two o'clock, which is the time when the pigeons come to be fed in the Piazza of St. Mark. It is all very soft, and lazy, and beautiful, and the letter which I received the other day from Mr. Allen, about things at Trinity, sounded far away. . . .

I wish you could see it all. The Queen is here, and every evening the young prince comes out on the Grand Canal, and hosts of gondolas are there with lamps and lanterns. Every now and then a company of singers in a gondola goes floating by, the fine band plays in the Royal Gardens, the people shout, "Viva Regina Margherita" under the royal windows, the ices of the cafés are really most delicious, and San Marco looks down upon it all in the moonlight and seems to smile. In the mornings, there are great cool galleries full of glorious pictures, and quiet back streets where the people lounge in the doorways and chatter round the fountains. Oh, it is very delightful, and I wish with all my heart that you all were here, so I do. . . .

BELLAGIO, July 30, 1885.

MY DEAR GERTIE. — It is a beautiful warm morning on the lake of Como, so warm that one does not feel like doing anything but sitting still and writing a lazy letter to a dear little girl in America. The water, as I look out of the window, is a delicious blue, and the sweet green hills on the other side of the lake are sound asleep in the sunlight, which they like. There is a garden of palm-trees and oleanders right under my window, and the oleanders are all in gorgeous bloom. A boatman is waiting at the marble steps, in case any one wants his boat; but I think he hopes that nobody will want it, for it must be awfully hot rowing upon the lake. This afternoon, when it gets cooler, I shall change all this and start up to the mountains, and by to-morrow night I shall be at St. Moritz, among the glaciers and snow-banks. But wherever I am, I am thinking how very pleasant it must be in the old house, and what a good time we will have when I get back there six weeks from next Monday afternoon. We will not make any plans for excursions, but just stay quiet on the big piazza, and now and then, when we feel very energetic, make a long trip to the corn-barn. Everybody must come and see us; we will not go to see anybody. . . .

Your affectionate uncle,   P.

WENGERN-ALP, August 12, 1885.

DEAR WILLIAM, — . . . A letter from the Wengern-Alp must go to you, for the view which is before me as I write brings back most vividly the day we climbed from Grindenwald, and sat and looked at the white beauty for an hour before we scrambled down to Lauterbrunnen and went on our way to Thun. I came up the same way yesterday afternoon, on a better horse than I had the day I was with you, and reached here just in time to see the evening light. This morning the sunrise was delightful, and now, as I write, I can see the glorious Jungfrau with its splendid snow; and the avalanches keep thundering all the time, and sending up their clouds of icy dust. I wish you were here!

. . . What terribly hot days you must have had! One of the great discoveries of the future will be how to deal with the temperature of the world, and cool a whole city as you cool a refrigerator, or warm a continent as you warm a house.

It seems as if the Americans were at home this summer, for I have seen hardly any. Dr. Osgood and his family and Mrs. Copley Green and her children were at Lucerne, and I went to see them at the Englisher Hof, after service at that English church where we went, you remember, one Sunday in 1877. Three weeks from to-day I sail; then, in ten days, I shall see you all. Affectionately, P.

CHAMOUNIX, August 19, 1885.

DEAR GERTIE, — Mont Blanc has put his head under a cloud, and there is nothing to be seen outside except a lot of guides and porters waiting for the diligence to come from Geneva. So before the dinner bell rings, I will send off my week's letter, and it shall be to you. Tell Tood that the next week's, which will be the last that I shall write, shall be to her, for she has been a good little girl and written me beautiful letters all summer. So have you. I got your letter here last night with the picture of the bird house in the garden on the side of the paper. After you get this letter, remember that you are not to do a single thing exciting until I get home, so that you will be all fresh and strong to play with me. . . . Only two weeks from to-day! Just think of it! Two weeks from now the beautiful Pavonia will be steaming away down the Channel, bound for North Andover, and three weeks from next Sunday I shall stand up in Trinity again.

You cannot think how splendid the great mountain was last night. The sky was perfectly clear and the moon was glorious, and the big round dome of snow shone like another world. The people stood and gazed at it and looked solemn. This morning it had changed, but was no less beautiful. It was like a great mass of silver. And so it stands there and changes from one sort of beauty to another, year after year, and age after age.

I think you must have a beautiful time this summer with the pony, and next year we must try to have one of our own. Make up your mind what kind and color he shall be, and we will look about and see what we can find when I get home. It must be a great sight to see Tood driving all by her blessed self, and all the fast horses on the road getting out of the way for fear she will run over them. . . . Perhaps you and she can drive me out to Cambridge, mornings in November, in the pony-cart. I wonder if I shall go there this year, and whether you will go with me. Good-by now. Affectionately, your uncle, P.

GRAND HÔTEL, PARIS, August 27, 1885.

MY DEAR TOOD, — It really begins to look as if I were actually coming home, for you see the Pavonia arrived yesterday at Liverpool, and she will stay there until next Wednesday, and then she expects me to go back in her. It seems very likely, therefore, that two weeks from day after to-morrow, I shall come ashore in Boston; then I shall see you and have the chance to thank you for all your pleasant letters, which it has been a very great delight to get, and which have very much relieved the weariness and troubles of my journey. I think that you are one of the very best letter writers for your time of life that I know, and when you drop into poetry it is beautiful. So I will thank you when I get home, and we will sit in the shadow of the corn-barn and talk it all over.

Paris is very bright and gay and pretty. Yesterday I went out to the Jardin d'Acclimatation (say that if you can), and the monkeys were awfully funny. How would it do to get three monkeys for North Andover, and tie them to a post in the side yard and see them play and fight? How would Tom like it? And do you think it would please Johnny, or would he only think they were some more Brooks children? I am afraid you have not seen much of Johnny this year. That is not wise. For he is a very brilliant little boy, and it would be a great advantage to you and A. if you talked with him. . . .

Your affectionate uncle, P.

ACROSS THE CONTINENT TO SAN FRANCISCO.

1886.

VICTORIA HOTEL, ALAMOSA, COLORADO,
May 6, 1886.

DEAR WILLIAM, — This is the first letter of the great journey, written in the midst of the tumult of Raymond tourists and cow-boys, who fill the office of this beautiful hotel, while we are waiting for our dinner. We are on the crest of the continent, a good six thousand feet above the sea, with Pike's Peak and a host of other snow-peaked giants of the Rocky Mountains in full view, and the queerest shanty-town to stay in that you ever saw. But what a day it is! Such atmosphere, sunshine, and great outlooks in every direction! To-day we have been up to the Toltec Gorge, riding through endless plains of sage grass, with queer little prairie dogs sitting, each of them, on the edge of his hole to see us pass. The Gorge is very fine and picturesque, not up to Switzerland, but with a bigger feeling about it, and altogether mighty good to look at.

. . . . A very pleasant journey brought me to Chicago Saturday night in the director's car, with the Baker party, who were pleasant people. Sunday I heard Professor Swing in the morning, Osborn in the afternoon, and a man whose name I have forgotten in the evening. I wonder how things went at Trinity?

Then came the ride to Kansas City, crossing the big

Mississippi at Rock Island and Davenport. Then there was the very beautiful ride across Kansas, and here we are in Colorado, with New Mexico close by. All has gone well. The excursion plan works nicely. The company is pleasant. The days are long and idle. There is a great deal to see, and impressions crowd fast and thick. On the whole it is a good success so far, and better things are promising ahead. It is not Europe, but it is big America, and one is feeling its bigness more and more every day. . . .

We must be all in the best condition for Andover by and by. I am looking forward to that.

Affectionately, P.

PALACE HOTEL, SANTA FÉ, May 9, 1886.

DEAR GERTIE, — It is very hot here, and the sun is shining down upon my window dreadfully. But the things one sees out of the window are very queer and interesting. The houses are built of mud, and almost all of them only one story high. Indians and Mexicans, in bright red and white blankets, walk down the street. Funny little donkeys are wandering about, with small children riding on their backs and kicking them with their small naked heels. There are some barracks across the street with a flag flying, and a few soldiers lounging in the shade. Up the street there is a great cathedral, whose bells are ringing for some service. We are over seven thousand feet above the sea, and the air is so dry that you are always thirsty and cannot get enough ice water.

How I should love to take a Back Bay car and come down to one of those lovely five o'clock teas, and drink, and drink, and drink lemonade for three quarters of an hour. . . .

To-morrow we start across the Desert to California, and when you get this I shall be at Los Angeles, which everybody says is just as beautiful as Paradise. How I wish you would take a swift car and join me there. We would eat oranges, and figs, and grapes, and apricots, and all the good things that make your mouth water when you think of them.

. . . I wonder how far your letter to me has got. About to Kansas City, I should think. Give my best love to everybody, and be sure I am your

Affectionate uncle, P.

SIERRA MADRE VILLA, NEAR LOS ANGELES, CALIFORNIA,
May 14, 1886.

MY DEAR WILLIAM, — I wish you could see how beautiful this place is. It is not exactly like anything I ever saw before, though there is something of Italy, and something of India, and something of Syria about it. It is a world of vines and oranges, with palm-trees here and there, the high hills and a few white peaks of the Sierra Nevada standing up behind. The flowers are gorgeous; masses of roses and hedges of calla lilies all in bloom, honeysuckles and heliotropes growing up like the sides of houses. It is as good a fairy-land as one can find anywhere in this poor world.

The way here over the Desert was dreary enough, but very picturesque and striking, and the descent of the long Pacific slope was very beautiful, with countless flowers and all sorts of strange shapes of hill and valley.

The great continent is crossed, and though we have not yet seen the Pacific, we are within a few miles of it, and shall get sight of it to-morrow when we go to Santa Monica, which is directly on the coast. The journey has gone bravely on, with no mishap. The "excursion" part of it is a decided success. It has reminded me always of an ocean voyage. The excursionists are like your fellow-passengers, — you get familiar with their faces, and learn to greet them in the morning. With a few of them you become acquainted, but you are under no responsibility regarding them, and make your own companionships just as you please. The comfort of it is delightful. There are no plans to make, no money to pay out, and no time-tables to be studied. Nothing but a little book to go by, and a man to tell you what to do. By all means, when you come to California be a Raymond Excursionist. . . .

YOSEMITE VALLEY, May 20, 1886.

MY DEAR MARY, — There never were such precipices and waterfalls, and so I am going to write you a letter. You see, it takes a two days' drive to get here; the roads are terribly rough, and when you come suddenly to Inspiration Point and look down into this glorious place, ringing with cataracts that come tumbling over the brink, and with a plunge of ten Niagaras burst into clouds of spray, it is like looking into a big green heaven inclosed with the most stupendous cliffs, so that the blessed cannot get out, nor the wicked get in. After you get here it is very wonderful. One cannot describe it any more than one can paint it. There is nothing like it in the world, and if it were not so many thousand miles away, we would come here from North Andover once every summer. But it is a marvel that one can only get once in a lifetime. You can see a bit of a picture of it in the corner.

I am writing this beautiful letter at the right-hand

side of the piazza, where the mosquitoes are very troublesome. To-day I have ridden an unfortunate horse up a four-mile hill, and seen another world of waterfalls and hills. I will describe them to you when I get home. The whole journey has been very funny and pleasant. There are people and places all along the road, at Chicago, Kansas City, Alamosa, Santa Fé, and Los Angeles, which I never shall forget. If you could only see the place where we spent last Sunday! The oranges made the whole landscape glow, and the roses and heliotropes made it fragrant. Tomorrow I start for San Francisco. Think of us on Sunday after next, May 30, at Monterey, and probably the first Sunday in June at Portland, Oregon. Have you heard they have chosen me Assistant Bishop of Pennsylvania? . . . Would it not be strange to go there again and end my ministry where I began it? But then it would interfere with our plan of retiring to North Andover in a few years, which is what I am most longing for and looking forward to in life. . . .

Just now a carriage-load of Raymond people, fellow-travelers of ours, went by. You have no idea how friendly and familiar we are with them all. There are men of letters and men of business, and women of all sorts and kinds. Some of them talk good English, some talk bad, and some talk what can hardly be called English at all. Some of them grumble, some of them smile, and some of them look too stupid to do either. The way they make up to each other, and have grown to be like brothers and sisters, is delightful. They are more or less scattered now, but they will come together again at the Palace Hotel at San Francisco on Saturday night, and then until we go, some of us, to Oregon, the company will see much of one another.

There is the queerest primitiveness of life in this blessed valley. Your landlord talks to you like a brother. He asked me just now if I was the father of a Mr. Brooks who was here ten years ago. . . . Then he appealed to us this morning to be prompt at breakfast, because his wife had been working over the stove ever since three o'clock (when the first stage went off), and was almost dead. So one finds himself part of the family, and the cares of the house are his. Yet, if it were Boston, I would leave it and come to Marlborough Street and get some lemonade. I wonder what you all are doing and how you are.

. . . Here comes another stage with a tired-looking party of Raymondites, who have been to see the afternoon rainbow on the Bridal Veil. Then a wild Mexican galloping by on his mustang, to show off before us who sit on the piazza. It is all very nice, but by and by it will be over and then

I hope you will be glad to see
Your very loving brother, P.

PALACE HOTEL, SAN FRANCISCO, CALIFORNIA,
May 27, 1886.

MY DEAR GERTIE, — What a good time we shall have this summer! . . . I will tell you all about the Pacific Ocean, and how fine it is to stand on the rocks and look way off to China. There is a great deal of China here. The other night I went to a Chinese theatre, and the way they howled, and grinned, and cut up on the stage was something wonderful. Their play goes on for a month, being taken up each evening where they happened to leave off the night before, so you hit it at one point, and it is very hard to make out what the story is. Besides, it is in

Chinese. There is no scenery, and the spectators (those that pay half a dollar) sit right on the stage and go through the dressing-room. The quarter of a dollar people sit in front of the stage, just as our audiences do. It was very confused, picturesque, and funny. Next week I am going up to Oregon, and shall be somewhere there when you get this letter. I wonder what that country is like. It always sounds as if people went about in furs and talked Ojibway to each other, but I dare say they do not. However, I shall see next week, and then can tell you. We shall sail through the Golden Gate, and have a lovely voyage up the coast to Portland, in a beautiful steamer. How I wish you would come, too. . . .

HOTEL DEL MONTE, MONTEREY, CALIFORNIA,
June 1, 1886.

I have written from such various places the last month, I fear my letters have been rather irregular in reaching you. I have written to somebody at your house every week. I have heard also most irregularly from you, but I have had several letters from yourself, and your father and mother, for all of which I am very thankful. They have been very good to get. . . . I am longing now to be quietly settled at the old place. Not that this trip is not delightful. Everything has gone perfectly, and much of the best is yet to come. We are spending a few days at this beautiful place, and to-morrow go back to San Francisco, stopping on the way to see the Floods at their famous palatial place at Menlo Park. I have already had five days at San Francisco, which were very interesting. . . .

Thursday I go alone by steamer to Portland, Oregon, and shall rejoin the party ten days later at Salt

Lake. The sea, on which we spend forty-eight hours, is a terror to most of the people, but I expect to enjoy it very much, and shall be glad to get sight of Puget's Sound and Vancouver's Island. The June days there will be delightful. Oh, if you could only be with me. . . . My next great delight is being with you all at Andover. My best love to everybody.

Affectionately, P.

     VICTORIA, VANCOUVER'S ISLAND, PUGET SOUND,
           June 8, 1886.

MY DEAR MARY, — I hope this Puget Sound sounds as far from Boston to you as it does to me. It has taken a long time to get here, and is my farthest point from home upon this journey. From this afternoon every step is homeward. Already the boat is lying at the wharf and I am writing in the cabin, while there is a racket going on, of the men who are bringing freight on board, and in a few minutes we shall sail for Tacoma and Portland. Lunch is ready on the table, or at least the preparations for lunch, but we must not have any until the steamer gets away. And I am very hungry, for I have been on a long drive over the country for the last three hours, trying to find out what this bit of Her Majesty's dominions may be like.

 I wish you and G. had been with me, for the drive was beautiful, and led to a dry dock at a queer little village, where one of the Queen's men-of-war was lying, looking very picturesque. The town itself is a big rambling place, with a pretty park outside, which they call Beacon Hill, just as if it were in Boston.

 The streets have queer folks, Indians and Chinamen, strolling about, which makes them interesting. There was a curious little Chinese girl, with a long pigtail, who came with us in this boat in charge of an officer who was taking her back to Victoria. She had been stolen from China, brought out to British America, thence smuggled to our dominions, and there a China man had made her marry him, and he was going to sell her again in San Francisco, when the law came to her rescue, and she was going back in great glee, leaving her husband behind her. She was not far from being pretty, and was certainly a very cunning-looking little thing, only fifteen years old, with flowers in her hand and the most comical and clumsy dress you ever saw. We left her at Victoria, and there seems now to be nobody of any interest (here the boat started which accounts for the joggling) except a horrid little boy, who looks out of the window and asks silly questions, for which his mother scolds him. His questions are very silly, but she need not scold him so, for he evidently gets his silliness by direct inheritance from her. I had a beautiful luncheon, rice, salmon, lamb chops, baked beans, and cherry-pie. There is nobody on the boat that I know. Coming up, there was a man from Jamaica Plain, but he left at Seattle, and I saw him no more.

The Sound is very beautiful, with its woody shores and snowy peaks beyond. Mt. Baker at this end and Mt. Tacoma at the other are majestic creatures, quite worthy to keep company with the Alps or Himalayas. I hate to turn back and leave Alaska unseen. That must be gorgeous, and it is so easy to go there from here! . . .

When I get back I will go to town Sundays, and the long weeks between, we will spend in the old house and have a lovely time.

I hope that you are all well and happy as I am, and as anxious to see me as I am to see you.
Ever affectionately, P.

MANITOU SPRINGS, COLORADO,
June 17, 1886.

MY DEAR AGNES, — You wrote me such a very nice and interesting letter, which I received the other day when I was among the Mormons, that I must acknowledge it by sending this week's letter to you. It is my only chance, for before next week's letter is written I shall be rushing across Kansas and Missouri on the way home, and should overtake my letter if I wrote one. So this shall be the last. . . .

I wish I could look in upon you at North Andover this morning, though this place is very pretty, the top of Pike's Peak very high, and the waterfalls are very noisy; so are the visitors, for it is a real summer place, like a White Mountain hotel. It would be pleasant, instead of breakfasting in a few minutes in the room next to this, to come into your dining-room and eat a great deal better breakfast than we shall get here. Well, it will come in two weeks.

I shall get to Boston Saturday morning. Then I must spend Sunday there. I have a meeting to which I shall go on Monday evening, so I may not get to Andover till Tuesday, and must come down again for Commencement on Wednesday and Thursday. That week will be a good deal broken up; but after that is over, I shall live at the old house all the time.

This is Bunker Hill day, is n't it? Little those people knew about Pike's Peak and Salt Lake City!

You must give my love to everybody, and some day write another letter to your
    Affectionate uncle,   PHILLIPS.

DENVER, June 20, 1886.

DEAR TOOD, — When I got here last night, I found the hotel man very much excited and running about waving a beautiful letter in the air, and crying aloud, "A letter from Tood! A letter from Tood!" He was just going to get out a band of music to march around the town and look for the man to whom the letter belonged, when I stepped up and told him I thought that it was meant for me. He made me show him my name in my hat before he would give it to me, and then a great crowd gathered round and listened while I read it. It was such a beautiful letter that they all gave three cheers, and I thought I must write you an answer at once, although I told A., when I wrote to her the other day, that I should not write to anybody else before my coming home.

Your letter is very largely about Johnny. My dear Tood, you must not let his going away depress you too much. I know you like him, and that he has been very good to you; but such separations have to come, and you will no doubt see some other young man some day that you will like just as much. You do not think so now, but you will, and he no doubt feels very bad at going, so you must be as cheerful as you can and make it as easy as possible for him. Remember!

I am on my way home now, and next Saturday will see me back again in Clarendon Street. All the dear little Chinese, with their pigtails, and the dreadful great Mormons, with their hundred wives, and the donkeys and the buffaloes and the Red Indians will be far away, and I shall see you all again. I am impatient for that, for the people out West are not as good as you are. I am going to preach to them this morning, to try and make them better, and it is quite time now to go to church. . . .

     Your affectionate uncle,   P.

A SUMMER IN JAPAN.

1889.

WALKER HOTEL, SALT LAKE CITY,
June 18, 1889.

DEAR WILLIAM, — This is the first letter of the great new series. It will not amount to much, but will let you know that we have come thus far without accident, discomfort, or delay, and are spending Sunday among the Mormons. The day is bright and warm, and we shall sit with content this afternoon in the great Tabernacle, and see the queer people go through their queer worship. In the cool of the evening we shall leave for Ogden, and sleep in the hurrying car which carries us to San Francisco, where we shall arrive at noon on Wednesday.

Everything here looks just as it did three years ago. The great Temple has grown, but is many years from its completion, and the Mormons and Gentiles who fill the streets are the same lank and loungy crowd. I do not want to live here, and do not see any danger that I shall have to. . . . We saw the mighty scenery of the Denver and Rio Grande, gazed at Pike's Peak, rushed through the Grand Cañon of the Arkansas, and reached here in time for a drive and a bed last night. . . . The heat has not been troublesome, and Japan does not seem to have such a sultry climate, after all. . . .

All begins well. May everything go well with you

until we meet again. My love to all, and tell them I am in North Andover in heart to-day.

PALACE HOTEL, SAN FRANCISCO,
June 20, 1889.

DEAR WILLIAM, — At last the great day has come, and we sail this afternoon in the City of Sidney. We have been to see her, and find she is a fine big vessel of three thousand five hundred tons, with large state-rooms on the upper deck, of which we have one apiece. There is only one other passenger besides us. We have not seen him yet, but he is said to be a Russian, and is the United States Commissioner for Alaska. We shall know him well before we get to Yokohama. The captain, first officer, and steward seem to be good fellows, and there is every prospect of a pleasant voyage. Everybody says that it is cool and smooth, and I do not think we shall find it too long. We have laid in some books, and there are big decks for walkee-walkee when we feel the need of exercise.

We shall hope to sail back by the City of Rio de Janeiro, leaving Yokohama on the 21st of August, due in San Francisco about the 5th of September. I hope this will bring me back to Massachusetts in time to get two solid quiet weeks at North Andover before the time to go to New York for General Convention. That will be good, will it not? . . . Thanks for your letter and your telegram. How often I shall think of you on the long voyage. My kindest love to all of you, and may we be taken care of until we meet in September. Farewell, farewell!

Affectionately, P.

STEAMSHIP CITY OF SIDNEY. 357

STEAMSHIP CITY OF SIDNEY,
July 8, 1889.

MY DEAR GERTIE, — You shall have the first letter from the other side of the world. We have crossed the Pacific and are within a hundred miles of Yokohama. We shall arrive at midnight, and to-morrow a steamer leaves there for San Francisco, which will carry homewards this letter. It is our eighteenth day at sea, and we are more than seven thousand miles from North Andover, — think of that!

It has been a good voyage, though the weather has not been bright. It has been cold and rainy till yesterday, but there has been no storm and not much rough weather. To-day is loveliness itself, but we are still wearing thick clothes, and the big ulster has done service most of the voyage. There has been almost no sitting on deck. We have read a great many novels, and looked for the sunlight, which we have hardly seen.

Besides Dr. McVickar and me, there have been two passengers and a half. First, a queer old Russian gentleman, bound for Kamchatka and the islands where the seals are found; a strange old creature, who has been all over creation, and seen everything and everybody, and is quite interesting. Besides him, there is a missionary lady and her baby, going back to Japan, but she has kept her stateroom most all the way, and we have hardly seen her. So we three men, with the ship's officers, have had the great steamer to ourselves. She is not like the Adriatic or Germanic, but she is a fine large ship and very comfortable. Plenty of room, plenty to eat, and everybody well all the time.

. . . The Kodak came out this morning for the first

time, and took the ship and the captain. There has been no sun for it before. . . .

Think of us seeing Fujiyama to-morrow.

Your affectionate uncle, P.

Tokyo, July 14, 1889.

ARTHUR DEAR, — Shall I tell you what Japan looks like to one on the sixth day after his arrival? I could not begin to do it if I tried, but of all bright, merry, pretty places, it is the prettiest and brightest, and if ever life anywhere is a frolic and a joke, it must be here. I do not think there can be a grim spot in all the happy islands. It is all so different from India. If India is a perpetual dream, sometimes deepening into a nightmare, Japan is a perpetual spectacle, now and then blazing into a mild orgie. I do not think there can be a place anywhere in the world more suitable for pure relaxation. It is just the country for a summer vacation, and the getting here is delightful.

After we left you that morning in New York, five weeks ago next Tuesday, we had a prosperous journey across the continent; and after two days in San Francisco, sailed across the Pacific, a long, wet, placid voyage of eighteen days, and landed at Yokohama with minds well emptied, rested, and ready for whatever might be poured in. The people looked so glad to see us. The jinrikisha men did not quarrel with our bulk; the foreign residents were kind and hospitable. In Yokohama I dined with a classmate of yours, John Lindsley by name, who is the agent of the Canadian Pacific, and has a beautiful house and pretty wife. Yesterday we came on hither, where to-day, in addition to thousands of heathen, I have seen Bishop Williams and many of the missionary people and arrangements of our church. It all looks very well, and the best of the foreigners tell good stories about missionary life and influence.

So Japan is a true success as the field for a summer journey. The weather so far is delightful, and the great Buddha at Kamakura is wonderful indeed.

I hope your summer is going delightfully. I am sure it is. My best love to Lizzie. . . .

Affectionately, P.

TOKYO, July 14, 1889.

DEAR WILLIAM, — This is the sixth day in Japan, and all goes wonderfully well. In a few days the steamer starts for San Francisco, and a word of greeting shall go in her to tell you that we landed safely from the City of Sidney last Tuesday morning, and since then have lived in Yokohama until yesterday.

We came here, and are now in the very heart of Japanese history and life. It is very fascinating. The brightest, merriest, kindest, and most graceful people, who seem as glad to see you as if they had been waiting for you all these years, smile upon you in the streets, and make you feel as if their houses were yours the moment you cross the threshold. They drag you round in their absurd jinrikishas as if it were a jolly joke, and are sitting now by the score along the road outside the window in all degrees of undress and all the colors of the rainbow, chattering away, making pretty gestures, as if good manners and civility were the only ends of life. I never saw anything like it, and the fascination grows with every new street picture that one sees.

The weather is delightful: mornings and evenings

are very cool and pleasant; the noonday is hot, but not too hot to go about; and every now and then tremendous downfalls of rain. Wednesday it rained as I hardly ever saw it rain before, and you would have laughed to see our experiences on Thursday, when we went into the country to see the great bronze Buddha, sixty feet high, who has sat for six hundred years in a great grove of pine-trees twenty miles from Yokohama. The railroad had been swept away by the rain, and we had to take to jinrikishas. The road was overflowed, and we had to get into boats and be ferried over the submerged rice-fields. Finally, I found myself on a coolie's back, being carried over a little torrent, which the jinrikisha could not cross. The coolie never will forget it any more than I shall; but we saw the Daibatzu, which is the gigantic Buddha's name. And I snapped the Kodak into his very face.

We have had most hospitable welcome from American and English people; almost every night in Yokohama we dined out, and here we have been given rooms at the club, which is a Government affair and most comfortable. To-morrow night we are to dine with the English Bishop of Japan, and there is more of courtesy and kindness than we can accept.

We shall have warmer weather, for everybody says the summer has not fairly begun. It will not be excessive. Indeed, the whole climate is not unlike the summer climate of New York.

To-day we have been looking a little at our foreign missionary work, and find it a very real thing, full of interest and promise.

Five weeks ago to-night I spent the evening in Marlborough Street. If you meet Dr. George Ellis, as we did that evening on Commonwealth Avenue, tell him

Japan is a great success; and with all love to M. and the children, be sure that I am

Affectionately, P.

NIKKO, July 21, 1889.

MY DEAR MARY, — You remember the Japanese have a proverb which declares that "he who has not seen Nikko has no right to say Kekko." Kekko means beautiful. You may have seen Keswick, Heidelberg, Venice, Boston, North Andover, and Hingham, but if you have not seen Nikko, the Jap does not believe you know what beauty is. I do not think he is quite right, but Nikko is certainly very beautiful.

We came up here from Tokyo on Friday, with three hours of railroad, to Utsunomiya, and then six hours of jolting over the worst of roads, all washed with recent rains, with long stops to rest the wretched horses at queer tea houses by the way. A most beautiful avenue of stately trees extends along the whole route, and we came into the sacred valley far up among the hills. Here are the most splendid temples in Japan. They are the great shrines of the heroes of the proud days of Japanese history. Their solemn bells are always sounding, and the richness of their decoration, the mystery of their vast courtyards, and the strange figures of their priests are most impressive. In Tokyo there is much of new Japan. We saw the university, the missionary operations, and the electric lights. Here it is all mediæval, and the works of man are as venerable as the hills. It is intensely interesting.

The jinrikisha men finally rebelled at Utsunomiya, and would not bring us over the washed and gullied road. One could not blame them, but it was inconvenient, for we had to take the roughest of carriages, and the horses would not have been allowed to be harnessed by any society for the prevention of cruelty to beasts.

Our traveling for these ten days in Japan has been a beautiful frolic. We have a capital guide and servant, a merry little fellow named Hakodate, who talks queer English, does everything that one mortal man can do for two others under his charge, and makes us very comfortable. He is the best guide, I suppose, in the country, has traveled with all sorts of distinguished people, and is perpetually proud of the size of the party at present in his care. If you come across a little French book called "Notes d'un Globe-Trotter," by a Mr. Daudiffret, you will find much about Hakodate under the name of Tatzu. Tatzu is his real name, but for some unknown reason he goes under the name of the town in the north of Japan from which he comes. That same French book is a very amusing account of much of what we are seeing every day in this delightful land.

. . . This Sunday morning is Sunday evening with you. I am just going to preach at a service in one of the houses here. You are sitting on the piazza. I wish I could spend the evening with you, and yet these hills are lovely, and so far the climate has been perfect. There has been no excessive heat. Now and then a bit of an earthquake, they say, but they are so little that there is no excitement.

It seems as if there were all pleasant things, until we meet in mid-September. Till then may we all be safe and well. My love to all.

Affectionately,   P.

NIKKO. 363

NIKKO, JAPAN, July 22, 1889.

DEAR JOHNNIE, — I wonder if it rains this morning at Marion as it rains at Nikko. The bells of the Buddhist temples sound through the thick mist, and the mountains hide themselves under the clouds, and we can see nothing of what everybody says is the most beautiful place in Japan. Before it clears I will talkee-talkee a little with you. After I left you, Hattie, Dodo, and baby at Springfield, I reached New York safely, and the next morning the great trip really began. We went on, and on, and at last, on the morning of the 8th of July, set foot on the land of the Rising Sun at Yokohama. The little Japs were very glad to see us. They brought their little jinrikishas down to the wharf, and pulled us through their little streets, past their little houses, to the big hotel. Ever since that they have been as good, civil, and delightful as possible. They are the merriest folk alive. Everybody smiles all the time. They smile when you speak to them and when you do not, when you stop and when you pass by, when they understand you and when they do not. They meet you with a smile at the steps of their little toy tea houses, and though they expect you to take off your shoes and enter in your stocking feet, that you may not hurt their pretty mats, and you have to sit upon the floor in most uncomfortable attitudes, still they are so glad to see you, and hand you the chopsticks, with which you are to eat your rice, in such a winning way, that you would not offend one of their inconvenient little prejudices for all the world.

The missionaries are good people and are doing excellent work. We spent one Sunday in Tokyo, and saw Bishop Williams and the mission buildings and one of the girls' schools. Most of the schools are in vacation for the summer, and many of the missionaries are here in this mountain place of cool resort. We held service yesterday in the house of one of them, which belongs to a Buddhist priest, and has the temple itself in the side yard. The priest looked at us as we went to church, but did not come into our meeting. If he had, he might have heard me preach in the morning and McVickar in the afternoon. Here, also, is your classmate Sturgis Bigelow, who with Mr. Fenollosa of '74, and Mrs. Fenollosa, has been living in Japan for years. They know the whole thing thoroughly, and since I began this beautiful letter (about the middle of the third page) we went with them and spent three hours in the Shinto temple of the great Iyeasu which is the most beautiful thing you ever saw. We are going to dine with them to-night.

About the time you get this, the 21st of August, we shall sail from Yokohama for San Francisco in the City of Rio de Janeiro, and about the middle of September I shall be in North Andover. Come and see me there, and tell me about your summer, and I will tell you all about mine, which is as jolly and queer as anything.

My love to the babies and Hattie.

Ever affectionately, P.

MYANOSHITA, JAPAN, July 28, 1889.

DEAR WILLIAM, — I will put into this letter a photograph of this pretty place, where we are spending a delightful Sunday. It is far up among the hills, and is Swiss-looking in its general mountain aspect. Thursday we left Nikko, after five days among its marvels, only made less perfect than they might have been by rather too much rain. But they were full of interest. Then we came back over a horrible road to Utsonomiya and by rail to Yokohama. Friday we took rail to Odza, then carriage and jinrikisha to this place. Yesterday we went to Hakoni lake and saw most finely Fujiyama, the great mountain of Japan.

The whole way was full of interest, through villages, past temples, and by one mighty Buddha carved out of solid rock, sitting by the roadside. To-morrow we go to Nagaia, then to Kioto, Nara, Osaka, Kobe, and by the Inland Sea to Nagasaki, whence we return to Yokohama to take the City of Rio home the 21st of August. She brought to us this week your letters of the 2d of July. . . . All this list of places can give you no idea of the perpetual interest of this strange land. The Kodak keeps snapping all the time, and I hope is getting some pictures which will be interesting. Every person in the street, every group upon the country road, every shop, and house, and tea house, and temple is as queer or beautiful as possible, and the people are delighted when you tell them to stand out in the sunshine to have their portraits taken.

Hakodate proves a jewel of a guide, and while he looks out ludicrously for his own comfort, is very careful also for ours, and orders the good native Japanese about as if he were a prince. We have not suffered from the heat more than we should have done on an ordinary White Mountain journey, and though the hottest part is yet to come, I have no fear that it will be excessive. The rains have bothered us a little, but on the other hand have kept the country very fresh and green, and the luxuriance is something wonderful. Rice fields are sheets of emerald and the bamboo groves are like fairy temples. The lotus is breaking into flower, and the low swamps are gorgeous with its great leaves and splendid flowers. Just now the talk is of the new Constitution of Japan, which goes into operation next winter, and will make the country as modern in its government as the United States itself. What will become of the Buddhist temples and the picturesque dresses, nobody can tell. Already young Japan affects skepticism and trousers, but the missionaries will have to set all that right. They are doing good work and have the respect of all true men here.

So much for Japan, though one might write about it forever. My thoughts run all the time to North Andover. You are about going to bed as we sit here writing and waiting for tiffin, which is served about one o'clock. I hope there is as cool a breeze blowing across the piazza as that which blows through this open hall, but I am sure that no such little Japanese waiting-maid, in kimono and obi, sits squatting on her bare heels in the corner. North Andover is best in the long run. My loveliest love to all.

Affectionately, P.

KOBE, JAPAN, August 7, 1889.

DEAR WILLIAM,—We are here at Kobe after a most delightful journey from Myanoshita, from which place I wrote you last. The prettiest thing about it was the visit to Nara, the old, old capital of Japan, and the seat of its most venerable worship. We left Kioto after dinner and traveled at night to avoid the heat, which was pretty terrible that day. We had three jinrikishas, one for each of us, and one for Hakodate, also one which went ahead with the luggage. Each of our jinrikishas had three men, one in the shafts and two pulling ahead. We left at seven o'clock, and reached Nara at one in the morning, thirty-three miles in six hours. The cheerful little men went on a steady trot most all the way, and seemed as merry as crickets when we arrived. Three times we stopped at teahouses and stuffed them full of rice, and then trotted off again into the night. It was bright moonlight the first half of the way, and the stars were splendid when the moon went down. We ambled along through rice fields and tea plantations, with villages strung along the road and people coming out to look at us all night.

At Nara, the hospitable people of the Japanese hotel were looking for us, and soon after our arrival we were sound asleep. Here we spent two days, in a perfect wilderness of splendid scenery, historical association, temple architecture, and curious life. There are tame sacred deer in the groves, and tame sacred fishes in the lakes. The trees are hundreds of years old, and the temples are older. And the beauty of the landscape is a perpetual delight. Here we spent Sunday. We went to a little missionary chapel of our church and heard our service in Japanese, and an excellent sermon in the same language by a native layman.

The white missionary in charge was off on his summer vacation, like the Rector of Trinity Church, Boston. After service, we sat in a tea house overlooking the lake, where it was cool. In the afternoon we strayed in the great temple groves and saw the priests at their curious worship; all night the drums were beating and picturesque heathenism going on in its remarkable way. Next morning early we left for Osaka, stopping to visit a most remarkable Buddhist monastery on the way. After one brilliant day at

Osaka, we came here, and to-morrow leave by steamer for Nagasaki, which will take us through the beautiful inland sea, one of the chief glories of Japan. That will be the extreme limit of our traveling.

From Nagasaki we come back to Kobe; then by sea to Yokohama, and after a few excursions from that familiar place, we shall be ready for the City of Rio two weeks from to-day. After that you know what will become of me until I present myself at the side door in North Andover. The Kodak is full. I cannot find anybody wise enough to change the old plates for the new, I cannot make the back come out to do it for myself, so I shall bring it home as it is; perhaps some of the hundred snaps which I have made may have caught something interesting, which the man in Bromfield Street can bring out.

It is hot, beautiful weather, no hotter, I should say, than we often have in Boston, and only slightly, for the most part, letting up at night. We are quite well, and the weather does not hinder our doing all we wish to do; the country is in beautiful condition, and the half-naked folks are brown as berries. And you are all well, I most devoutly hope. Letters will come to-day, but they will not bring advices very late. My love of loves to all of you.

Affectionately, P.

KIOGO HOTEL, KOBE, August 9, 1889.

DEAR TOOD, — The mail came this morning, and brought me beautiful letters from your father, mother, and *you*. Before we start for Nagasaki, in the beautiful steamer Tokyo-Maru, there is just time to write a beautiful line to you, and send these beautiful pictures which have just come in from a beautiful photographer's shop at the corner of the street. Mr. McVickar sends his love to you with this, and so does Hakodate, who sits in his native fashion on the floor at Dr. McVickar's feet. He is a good, wise man, and when you come to Japan you must have him for your guide.

I am glad you are having such a good time at North Andover. Look out for me there soon after you get this. My loveliest love to all.

Your loving uncle, P.

STEAMSHIP WAKAMOMA-MARU,
August 13, 1889.

DEAR GERTIE, — The Parthia sails this week for Vancouver, so there seems to be one more chance to send a letter from Japan before we leave, and it shall go to you. We are sailing along the southern coast, between Kobe and Yokohama, with the pretty, hilly shore in clear sight. We should see Fujiyama itself if it were not quite so hazy. This afternoon we shall be in Yokohama, then we shall probably go off into the country to Kamakara and Enoshima, and a few other pretty places, for the one short week that remains before the "Rio" comes along to carry us away from this delightful land.

Since I wrote the other day, we have been from Kobe to Nagasaki and back, sailing twice through the Inland Sea. It was very lovely, almost as pretty as Lake George itself. The days were warm and breezy, the nights had glorious moonlight, and I only wished you were all here to see the pretty sights. Queer junks were lounging on the water about us, and funny little villages were on the shore, and curious Japanese people went pattering about the steamer's deck. None of them were as nice or well dressed as the little girl I send you, seated between her cherry-trees, but they were her poorer sisters, and she will give you some idea of what looking folk they are. I am quite sure I have seen her a dozen times, as I have gone in and out of their ridiculous little houses.

And so this fun is almost over! In three weeks we shall be in San Francisco. . . . It will be hard to realize that this life, which we have been seeing so constantly for these five weeks, will be still going on. The priests praying in the temples, the girls chattering over their tea, the jinrikishas running round the streets, the jugglers performing in their booths, the missionaries preaching in their churches, the merchants squatting in their shops, the women toddling with their babies, the boys swimming in the streams, and everybody as merry and good-natured as in a world of dolls. It will be quite as good to remember as it has been to see.

When you get this, begin to look out for our arrival at the Golden Gate, and have the corn barn ready for a pleasant little smoke soon after. My best of love to everybody. How pretty the piazza at North Andover must look this pleasant morning! Good-by, dear Gertie. Your affectionate uncle, P.

STEAMSHIP CITY OF RIO DE JANEIRO,
August 28, 1889.

DEAR ARTHUR, — Japan is far behind us. We are almost halfway across the Pacific Ocean. McVickar is on deck talking to some English people, and I remembered the letter which I was very glad to get from you just before I left Yokohama last week. I want to answer it, first to thank you for it, and then to say how sorry I am that I must not allow myself to think of accepting your kind invitation to visit Minnequa on my way across the continent. It would be a very pleasant thing to do, but I shall not much more than get home to Boston for Sunday, the 22d of September, and I have promised myself to preach there on that day. Then I shall have one quiet week at North Andover to get my wits and clothes in order before I start, on the 2d of October, for the great campaign of General Convention. It will not do to try and get in anything besides, and the first that I shall see of you and Lizzie will be when I appear at breakfast on the morning of October 3, and we go together to the great opening service at St. George's. It was very good and thoughtful of you to propose the visit, but it must not be.

This is a good, slow, steady steamer, with a very multifarious lot of folk on board, and all is going very pleasantly. We shall have two Thursdays this week, picking up the lost day which we dropped here in the mid-Pacific two months ago. But, in spite of that, we shall not be in San Francisco until Friday of next week. Then we are going up to Vancouver and home by the Canadian Pacific via Winnipeg, St. Paul, and Chicago. It has been a great success, — the worst thing of the summer being the steamboat ink with which I am trying to write this letter. I hope that all goes well with you, and that Minnequa is gayety itself. Well, well, another winter's work draws very near!

My kindest love to Lizzie, and counting on much talk in October, I am, Affectionately, P.

STEAMSHIP CITY OF RIO DE JANEIRO,
Pacific Ocean, September 6, 1889.

DEAR WILLIAM, — We shall be at 'Frisco tonight, then I will send this last letter of the summer, which will tell you we are safely across this mighty pond, and that I shall be with you before two weeks more are passed. We have had a slow voyage, because the ship is not a fast one, needs cleaning, and has not been pressed. We were also one day late in leaving Yokohama, owing to the severe storms raging in the Chinese Sea, which were expected to delay the steamer in arriving at Japan. The whole voyage has been calm and peaceful. For days and days the ocean was almost without a wave, and at her worst the ship has not rolled enough to hurt the weakest traveler. We have about twenty first-class passengers, a curious lot, Americans, English, Scotch, French, German, Russians, Japanese, and a whole lot of queer Chinese in the steerage, who cannot go ashore in San Francisco, but will be passed on to Mexico and other places which do not yet refuse to take in the poor Celestials. The voyage has not been dull or tedious, but it will be rather good to go on shore early to-morrow morning and telegraph to you that I am safely here. We shall spend Sunday in San Francisco, and in the evening start by way of Sacramento for Portland and Puget Sound. We shall probably arrive in Boston Thursday, the 19th, and then for a quiet, delightful week at North Andover before the General Convention at New York.

I hope to hear to-night that all is well with you. If I hear that, the summer will be perfect. It is five weeks since your last dates, and one cannot help feeling a bit anxious. I believe all will be well. You shall hear from me, by and by, just when I will arrive. Until then, be sure that I am anxious to get home, and with the best of love to all, count me

Affectionately your dear brother, P.

SUMMER OF 1890.

LUCERNE, August 25, 1890.

DEAR JOHNNIE, — You were mighty good to write me such a fine, long letter. Although you will not get this answer much before I come myself, I cannot help thanking you and sending you all an affectionate greeting this rainy morning. It is our first real rainy day. The summer has been free from blighting heat and blasting tornado, such as has devastated things at home. To think of South Lawrence getting all blown to pieces! I read about it in the " Journal de Genève," and trembled for the corn barn. What a pity that I have lost your visits to the old house. It must have been delightful both for you and for Andover. . . .

This has been the quietest of little journeys, but very pleasant indeed. The streets of London looked just as we left them ten years ago, and the great white hills were waiting for us in Chamounix and Interlaken. Of course the people whom we wanted most to see were gone from London, for the season was over before we arrived, but I had a delightful little visit with Tennyson in his home at Aldworth. He has grown old, but is bright and clear-headed, and may give us some more verses yet. Just after I left England, Newman died, and the pulpit and press have been full of laudation and discussion of him ever since. He was a remarkable man, by no means of the first class, for he never got at final principles nor showed a truly brave mind; but there was great beauty in his character, and his intellect was very subtle. . . . What a wild scene of frivolous excitement Marion seems to have been! I do not wonder that you, H. and the children had to take to the water, to escape the land. Be sure and all keep well and safe till we come back, and then for another year of the old familiar, pleasant work. My kindest love to all of you.   Affectionately,   P.

LAST JOURNEY ABROAD.

1892.

H. M. S. MAJESTIC, June 27, 1892.

DEAR MARY, — I miss my old companions very much indeed. It would be very delightful if you and G. were on deck to-day, as I am sure you would be if you were on board. The day is delightful, and the big ship is going splendidly. She is a magnificent great thing, and could put our dear little Cephalonia into her waistcoat pocket. Her equipment is sumptuous and her speed is something tremendous, but I do not know that I like her as well as the old-fashioned little boats which seem more homelike, and where one knows how to find his way about. . . . Our captain is Purcell, who commanded the Adriatic when G., you, and I once sailed on her. He has given me the use of his deck-room during the day, so I have a lovely, quiet time . . . . Mr. Howard Potter and his family, and Dr. and Mrs. Watson of Boston, with whom I sit at an extra table in the hall which opens on the deck, are about all of whom I see anything.

Yesterday we had service, and I preached in the great saloon in the morning, and in the evening I held a service for the second-class passengers, of whom there is a multitude. There is no gong for meals, but two rosy little sailor boys march through the ship with bugles playing a tune to call us, which is very pretty indeed. Wednesday morning we shall get to

Queenstown, and that night I hope to dine and sleep at the Adelphi, where I will eat some mushrooms in your honor. Then I go to London, where I shall be on Thursday night, and ever so many nights afterwards, I trust. It looks very nice, but indeed I should not have been disappointed if the Majestic could not have taken me, and I had been left in North Andover for the summer, as I expected when I saw you last. May it be a beautiful summer to you all. . . .

Yours affectionately and majestically, P.

WESTMINSTER PALACE HOTEL, LONDON,
July 4, 1892.

DEAR GERTIE, — I have the same old rooms, the big parlor and bedroom on the second floor; the bootblack boy is across the way, the smiling youth is on the sidewalk, the big porter is in the hall, and everything is just the way it used to be, only I miss you very much indeed, and wish you would take the next steamer and come out. You must not take the City of Chicago, because she was wrecked, and it would not have been nice to clamber up the side of that steep rock on a rope ladder. You had better take the Cephalonia; or, if you cannot get her, the Majestic, which is a splendid great boat, with a great deal of room and all the luxuries of which you can conceive, and she comes over in no time. . . .

All your friends are well and asking after you. I dined at Archdeacon Farrar's Saturday night. Lady Frances Baillie was there, and so were the Bishop of Rochester and his wife; he used to be Dean of Windsor, you remember, when we went there once. Yesterday I preached in the morning at St. Margaret's, and in the evening at the Abbey, and there were a great many people in both churches. And now to-day, for I have been out since I began this letter this morning, I have been running all over town, and last of all have been to pay my Fourth of July respects to Mr. Lincoln, the American minister. Do you remember when we went to see Mr. Lowell one Fourth of July, and you sat all the time in the carriage?

There is a splendid new Velasquez at the National Gallery. The National Gallery has bought it since we were last here, and the people for the first time have a chance of seeing it. . . .

I am going now to dine at Dr. Sewall's, to-morrow at the Abbey, Wednesday at Mrs. Synge's, Thursday at the Dean's, and so on every day. How is Tood? Everybody is expecting her, and wondering why she did not come over this year. They can hardly wait to see her. Last Saturday there was a garden party at Lambeth Palace, and everybody looked happy, and some of them very pretty. Next week I am going to see the Tennysons, and the week after I go to see our friend the Bishop of Rochester, who is now the Bishop of Winchester, and lives at Farnham Castle. . . . I am coming home on the Pavonia with Uncle John and Aunt Hattie on the 8th of September. Now I cannot write any more, but send my love to everybody, and am   Your affectionate uncle,
P.

WESTMINSTER PALACE HOTEL, LONDON,
July 11, 1892.

DEAR WILLIAM, — I did not get any time to write yesterday, because there was preaching to do all day. In the morning, I preached at a great big church in Chelsea, and went home to dinner with the minister.

Then I came back here and went to sleep in the afternoon, and had a beautiful time. In the evening, I preached at St. Peter's, Eaton Square, a large and fashionable church; went home to supper with the minister, and found a number of people, quite a Sunday evening supper party. . . . I am only going to preach once more, next Sunday morning, for Haweis, to whom I have owed a sermon ever since he preached so remarkably in Trinity. When that is over, I shall do up the sermons and the Episcopal robes, and not open them again until I get to North Andover and preach for Mr. Walker.

This morning, I had a long call from Father Hall, who looks well and hearty, and seems to be enjoying things over here, and to have no thought of coming back to Boston or America. It was pleasant to see him again.

John and Hattie are somewhere in England. I heard from John when they arrived at Liverpool, and he expects to bring up here next Saturday night. They seem to have had a very comfortable and prosperous voyage. Arthur is now upon the ocean, and will be here, I suppose, some time near the end of the week. McVickar is somewhere on this side, but has not yet shown himself.

I think I shall go to the Continent on the 25th, two weeks from to-day. I do not know where I shall go, or what I shall do. I would like to go over the Stelvio again with you, and if you will come out we will do it. If you do not come, I shall go alone, probably as far as Switzerland, perhaps to Venice. . . .

Yours affectionately,   P.

LONDON, July 17, 1892.

DEAR WILLIAM, — . . . I have just come back from preaching for Mr. Haweis at his church in Marylebone, and have promised to take luncheon here with Arthur at half past one, and then go and hear Farrar preach at the Abbey at three. Before he comes I will begin my Sunday note to you. I am not going to preach any more. Next Sunday I shall be here with Johnnie, and we will go and hear some of the great men whom this big city can supply.

. . . Yesterday I spent at Lord Tennyson's, going down with Farrar in the morning and getting back to dinner. The old man was in beautiful condition, gentle, gracious, and talkative until he went for his snooze, as he called it, after luncheon. He read us some of his poetry, and talked about it in the most interesting way. Lady Tennyson is a beautiful invalid, and the young people, Hallam, his wife, and children, are delightful.

We have been to the afternoon service at the Abbey, and had a pleasant anthem and a fine sermon from Archdeacon Farrar. The whole thing goes on, you see, very much after the old fashion, and is very good. After another week I shall be glad to be away, and then I shall think of you, in Paris and among the hills. . . .

WESTMINSTER PALACE HOTEL, LONDON,
July 24, 1892.

DEAR TOOD, — . . . Yesterday we were at the National Gallery and saw the Botticellis, Giorgiones, Tintorettos, Titians, and others. The afternoon before, we took a fine drive in the Park and had a lovely time. This afternoon we have all been to

Westminster Abbey and heard Archdeacon Farrar preach a fine sermon. Right in the middle of it a girl went wild and shrieked at the top of her voice, and they had to carry her out neck and heels. Don't ever do that, will you? . . .

I am going to leave Tuesday morning for the Continent. I do not know where I shall go, but I think Dr. McVickar will go with me, and we shall find some snow mountains somewhere. I am very sorry about the electric railway at North Andover, and the trees. Perhaps we cannot go there any more after this year. Where do you think we had better go? I went the other day to the Bishop of Winchester's. He lives at Farnham Castle, an awfully old affair, with keep, drawbridge, and dungeons underground, and a park of three hundred acres and deer in it.

D. and B. have grown up to be young ladies, and D. sits at the head of her father's table. I am glad you are reading so many nice books. You will know all about things when you come abroad. How are all your friends? Dear me! it sounds very far away, but I shall come home by and by, and we will get a few days in the old house together before we break up and call the summer done. . . . Good-by, my love to all, and I am

Your dear uncle, P.

ST. MORITZ, ENGADINE, HOTEL KULM,
August 7, 1892.

MY DEAR MARY, — . . . It has been a very good week. Last Sunday we spent at Trouville. That means Dr. McVickar and I. Monday we went to Paris and put up at the Grand Hôtel. It looked very bright and familiar, just as it did when G., you, and

I were there. You and G. were not there this time, for which I was very sorry.

Tuesday evening we took the Orient Express for Munich, the train which you know we thought of taking, but did not, from Strasburg to Paris. It was very swift and comfortable, and brought us to Munich at noon on Wednesday. We stayed at the Baierischer Hof. . . . Thursday morning we took a train to Innsbruck, but did not go by the Achensee. As we passed Jenbach, we saw they had a railway from Jenbach to the Achensee, with queer, tilted-up cars, like those that go up the Pilatus. Friday morning we took the rail to Landeck, and then a carriage for a two days' drive up the valley of the Inn, which brought us here. . . . We slept at the Tyroler Hof, where A. and L. and G. and you and I were five years ago. . . .

This is a glorious place, and the weather is superb. We shall stay here for several days, and then I do not know where we shall go. . . . I wish you were all here this afternoon, for the snow mountains are very fine. . . .

LUCERNE, August 14, 1892.

DEAR GERTIE. — I passed the Restaurant Titlis this morning, and thought of you and the night we spent there before they moved us to the pretty Entresol in the Schweitzer Hof. The Schweitzer Hof now is full, and we are lodged, Dr. McVickar and I, in the top story of the Lucerner Hof. Last night there were the band and the fireworks in front of the Schweitzer Hof, the old way. . . .

We came here yesterday over the St. Gotthard from Lugano, on the lake of Lugano. There we had spent a day, climbing up Monte Generosa by a queer old railway, like that which climbs up the Mount Pilatus, which I can see from my window now, if I almost break my neck by twisting round the corner for a view. We came to Lugano from Cadenabbia on the lake of Como, and to Cadenabbia we had come by the Maloja Pass and the beautiful lake from St. Moritz, whence I wrote last Sunday; that is thus far our journey. . . .

Oh, I wish you were here, and that we were to go over the Brunig to-morrow to Interlaken, M. and you, and I. But you can see how it all looks. The lake, the boats, the flags, the people, and the hills around it.

I send my best love to you all, and by and by will see you at North Andover.

Yours affectionately and affectionately, P.

HOTEL VICTORIA, INTERLAKEN,
August 21, 1892.

DEAR W[,]LIAM, — There is no letter this week, from any of you, for which I am very sorry. I hope you have not grown tired of me, and given me up altogether.

Do you remember Grindenwald and the Bear Hotel, on whose balcony we sat one long afternoon, waiting for the rain to stop, so that we could ascend the Wengern Alp? M. and G. and I went to the same Bear Hotel two years ago, and sat in its hospitable courtyard, drank coffee, and had our photographs taken by a low-spirited practitioner a little way beyond. I went over there yesterday to see the ruins. It was burnt down on Thursday, the Bear Hotel, the photographer's shop, and pretty nearly the whole village, a hundred houses in all destroyed, and ever so many wretched peasants thrown out into the cold world. It is quite awful. You will never see the Bear Hotel again. They have a railway from Grindelwald to the Wengern Alp, and down again to Lauterbrunnen, so there will be no more pleasant horseback rides across the meadows and down the steep descent upon the other side.

It has been a lazy week. I tarried in Lucerne until Thursday. The days were hot and lovely. McVickar left me on Tuesday and went to Paris, where he must have been hot and wretched for the last few days. Thursday I took train and came over the Brunig here. Now I am expecting, to-morrow, the 22d, John and Hattie. They are at Lucerne to-day, having reached there last Friday. . . . Their time in Switzerland will not be very long, but I think they have enjoyed everything pretty well. You cannot go very wrong in Europe. When they have joined me, I think we shall go to Thun, Berne, Martigny, Tête Noire, Chamounix, Geneva, and so to Paris, where we shall get a few days before it is time to go to London, Liverpool, and the Pavonia.

These are sad tidings of the riots and fightings in Buffalo and Tennessee. It is good that violence should be put down by military force, but that does not solve the problem of how the great men are to live with the little men, and what is the function of government as regards them both. Only time and events and the slow progress of mankind will settle that.

Meanwhile, I send you all my dearest love and am
 Ever and always yours affectionately, P.

HOTEL D'ANGLETERRE, CHAMOUNIX,
August 28, 1892.

DEAR WILLIAM, MARY, GERTRUDE, AGNES, AND TOOD, — This is the last letter I shall write to any of you on this journey, because next Sunday it will be within four days of the sailing of the Pavonia, and it will not be worth while to write. This fun is almost over. John and Hattie joined me last Monday at Interlaken.

. . . Tuesday we went to Lauterbrunnen and the Trummelbach, and had a fine, bright, sunshiny day. Wednesday we loafed about Interlaken all the morning, and took the boat and train in the afternoon for Berne by Thun. It was not clear when we reached Berne, so we did not see the great view of the Alps, but saw the bears in their pit. I showed the old woman on the terrace the bear which I bought of her for fifty centimes two years ago and have carried in my pocket ever since, which pleased her simple soul very much indeed, and pleased mine more. She thought it very pretty of me to have taken such fond care of it, and she offered to make it brown and young again for nothing. But I did not want her to do that, and told her I would bring it back again in two years more to see her.

We went back to the Berner Hof for dinner, and in the evening to a Beer Garden and heard music. Thursday it rained hard, but we came to Martigny by rail, and after we reached there in the afternoon it was pleasant enough for us to take a drive and see the Gorge de Trient. Friday we drove over the Tête Noire. It was a beautiful day, and the views were prettiest and best. Saturday the mountains were as clear as clear could be, so we are lucky.

An Oxford professor tried to go up Mont Blanc Thursday in the storm, and died of exhaustion. Yesterday, through the telescope in the hotel yard, we could see them bringing his dead body down over the snow, and I suppose it arrived here late last night.

The only high ascent made by our party, and that was entirely successful, was John's going with a mule and a guide to the Montanvert, crossing the Mer de Glace, and coming down by the Mauvais Pas. The journey was accomplished without any accident, and the climber reached the hotel about three o'clock in the afternoon, not much fatigued.

To-morrow we go to Geneva (Hôtel de la Paix), and the next day shall take the long, tiresome ride to Paris; after that you know about what will happen to us, until you find us in your arms again. . . I am very well indeed, thank you, and shall be glad to see you all again. Yours most affectionately,   P.

www.ingramcontent.com/pod-product-compliance
Lightning Source LLC
Chambersburg PA
CBHW032017220426
43664CB00006B/281